WHAT EVER I
WHAT ı ..

Paul K. Lyons spent many years as a Euro-journalist, writing about energy, environmental and transport policies. His business publications were among the first to focus exclusively on these issues from an EU perspective. His experiences in Brussels led him to write and publish *Kip Fenn – Reflections* (re-published in paperback as the *Not a Brave New World* trilogy). This is the bold fictional biography of a high-level UN official who lives throughout the 21st century working to improve inter-national co-operation and reduce the rich-poor divide. Lyons was an early enthusiast for psycho-geography, with his online book, *London Cross*, describing a 30 mile straight line walk across Greater London. The History Press published his two local history books: *Brighton in Diaries* and *Brighton & Hove Then & Now*. Most recently, his passion for diaries has led him to create three diary websites, all freely available and non-commercial: *The Diary Junction* (a database of 500 diarists), *And So Made Significant . . .* (possibly the world's greatest diary anthology), and *The Diary Review* with over a thousand news-type articles on diaries and diarists. His own colourful diaries, spanning more than half a century, can also be found online. In late 2018, Wiley-Blackwell published his comprehensive essay on diaries in *A Companion to Literary Biography*. He has one adult son, and now lives in Brighton with his wife, Hattie, and their two young sons.

WHAT EVER HAPPENED TO WHAT I WROTE

PATCHWORK OF A WRITING LIFE
PART TWO

Paul K. Lyons

PiKLe
PuBLiSHiNG

Published by Pikle Publishing 2024

ISBN 978–0954827076

Pikle Publishing
44 Shaftesbury Road, Brighton BN1 4NF, UK

www.pikle.co.uk

Wrapped in a yielding air, beside
The flower's soundless hunger
Close to the tree's clandestine tide
Close to the bird's high fever,
Loud in his hope and his anger,
Erect about his skeleton,
Stands the expressive lover
Stands the deliberate man.

W. H. Auden *As He Is*

For Adam, JG and Albert

WITH MANY THANKS TO HATTIE AND ADAM

CONTENTS

Introduction – What ever happened to what I wrote?   1

1   Adam Co-op – An idiosyncratic way of parenting   4

2   The Office – Success, fraud, failure   24

3   Evolution – In thrall to natural science   44

4   EC INFORM – A business of my own   61

5   Adam – The joys and privileges of fatherhood   84

6   Music – Where life is better   107

7   Health – To balance mind and body   125

8   Fiction – Yah boo sucks, you agents, you publishers!   141

9   Diary – Five million words long, deep, wide   161

10   Kip Fenn – Magnum opus or white elephant?   179

WHAT EVER HAPPENED TO WHAT I WROTE?

My life, conveniently and fittingly, can be divided into three chronological periods. I wrote about the first of these, from birth to the beginning of fatherhood, in my first memoir, *Why Ever Did I Want to Write*. Looking back on my youth, I re-discovered it as full of colourful, exciting experiences, with much travel – emotional, geographical, spiritual and intellectual. I had the good fortune, as I see it, to be literate and able to digest those experiences, and to record them in diaries.

Becoming a parent is for most a life-changing moment, and it was for me too, launching the second period in which I 'settled down' to some extent, became far more responsible, serious, as befits anyone who has charge over another life, or other lives. Decisions, of multifarious types, once made with egotistical drive, were now to be taken with due consideration of family. This volume, thus, covers the 20 odd years from Adam's birth to his leaving home, a period in which my primary purpose was parental. As for the third period – one in which I have become very happy and content, yet wrestle against diminishing physical fitness and mists of mental jadedness – well, I doubt I will feel any impetus to prepare a third memoir.

You may well ask – as I have myself – why I bother with a second memoir. After all, my adventuring came to a relatively abrupt end in 1987 on returning from Brazil, and with the arrival of Adam. I had lots to write about in a first memoir, what with my mixed-up family background, round-the-world travels, love affairs, theatre and psycho-social experimenting . . . much of it now reminiscent of a culture that has changed so much since the 1970s and 1980s. But life with a baby and a full-time office job? Surely not memoir material. Well, I will have to leave that for you to judge. I explored – in the first memoir – how I came to be a writer, a label I could apply to my occupation as a journalist, and to my primary leisure activity. In this memoir, I intend to explore more thoroughly what I actually wrote, and how I wrote it, again, as in the first memoir, using themes to direct the focus of each section.

Two chapters are largely devoted to Adam. Chapter one – the most difficult to write – looks at how Bel and I managed our relationship as parents. We had taken the decision – I thought it courageous, others thought it foolish – to have a child, yet without any intention to live together. Nevertheless, because of Adam, our joint and joyous commitment, Bel and I stayed together, a sort-of couple/threesome for the best part of a decade, occasionally in the same house, but mostly not – Adam moving between us naturally whenever necessary. There were trials a plenty no more or less, I suppose than for those in wedlock, but – unusually, I suppose, I've a wealth of diary material to help me unpick the responsibilities, tensions, arguments, as well as to colour in the joys and fun of parenthood. In a second chapter, I look more directly at Adam's later development and the relationship just between the two of us, not shying away from some of the difficulties I experienced as Adam moved through his teens.

I devote two chapters to my working life as a journalist/editor, one covering the five years I worked for Financial Times Business Information (FTBI), and the other covering the decade or so during which I ran my own small publishing company – EC INFORM. So much writing, such a lot of words I wrote. I flourished at FTBI, producing my first business books, launching new initiatives, and managing a small team of assistant editors. Increasingly, I was drawn to the political and legal developments in Brussels, and when I started my own newsletter business it was aimed exclusively at those wanting detailed news about the European Community's activities. My EC INFORM years were generally very busy. I was spending several days every month in Brussels, and most of the rest of the time I was writing articles to fill the monthly publication. After several years, I employed an assistant, and we launched a second newsletter. I made a living, but the business – in competition with FTBI – was never profitable enough to expand further. I wrote and published books, too, but again these were not as successful as those I'd written under the FT banner.

I've studied and read a lot about science over the years, especially evolution and consciousness, and there's plenty in my diaries on the subject. I was so keen indeed that, in my 30s, I completed (part time) an MSc in biological anthropology. For it, I wrote a decent thesis – the only significant piece of academic science work/writing I've ever done. It did not seem out of place to draw on my diaries and the thesis itself for a chapter on these studies and thoughts.

As I write now I am into old age and creaky bones, but for this second memoir I wanted to celebrate a lifetime of reasonable good health, and thus I have devoted a chapter to the subject, encompassing cycling for transport, hiking, swimming (what is now called 'wild swimming'), volleyball, yoga-ish exercising (especially outdoors). For another chapter, I've trawled my memory and my diaries with the aim of describing how music has enriched my life (far more so than art, for example).

Finally, I am including one chapter on the how, what and why of my lifetime diary habit, and two chapters specifically about my creative writing. One looks at what I wrote in terms of novels, short stories, plays (some for children) – all of which failed to find interest from agents or publishers – and psychogeography-type works that I published online. The second is a meticulous (blow-by-blow) examination of how I came to write a very ambitious novel called *Kip Fenn – Reflections*, how I came to the decision to publish it myself, not once but twice, and how, ultimately, I found more use for the boxes *Kip Fenn* was packed in than for the volumes themselves. A failure it was, in terms of the publishing universe, but what a terrific failure! Many years later, I could be no more proud of *Kip Fenn* than if it had won a Booker Prize.

Chapter one

ADAM CO-OP
AN IDIOSYNCRATIC WAY OF PARENTING

Again – as in the last chapter of my earlier memoir – I must face up to a conflict of interests. Then, it would not have been possible to reflect meaningfully on my life, nor to present the story of it adequately, without writing about Bel. But she herself did not want me to. I did not compromise over the truth, as I saw it, of how we arrived at a point of deciding to have a child together. In any case, our son, Adam, ever even-handed between his very different parents, read over the chapter, and without actually approving my decision to publish, let me know he thought it a fair treatment.

Now I am back with the same dilemma, even more tangled, for there is far more to tell. I mean, whatever interesting narrative might be told about two parents in the run up to the birth of a child, there's a much longer and more complex narrative to come concerning their relationship and how they managed their parental love and duties. Bel and I loved mostly but fought too often for the next dozen years or so, mostly living apart yet still in the closest of relationships. How we managed is the difficult subject of this chapter. Whatever highs and lows came before, now with a dependant life in our hands, there were richer highs and deeper lows. We both sacrificed parts of our selves, our lives, but we were often extremely happy. Again, Bel would wish none of this were written down, but – as I said before – I am writer, it's what I do. This time round, knowing her position, I have not consulted her; she would wish it thus.

As it happens, I already have more detailed, banal and intimate written material about our three lives than any writer could ever wish – first hand, uncensored. My own diaries! Too much. As I start out on this new chapter of my life, I already feel daunted by the challenge of being accurate, fair to us all, and interesting.

I believe it was a courageous decision, though others thought it foolish, for both Bel and I in different ways, to decide consciously to have a child out of wedlock and with no intention of living together. Neither of us had lived or were living conventional lives, constrained or driven by social mores, but, nevertheless, we did have social frameworks of family, friends, and work colleagues who might have found it a confusing decision. For Bel, the risks were certainly greater, as they generally are for women, her life so quickly becoming restricted by the major duties of child rearing. For me, the risks of this unconventional venture were less, I suppose. Being a father, of whatever kind, would impose restrictions on my freedom – a freedom I'd come not only to value but to need.

Although we had tried, off and on, to be a couple, it wasn't an ar-rangement that suited me or my temperament, and Bel understood that. An onlooker, not privy to the history of our relationship, might presume that Bel, consciously or unconsciously, hoped that a child would lead to coupledom. But I am fairly certain this was not the case. When she was pregnant and I was still in Brazil, she feared – although I didn't know this at the time – that I would have very little to do with the child, and she was preparing herself mentally for such a situation.

Nevertheless, because of Adam, our joint and joyous commitment, Bel and I stayed together, a sort-of couple – I coined the term Adam Co-op to describe and define the relationship – for the best part of the next dec-ade. Early on in this period, I tried to exploit (not in the negative sense of taking liberties, but in the sense of utilising) the fact of our separate lives – that I had so insisted on – to form other relationships, only two in fact, and neither significant. But with working life so busy, my emotional world full of Bel and Adam, and intimacy with Bel still lovely, the libertine in me more or less vanished. There were years, I would say, of us slowly slipping further and further apart (as compared to the intensity of our best times), but it would be Bel who first formed a serious and long-term relationship. I didn't mind, it was right and proper for her to do so, which is not to say I didn't make life awkward for her vis-a-vis Adam and who he was living with on a day-by-day basis. Meanwhile, I was left in a morass of my own making, sinking into an unwanted life of celibacy – not to be rescued from it, in fact, until Adam had left home.

I returned to the UK in March 1987, and Adam was born some four months later, on 4 August. I had reinstalled myself in my terraced house in Kilburn, at 13 Aldershot Road (my brother had moved out and bought his own place), and Bel was living in a small garden flat just five minutes walk away. By then, I had already purchased a second home, a small ter-raced house in Aldeburgh, Suffolk, where Bel and I had been spending weekends. I wrote in my diary: 'I love Aldeburgh more than any other single place, I love to be in the country, by the sea. [...] And perhaps most importantly it can be a place where both Bel and I can be together with our child. Bel will also have somewhere to go to be away from her flat, somewhere more spacious, more healthy where she can stay for a week or more at a time with no cost and no compromise.'

We'd had a busy day on 3 August, an auction and garden centre at Woodbridge in the morning, and me digging over our small garden in the afternoon. Early evening we drove to Thorpeness beach to walk along the pebbles, arm in arm, enjoying the land and seascapes. Bel said the colour in the sky was pink, I maintained it was orange. Back at the cottage in Aldeburgh, Bel prepared salads while I made cheese and herb pizzas, and cooked a tin of soup with fresh courgettes. A little while afterwards Bel went upstairs to prepare for bed. A few minutes later she called out, I could hear distress in her voice – her waters had broken.

We made the decision to drive back to London and the Royal Free Hospital where Bel had planned to give birth. On the way, Bel's contractions were coming on rather quickly, but we had no clock or watch to time them, so we couldn't judge how urgently we needed to be at a hospital. However, it was late at night, and there was little traffic on the A12 so I was able to drive at a steady 60mph. This allowed us to count the miles (equivalent to minutes at that speed) between contractions. We stopped at a telephone box to call the Royal Free and were told to take it easy, no need to panic. We arrived at 1:30, and Adam was born around 7:30.

Bel and I had come to an early decision on names, and I'd been writing about our unborn baby as Laura/Adam in my diary. Laura came into our minds, largely I think, from the famous book/film noir written by my grandfather's second wife, Vera Caspary. And Adam came to us from George Eliot's 18th century rural novel, *Adam Bede*. Intriguingly, in the weeks before Adam's birth, I was reading A. J. Cronin's novel *The Stars Look Down* which my grandfather Igee Goldsmith had made into a successful film, and therein I found a Laura and Adam Todd – Todd being my mother's maiden name. Bel and I also agreed that he/she should have Bel's surname rather than mine – this was not a difficult decision for me, as I'd never felt any affinity with Lyons, my stepfather's name.

Adam was born on 4 August some two weeks early but in perfect health, or so we thought. A first trial for two proud parents came later that very same day. By the afternoon both Bel and I had began to worry that Adam hadn't woken up during his first bath, and that he wasn't waking to feed. Bel had asked to talk to a midwife several times, without result, so now she grabbed hold of the tiny life and went marching through the wards to find a doctor. It was quickly established that Adam's blood sugar level had dropped dramatically (he should never have been bathed without this being checked), and he was whisked off to a special care unit, and put on a feed drip. An anxious few days followed; Bel was allowed to sleep in a camp bed next to Adam. By the third day, she was breast feeding regularly, and on day five they were both allowed home.

Some years earlier, I'd been given – by Harold, one of the stars of my young life – a large diary book, with a gold-designed padded front and back, and high quality plain paper inside. It was larger than my usual journals, and fatter, and I'd not found any use for it so far. But Adam's birth called out to be marked in my diaries in a unique way, so I decided to use this special book and write my entries as if they were letters to him, starting each entry with 'Dear Adam, . . .'. The first entry is rather short, starting with 'Dear Adam, you are born. You are nine hours old.' A few clinical details follow, before it concludes with, 'Your father is tired and finds it difficult to concentrate on writing but there is so much to tell you.'

And here, eight months later, is the very last entry.

> 3 April 1988
> Dearest Angel Heart, I plan to finish this book tomorrow when you are eight months. The next one will not be written to you, but I suspect you will play a large part in its contents.
>
> To think, when I started this book you were a sleepy foetus thrust into the world rudely without any choice in the matter. Now you are eight months old – a crawler, a smiler, a food gobbler and a milk sucker. You have been so well behaved these few days and given me pure joy. Sometimes I watch you and can barely keep from tears. Sometimes you sit on my lap when I read the paper and try to eat the bits I haven't read, sometimes you scamper along the floor to get close to me if I'm also lying on the floor. Sometimes, when I'm standing you grab at my trousers and climb up to my knees. You feel very insecure but if I'm careful and move very slowly you will take hesitant steps in time with my knees.
>
> How you love to be naked, when you are all warm and dry after a bath, you smile and giggle away as we play with you. And then how you wriggle when we try to dress you.'

The eight month diary, of course, documents obsession with our young baby, the joy of him especially, as well as many anxious concerns over his well-being. I was particularly stressed for a while over various unnatural movements Adam would make, muscle spasms, twitches, especially when we realised after some weeks that he didn't seem to be growing, and might have been underfeeding. These movements, it seemed to me, were very similar to those made involuntarily by a close friend I'd had in New Zealand with a degenerative disorder. I feared they were being caused by the hypoglycaemia he'd experienced as a new born, and might develop into a lifelong disability.

> 13 October 1987
> Dear Adam, Some sort of celebration is in order, you are 10 weeks old today. I wouldn't say yet that you have a clean bill of health. Bel and I remain quite worried about your tendency to make funny faces. You really do screw-up your mouth and often lift and tense your arms as well. I thought you had stopped but this weekend in Aldeburgh you seemed to be doing them all the time. And your Mum has discovered that one of the causes of spastic paralysis is low blood sugar level at birth! We are not afraid. What will be, will be. Your Mum cried a couple of nights, and I was tearful and sad at the weekend. But I know that a

mild disability (and there is no question of you being severely handicapped) can often enhance a person's life, for that person is more able to keep a mental perspective on the joys of living.

But oh thank god your Mum did pick you up and race off through the ward to find a doctor. I might have just let you sleep on through the night.

Our fears proved groundless soon enough, but here's more from that diary entry, evocative of our days in Aldeburgh.

13 October 1987
We had a lovely weekend in A. Saturday morning, as usual, I strapped you to my front and we marched off to the village, leaving Bel to grab a bit more sleep. I am always singing to you.

Early on Saturday morning
Early on Saturday morning
Adam and Daddy are walking to the breadman
Early on Saturday morning
Early on Saturday morning
Adam and Daddy are walking to the breadman to buy bread and cakes

I love the moment after we've marched along Alde Lane, I think it is, and turned left and arrived at the top of the Town Steps. From there we can see the sea stretching beyond the Aldeburgh roofs in a vast and beautiful panorama, a wonderful stirring sight. We dance down the steps and along the high street navigating by means of the smell of fresh bread issuing forth from the bakery. We join the inevitable queue for the delicious baps, granary bread, pastries and pies. Then we walk back along the High Street to the newspaper shop to buy a copy of the *East Anglian Daily Times*. Maybe then we go to the beach for a quick close-up fix of the ocean otherwise we head back home, licking our lips at the thought of butter-soaked baps and a fresh cup of tea.

On Sunday, you and I make a similar trip, only this one is for the Sunday papers which, if the weather is fine and we're both well wrapped up, we take to the beach wall where I sit and read for a while. This particular Saturday, we met your mother all togged up and running. Yes, jogging down to the sea. Her first run since you were born. And when she got back, she revealed she had also swum in the sea.

We spent most of every weekend together, alternating between being in London and in Aldeburgh, but the first couple of years with Adam would prove to be the most difficult for the two of us. Becoming parents puts astonishing pressures on people, for all kinds of different reasons, and in our case uncovered cracks in our relationship and personalities, the same ones perhaps that had always led me to believe it would be too difficult for us to live together as a couple. It would be fair to say we argued a lot, and that I was the protagonist most of the time. Here's a self-critical analysis I wrote on the first day of the new year.

1 January 1988
At moments when I am being particularly oppressive, and I can see that Bel is shrinking away from every word I am saying, I feel it becomes all the more

urgent that she listens to me, then suddenly I see in her eyes a real fear. In these moments I realise that she cannot listen to what I am saying, understand it, or in any way comprehend my logic, because she thinks I am – for want of a better word – mad. And yet I think it imperative she understand what it is I am trying to say and that her shrinking away, her tears, are often a defence from the meaning of my words sinking in.

How can her mind cope with all these insults to her being. As I go over the top – which I have been doing – so she must surely lose confidence and trust in me. Increasingly, her mind will shut off against my words. Mostly in our relationship I have been in control – words and actions have been deliberate. But, as we spend more time together because of you, so this is increasingly difficult.

And now for my major failing: the very same traits in Bel that I love are those that now irritate me, and I appear unable to control my impatience. It annoys me that Bel never instigates excursions, walks, new developments on the house, or garden, that she doesn't provide intelligence into our conversations – new facts about a place we should visit, or about Aldeburgh or about books to read etc. Sometimes it seems that just everything comes from me. If I point this out, and she then makes a special effort, she can be more decisive – but this soon lapses.

And so you see, my son, there are lots of things going on between your parents all the time. In general, overall I must make a concerted effort not to nag so much, to allow time and space for Bel to have and implement ideas (I do already try very hard – giving her hints and direction in my quiet ways) and to be more encouraging to those ideas. I think Bel must make a determined effort to impact more into our time together at Aldeburgh, and to do so more consistently, to think about the house and garden and not just sit back and wait for me to make decisions. But, I think we came to those conclusions some weeks ago already. Implementing them is difficult.

If a casual observer might have diagnosed Bel as showing signs of post-natal depression and me as having a 'for God's sake, pull yourself together' attitude, they would only be echoing my own knee-jerk reactions to many of our arguments. But this would be too crude a way of judging the situation we found ourselves in. Yes, on many occasions I could have been kinder, and Bel could have taken more positive, practical steps to keep herself from sliding into periods of inertia. And while Bel was ill-equipped to deal with the strength of my certainty about so many aspects of bringing up Adam and our lives together, I was ill equipped to handle Bel's unwillingness to look forward, make changes, nor her inability to take up the ideas I was putting forward. We were ill-matched, always had been, as I knew, and being forced together into making joint decisions for the welfare or our son, only heightened this rift between our characters.

One of my ongoing concerns was that Bel lived in a cramped one-room flat (with a small garden and tiny kitchen). I knew it well, of course, since my Australian friend Harvey had lived there first. When he left, having been tried at the Old Bailey for blackmailing his landlord's agent

(*Why Ever* – Chapter eleven), I'd arranged for Bel to move in. Previously, she had been living in a bedsit, so this small flat felt like a palace to her at first. But, with a baby, I began to feel it was too small, too cramped (the bath was in a cupboard in the kitchen), and that Bel should be thinking about finding somewhere more suitable. Also, I worried hugely about the fact that Bel had no interests beyond Adam, nor any idea of what work she might do in the future.

Even through the worst of these early days of our parenting, Bel and I continued to love and laugh, if less so than pre-Adam. I guess it was living apart that – in the long run – allowed our small unconventional family not only to survive but, often enough, to thrive for as many years as it did. One consequence of the arguments was that we learned to spend (even) more time apart, so that some weekends I would look after Adam on my own, always a joy. During the week, I was busy at work (with much travel involved), socialising with friends or my lodgers, as well as pursuing my literary ambitions. Nevertheless, there were many a weekday evening when I would visit Bel and Adam, or vice versa. And then, for a time, I also looked after Adam one day a week, working from home, to give Bel some freedom.

I came to intellectualise our relationship as a kind of co-op centred on Adam. In our case, the Adam Co-op consisted of just two adults, but I could imagine how the concept could be socially useful. Years later, I included the idea of children-centred co-ops in a novel – *Kip Fenn – Reflections* (Chapter ten). Here is how I wrote about it in the fiction.

'*Co-ops, in a recognisable form, began around 2010-2015 as an alternative model for raising children. The concept originated in the UK, but spread more rapidly in the Netherlands, Scandinavia and the US. Although no country yet recognises the legality of co-ops, both Finland and Norway are looking at the possibility of legislation. In the US, the Christian fundamentalist movement is too strong to allow for political recognition but co-op arrangements have, nevertheless, won important battles in the courts.*

The idea with a co-op is for a group of people, usually the mother and father (but not necessarily) and other relations/friends, to make a firm commitment to a child and his/her lifetime development and well-being. Thus, rather than a child being brought up in a family centred on the life and wants of the parents, he or she is brought up in a co-op entirely focused on his or her needs. Some sociologists believe the child co-op system is more suitable for a culture in which long marriages are now the exception rather than the norm, and in which individuals often choose to have children with different partners. Other experts believe the propagation of such ideas can only harm us by further undermining marriage, one of the cornerstones of Western society.'

The relationship between Bel and I hitherto had been a very caring one. Now, though, with a child between us, I had a much enhanced interest in Bel's wellbeing – but a more complicated one. I was of the clear opinion that Bel's role as a mother – certainly the biggest job she had ever undertaken (as was mine as Adam's father) – was likely to be more fulfilling for her, and much better for Adam in the long run, if she could find some direction in life, meaning a work path and interests beyond the immediate world of her baby. She felt this too, but less urgently than I.

Bel had left school at 18, and had worked as a library assistant in south London. Finding that work unsatisfying, she opted for a back-to-nature lifestyle, as a gardener with a sideline studying Zen Buddhism. I'd met her then, in the late 1970s, but by the mid-1980s, she was finding herself depressed without knowing exactly why, until that is she realised she wanted more out of her working life. And the only way to achieve this was to go to university. With a degree, and only with a degree, could she further her newly worked-out aim to become a Chartered Librarian. She had begun to investigate degree courses and how to acquire the entry requirements while I was in Brazil. But this had only prompted her to think more carefully about my proposition that we have a child together, and deciding eventually that it would be more practical to have a child first and study later.

As the first year of Adam's life unfurled, I was hoping that Bel would return to considering her future, not only in terms of studying but in terms of finding more suitable accommodation for a mother and child. She found a media studies course at Brighton Polytechnic (destined to become Brighton University) with librarianship modules. Such a move, to Brighton, would have consequences in that I'd be separate from Bel and Adam during weekdays, but, I felt, this could be compensated for so long as we were together all and every weekend, whether in Brighton, London or Aldeburgh. Because this would entail Bel a) moving, and b) making concrete progress towards her future, I was very much in favour of the plan. Although initially Bel could rent in Brighton, we planned to sell the Aldeburgh house to finance a home for the two of them (and me at weekends) in Brighton.

Adam's first birthday passed, and with it any hope that Bel would be moving that academic year. In October 1988, I signed up to a part-time Masters degree at University College in biological anthropology (Chapter three). This was despite my relatively newfound responsibilities as a father (being one of only two members of the Adam Co-op), and with a heavy workload at FTBI (Chapter two). One factor in my making the decision to enrol for the degree was that Adam would be eligible to attend the University College creche (for staff and students) conveniently located close to where I'd be attending lectures and tutorials. This would free up my one day as his carer, and a second day for Bel. On visiting, we loved the place. I wrote in my diary: 'The place is so nice. I warm up inside when I think of Adam going there.' Mostly, I think, I was relieved that Adam would be experiencing a new place, new people, and not stuck – as I saw it – in Bel's small studio every weekday.

With Adam at nursery half the week, Bel experienced some relief from the physical and mental burdens of being a new mother. This allowed her to give a little more attention to her future, and to study for whatever entry requirements she didn't yet have. She applied to Brighton Polytechnic, to start in September 1989, and was accepted. Apart from the librarianship component of the degree course, another major attraction of the polytechnic was that it also had a thriving, subsidised nursery for use by staff and students, on campus right next to where Bel would be studying. That summer – 1989 – Bel eventually found a house to rent in the Hanover area of Brighton. It seemed the Adam Co-op was back on track, looking forward to better times.

Moving Bel and Adam into the Brighton house came at a busy time for me. I was in Bulgaria for a week, for work (and taking the opportunity of meeting my uncle Mike's second wife, Claudia), and my brother Julian got married to a nurse called Sarah. I wrote in my diary: 'Although, in many ways I do really despise the need for such pomp and ceremony and would never choose it for myself (I remember not even showing up for my degree award ceremony) when someone as close as my brother asks me to be best man, it seems only right to carry the thing off with all seriousness. Indeed, I was proud to be Julian's best man, but anxious as hell about having to give a speech. The wedding had its moments – I mistakenly allowed one of the tiny bridesmaids to wander off down the aisle at a crucial moment, and a jar of flowers was knocked off its stand – but there was general agreement that all had gone very well. Also in my diary, I noted some interesting observations vis-a-vis my relationship with Bel.

One of Sarah's relations was talking to Bel as though she had won a prize for feminism, telling her how strong she must be to have a baby on her own, saying she wanted to get to know Bel better. Contrastingly, we heard another relation shout out, 'Do you always go home together?' It was a seedy remark and seemed to be the tip of an iceberg of thoughts about us. Nevertheless, Bel and I were quite a couple during the evening, we joked a lot, we laughed, we danced here there and everywhere, and Adam was on such good form too.

And then Bel and Adam were gone, gone from all my weekdays. I was a weekend dad. I wrote about this in a letter to my Australian friend

Harvey (in which also, incidentally, I summarise very succinctly the state of the relationship between Bel and I): 'Although I have pushed Bel into moving to Brighton to do this course, I am left sad and distressed. Until now (for Bel and Adam have just moved) I have spent much time with Adam. Two or three times in the week, he would be here. Now I will only see him at weekends, and he gives so much joy. I was nearly in tears saying goodbye to him yesterday. Strange powers. Bel and I continue much as ever. There were some fairly bad times during the first two years: Bel was often seriously depressed as a consequence of the responsibility of motherhood, but would not really admit it to herself. I am the last remedy for depression, expecting people to be able to pull up their own bootstraps, thus, although I did much on a practical level, I could not really provide the emotionally-supportive prop she needed so much. Given the strange nature of our relationship, though, I rarely lost control, and only once, for a few weeks, did I really think we had lost our marbles – and that is very frightening when there is a child at stake. [. . .] On many of the important aspects of bringing up a child, Bel and I see clearly in the same direction, which helps matters enormously.'

The Adam Co-op moved into a productive period. As a base pattern, we alternated our weekends together between Brighton and London/Aldeburgh. On the Brighton weekends, I was often to be found driving from Kilburn directly south in the middle of the night, so as to avoid traffic and to pick up one of the very few free all-day parking spots near Bel. I'd stumble into Bel's bed for a couple more hours sleep, before going to a market or the beach or the library. I'd drive back late on Sunday night. On the alternate weekends, Bel and Adam would travel at more reasonable hours by train. At first, we'd almost always head on up to Aldeburgh for the weekend, but within the year, we'd found a buyer for the tiny cottage in order to buy a property for Bel to own in Brighton. In fact, I gifted the Aldeburgh house to Bel who then could legitimately claim it as her main residence, and in this way we avoided paying capital gains tax when we sold it.

We'd only had the Aldeburgh house for three years, but it had served the Adam Co-op very well, and, in any case, my history with the place had begun years earlier. Now that the house was being sold, I became rather nostalgic.

9 May 1990
We did all the usual things; I bought rolls for breakfast (we took all our meals in the garden since the weather was so fine); we drove to Leiston to deposit Adam's cot at a charity shop, for food, to look in the junk shop and potter around (I bought a few potting trays for cuttings); we strolled around Aldeburgh High Street in the afternoon, commenting on any changes and the number of people and debating how early we could go to Craggs for tea. Bel actually went home

to sleep for a few hours in the afternoon, while Adam and I rested on the beach calm and quiet just like the sea water a few feet from our feet. Adam happily played with stones while I closed my eyes and encouraged sad feelings.

All weekend I was breaking into a sort of dirge: no more Aldeburgh, no more bread rolls, no more tea at Craggs, no more blue garden [I'd planted only blue-flowering plants in our small front garden], no more walks by the North Sea, no more trips to Leiston, no more Leiston Abbey, no more fish and chips, no more jumble sales, no more trips to Southwold, no more walks along the railway track, no more Snape Maltings, no more early morning swimming. I would just say whatever came to my head. In a way I was trying to exorcise the sad feelings that must surely come with this end. I don't think I have felt suffi-ciently sad, perhaps I have not fully comprehended that there will be no more weekends in the country.

On my long Sunday morning walk along the Sea Wall I did manage a tear or two for a few seconds [. . .] So much bird song. Frogs and snails on the path in my way. So beautiful walking solitarily along the wall sweeping round the bends of the estuary following its rhymes and reasons.

With the proceeds from the house, and additional funds I pro-vided, Bel bought a characterful three-storey terrace in North Laine (with a yard backing onto a Chinese dumpling parlour!). Bel and Adam moved in during that summer. I reported to my diary that Bel was 'thrilled' with the house. It was so convenient, easy access to buses for college, shops nearby, the station but two minutes walk. There was also a park with playground and paddling pool very close, and we were only 15 minutes from the beach. When I started to take the train more often, it was always a joy to stroll out of the station knowing how soon I'd be with both Bel and Adam. I bought a bicycle, and a little seat to fix on the back to carry Adam. While Bel was studying or working on assignments, Adam and I could explore freely and further afield, especially along the sea front towards the Marina one way and the farther reaches of Hove and Shoreham Harbour the other.

And so our Co-op life was set, and fairly stable for the next couple of years. With the Aldeburgh house gone, we took a few holidays to-gether in the West Country/Wales – and would continue to do so until the mid-1990s. These had a familiar pattern to them. In the first couple of days I'd get increasingly grumpy, feeling resentment towards Bel that I was the one always doing everything, planning every outing, doing all the driving in every sense. I wanted Bel to bring more, something, any-thing to the party, so to speak. Although I knew this was mostly unfair, since our relationship had long been moulded thus, I couldn't seem to change my behaviour. Usually, by the second or third day, I'd have vented sufficiently (for what I don't know) to re-establish a happy at-mosphere between the three of us, which would then last through the holiday, busy with adventures of one kind or another. These short, sharp periods of resentment – surface rumblings of the ongoing deep fissure between our ways of being, our hopes for the future, our mental preoccupations – emerged more readily, I suppose, when we were together for longer periods .

And now I must come to look again at my own morality, and I'm likely to find myself wanting. Although I consider myself a person with decent moral standards (which must have come from my mother, as there's little evidence of being taught any by my fathers), it would be true to say that I've been able to live my life in a fairly free way, avoiding moral dilemmas. I consider myself honest, fair, not generous in a giving-to-charity sense but in other ways, not caring for sick animals or distant peoples but for those around me. But when it came to relationships, I had been promiscuous. There were two reasons for this, I believe. It was a liberal time, pre-herpes, pre-AIDS, when people were far more relaxed and open about their relationships (and I was still shedding my hippy skin). And, secondly, as a young man I did not take relationships seriously, they were like a game to me. I never felt grown-up, and I never imagined my girlfriends did either. My relationship with Bel had started during this period of my life, and had persevered for several years. One time only, before Adam, did I feel I was bypassing my moral compass with Bel. This was in the mid-80s at a time when we'd become monogamous by default rather than design. But then, very close to my leaving to live in Brazil, I used a week of my holiday time to spend in Switzerland chasing an affair rather than to be with Bel – I got well paid, in karma terms, for this deception, as explained in my earlier memoir.

On returning from Brazil, evidently, my relationship with Bel had become a far more serious affair. While we might have been stretching social mores with our alternative parenting model, there was nothing immoral about it in my book, and, as I've explained, Bel and I were very close as a couple, often joyous and intimate when together as a family. But despite ten years friendship, in one form or another, we had never managed, as a couple, to make friends with other people, or to develop anything like a social life together. I could not accept this as a long-term fate – and this was clearly one part of why I never felt we could or should live together. I wanted more – always had done – I needed to be free to develop more interesting relationships of whatever kind. In the past, I'd always been careful – without being dishonest – to shield Bel from knowing about some other social parts of my life, and she had always – deliberately – remained uncurious. I imagined, I believe, that I could carry on (yes, 'carry on' very good!) in a similar way even with my new found responsibilities.

For a couple of years, I found my life so busy and satisfying, with Bel and Adam, work and travel, studying, and a fair network of friends that I had little time or energy to spend on looking for new relationships, however much I might have fantasised about them. And, in time, I came to realise how I was no longer the same person that could fall in and out of love on a daily or weekly basis; moreover my relationship with Bel had become primary, not to be devalued. Also, truth be told, I'd always been shy, cowardly of rejection, and my work/lifestyle no longer offered up the kind of easy opportunities for free love and sex, let's say, that had been so readily available in the alternative social scenes of my 20s. In fact I was about to embark on a ten-year period during which Bel and I were faithful to each other. But before that period began, I did chance into two relationships both of which challenged me, in a moral sense, more than any of my earlier behaviours towards Bel.

At the time Bel and Adam moved to Brighton, I had two lodgers – Carol was a dancer, working in the West End production of *The Phantom of the Opera*, and Rupert was a Danish architect – living in my Aldershot Road house. They were the best lodgers I ever had, in the sense that the three of us became great friends, and spent time together when we could. Carol and I were particularly flirtatious around the house, and then one day, well, she seduced me . . . I'll let my diary cover this.

> 20 October 1989
> Yes I did briefly mention above that I had been seduced by [Carol]. She swears she has never done any such thing before; which makes me wonder how much was really my own quiet suggestion and teasing that led her to take so many bold steps all in a line. The first was the note of some ten days previously [. . .] we settled down for a chat. I'm sure I must have had it mind to sleep with [Carol]; but in some perverse way I conversed and acted in such a way as to leave behind all responsibility. She wrote the note saying she fancied me; she asked for a hug as I was going to bed, a hug that led to kissing and more on the sofa; and then when I finally managed to pull myself away and go to bed (thinking of my heavy workload and a trip to see the *Magic Flute* on the morrow) it was [Carol] who after much hesitation tiptoed down the stairs and came into my room wanting another hug. Once in my bed there was little hope for me.
> Oh dear diary how many years is it since this man found himself describing an experience with a new sexual partner?

It was a disgraceful breach of trust with Bel, I'll admit now, as lust trumped morals. Bel and Adam were, obviously, regular visitors to the Aldershot House, and Carol was often there at the same time. She was very discreet, as was I, but in time she wanted more from me, and this led to arguments. One took place in the lounge while Bel was sleeping in our bedroom, and I recall my anxiety level skyrocketing as Carol's voice got louder. She moved out of the house soon after, and I regretted losing her friendship. I never found out if Bel had known or not. Certainly nothing in her behaviour towards me indicated that she had.

Otherwise, I was certainly not faithful in intention. I was always hopeful, whether trying out London's social clubs (to which I had a deep aversion, and trying them out only deepened that) or because of chance encounters when out and about. I even tried a Lonely Hearts advert one time (as I had when in my 20s). But here, from my diary of course, is the frankest synthesis. 'The truth is simple, my incorrigible soul needs new love, my maturing lust needs passion, but I do not have the necessary seductive skills [. . .] I have become so shy and retiring unable to take risks.'

One brief affair did come my way in Brussels. By then I was travelling frequently to the city, where I would stay a few days every month in a small flat I'd rented on a long-term basis. The liaison was with a journalist colleague, I'd known for years, I'll call her Lorraine, who also travelled backward and forwards to London, where she had a long-term boyfriend. As with Carol, I was not the prime mover. We were in a club and had been flirting for a while before she told me she'd fancied me for years. Before long, my diary notes, 'we started kissing; well snogging, actually, like teenagers'. We went back in the early hours to my apartment. My diary again: 'It is worth noting that [Lorraine] kept on saying how embarrassed she was to have been so forward with me. But when I asked if she gets propositioned all the time, she said yes all the time. But it's really not different for you than it is for a man like myself who finds 'making a pass' at women really difficult. [Lorraine] couldn't understand why I'd never made a pass at her in all these years. I just don't make passes, I told her.' Within weeks, [Lorraine] had returned to live in London permanently, and there was never a hint of us trying to maintain the relationship on home turf.

I did not judge myself morally wrong over this liaison (as I had done over the one with Carol), conducted as it was at a safe distance, geographically and metaphorically, from my life with Bel. As I've tried to explain, it was what I expected of myself and my life. But I mention it here and now only because it proved to be a last hoorah, the last fling of the adventurous traveller, the hippy lover, the curious and angst-full young man I'd once been. Ultimately, I'd shed all those skins in favour of a stable, safe life as part of the Adam Co-op. It would be ten years – five years after my friendship with Bel drifted away from intimacy – before I found myself in a new relationship again (long after Bel herself had formed a new and lasting relationship).

But before this, before Bel and I accepted our separate futures, we passed through two significant trials. The first of these was over

whether we should have a second child together – this was Bel's suggestion – and the other, a related issue, was over where we should live (we
both wanted to move out of London), and whether we should live together or in separate homes. Through 1993 and 1994, I would say, the
Adam Co-op was struggling to find the best way forward (the issue of
schools, for example, was looming), as were Bel and I struggling to get
some direction in our own relationship.

> 3 September 1993
> 'Have been trying to think very hard again about the future and I seem to be
> swinging towards the household model – setting up home with Bel and having
> another child. On the one hand, it frightens me terribly to have the future so
> predictable (at least with regard to the positive side of life – there are always
> unpredictable negatives) but on the other I cannot even perceive what else it is
> I want in terms of daily life and living.'

I'd always felt that our decision (Bel's and mine) to have a child
and bring him up together yet in separate homes was a compromise. I
would have preferred, as would Bel, to have brought up a child/children
as part of a traditional family. But, equally, I was convinced – from experience – that Bel and I could not live together well, and that having Adam
together in the way we did was a positive action, if not ideal. There was
enough love and joy and trust in our relationship to bring up a child well,
to give him/her all that they needed and more. Thus, given our personal
limitations and the mis-match in our personalities, the Adam Co-op was
the best we could do, relative to some imagined ideal. I'd always felt it
would not be wise or even possible to have a second child in the same
manner. For stability, and many practical considerations, two or more
children would need a single home with both parents. Nevertheless, as
can be understood from the diary entry above, I was considering
whether we could revert to a traditional model – but largely for negative,
not positive, reasons.

How this came about is not so easy to explain. Bel and Adam had
moved back to London, and were living with me in Aldershot Road. But
there was still space for a lodger, and I came up with a plan – that worked
quite well – of offering a reduced rent in exchange for Adam-caring duties, like transporting him to or from school, and occasionally caring for
him during the evenings. Adam, who'd started his school life in Brighton,
had been enrolled at a brand new school in Kilburn. Unfortunately, its
flashy modern design and equipment did not make up for inadequate
teaching and discipline arrangements, so we'd moved him to a Victorian-
era school in West Hampstead, which had a playground the size of a postage stamp. But there he thrived – while Bel and I worked out our futures.

At the end of 1992, after five years at FTBI, I'd left to launch my own newsletter publishing business (from the house in Aldershot Road – see Chapter four). Bel had completed her degree. She was now working towards gaining her Chartership, and had started employment part-time as a librarian for a large charitable organisation. But, we both wanted to leave London permanently, partly to give Adam a healthier environment and more of an outdoor life, and partly because – after spending so much time by the sea, in Aldeburgh and Brighton – we'd come to value the benefits of life away from the city. But where to go, and how to manage such a move, together or apart?

Having accepted the idea in principal that Bel and I could have a second child, could live together as a married couple, I needed to work out how best this should be managed. If we were to move to the country, a small town or village in Surrey perhaps, I reasoned, Bel would need to drive. It wouldn't be feasible, I felt or desirable, for me to be the only one able to drive to the shops, to schools, to friends, to sports etc. Bel professed some fear of driving but accepted my point, and promised to take lessons. I took her out sometimes, though I clearly wasn't very good at instructing her. Time passed, and still she didn't take the issue seriously enough to start lessons. I became increasingly anxious about this, and fractious too. I wrote in my diary: 'I have never directly told Bel that driving lessons are a condition of me going ahead with having a [second] baby but I have said over and over again that I do not see how she could manage logistically with a young boy and a baby living outside of an urban environment unless she could drive. I have said this over and over again. Today she said she would go ahead with driving lessons.'

Six months later, with a degree of nagging from me, there was still no sign of her taking lessons. I was, metaphorically, tearing my hair out. My diary again: 'Why, I ask her [. . .] do you so strenuously refuse to do something that I have said I think is so important. If what I was asking was truly stupid, truly selfish, surely even then as my partner of such long standing you would consider doing it to appease me. [. . .] . And it is not really a question of you disliking being bullied, I say in response to her only apparent argument, because I first asked you nearly a year ago to take up driving lessons. [. . .] In time, I became really rude, and hypercritical. Every now and then I would rant for five minutes and then go dark and quiet again for 24 hours. I wouldn't even look at her unless we had something specific to discuss.'

And then this.

Thursday 23 June 1994, Brussels
I bought Bel a small bunch of cornflowers after the first driving lesson, the first flowers I have bought her in ages, but she said she didn't approve of why I'd

bought them and that sparked a discussion which left me shouting again. Several times in the last two weeks she has said that she has decided to move out by the end of the year at the latest. And then a few days later in an argument she confessed that she had only begun the driving lessons because 'I was so distressed'. I said there was absolutely no reason to do the driving lessons if she was moving out, did she not understand that, as far as I am concerned, she only needs to learn to drive if we're going to have another child. She refuses to accept this connection and insists that my horrible behaviour over the last few weeks is just how I behave sometimes and connected to my need to dominate her. This is despite the fact that she has agreed on several occasions she had never seen me like that before, and that I myself was constantly telling her I was behaving badly (itself a first) and that it was entirely directed to the business of driving lessons.

Any how for me, that was the last straw. Even though she has started the driving lessons, her refusal to accept any responsibility at all for the chaos of the last few months is just not acceptable to me. The fact that she made the decision to move out and give up on any joint future at the same time as starting driving lessons is itself so obvious – but she will not reflect clearly, she will drive herself into hell rather than admit a mistake – it is a quite extraordinary phenomenon. I have now given up caring about any joint future and that means that I will be able to relax at home, and I have promised that the tension in the house will ease.

By August, then, we had a plan. Bel had been offered a librarian's job (within her charity) at a place near Guildford, so that provided us with a locus. I would buy a house nearby, one big enough to run my business, where Adam and I would live. Bel would move in with us, and then look to buy herself a house nearby. Once installed, as such, Bel would look after Adam whenever and as much as they both wanted, and certainly every other weekend, sometimes during the week, and always when I was in Brussels. As things panned out, Bel moved first to Surrey, where her new job was starting, and rented a cottage not far from Guildford. That summer – 1995 – I got very excited about a property near a village called Elstead (10 miles from Guildford, 5 miles from the nearest station for London). The central portion of a large mansion (converted into three attached houses) had a large amount of space, a vast garden, great views, stacks of character. The property had been repossessed, and there was some urgency to the sale. I got on well with the agent, Henry, and he gave me help with where to pitch my offer. However, he had so many potential buyers that he was obliged to set a deadline for final bids – a process I'd never come across. I was on edge for days trying to decide how high I should go, and then for more days waiting for the result. I lost out. Henry told me I'd come second, and that if the sale fell through he'd be in touch – he said he'd known these things to 'bomb down the line' so to speak. It didn't, and I mourned the house for a while, at least until I found El Rosco.

Thanks to this experience, Bel and I became interested in Elstead, especially as it had a junior school (run by a Miss Loveluck!). Henry got in touch to tell me about a four-bedroomed detached house with a large garden, some 50 metres from the school. The property was a bit run down, and we rejected it rather quickly. But Henry was an astute agent, as attentive to the need of potential buyers as he was to his own clients. A month or two went by, and he rang back, suggesting I have another look at El Rosco. I did, and this time I saw beneath the ugly and dated surface decoration to a house well-built of high quality materials (all the internal doors, for example, were covered in hardboard, but were made of a beautiful pitch pine, and one room still had its original quarry tile floor). Moreover, as no one else seemed to be interested in the property it was going for a relative song. Although there was plenty happening in my life at the time, it was good, very good, to be moving, finally, with a new chapter of my life, of our lives, starting. It took until mid-October for the sale to be completed – though it took another nine months for us to sell Bel's Brighton house (several sales had fallen through over the years) and my Aldershot Road house.

I had succumbed hook, line and sinker to the idea of living in the country, and Elstead proved an ideal location, yet I was far from psychologically adapted to a permanent life outside the city. Uppermost in my projections were a concrete anxiety about being cut off from every day friends, culture and society, but also there was a vague paranoia about being less anonymous. I had been dealing with the first of these for a year or more, I would say, and had come to an acceptance that I was no longer the person I was or, occasionally, still thought I might be. Since Adam had magically appeared in my life, and since I'd started my own business, my social-cultural life had stagnated. And a forensic examination of my recent comings and goings revealed that I could service whatever remnants there were of the busy social-cultural life I used to have with occasional trips into London (which was barely 30 minutes away by train). As to the paranoia that the Adam Co-op would be the focus of village curtain twitching, and that somehow my lifestyle might be constrained by worrying about neighbours and their mores, well, it was only time, really, that healed that self-absorbed agitation.

By Christmas 1995, we'd moved into El Rosco, though I'd had the house renamed as Russet House. I'd wanted to revert to a simple number address, but the Post Office had informed me this wasn't possible, so I'd had to choose a name that would give my business address a semblance of respectability. With red-brown hanging tiles, and brown-painted window frames, the house did look a russet colour. And to confirm the name's suitability, I planted a russet apple tree in the garden.

It took another couple of years for our lives to properly stabilise, though busy they were. In 1996, we sold the Brighton and Aldershot Road houses, but it was not before mid-1997 that Bel finally bought her own house, 150 metres or so from Russet House. Until then, Bel had her own room in Russet House, and the garage was full of her furniture. The Adam Co-op adapted to the new situation, with Bel, now driving (yes!) to work every day, and me working in the Russet House office with a young journalist, Theo, I'd employed to help me set up a second EU newsletter. Adam's school was so close he could walk there on his own in a minute, just a shame the schooling was so poor (see Chapter five).

By September 1997, I could explain to my diary that the Adam Co-op had – finally – reached a point of stability.

> 6 September 1997
>
> Bel and I had a summit the other evening and we have tentatively agreed to an Adam-sharing arrangement. Essentially he will be here at Russet House from Sunday morning through to Thursday morning, and at Bel's from after school on Thursday through to Sunday morning. The weekends, however, will remain highly flexible, so that Bel might have Ads more one weekend, like this weekend when I am on production, and less the following the weekend. And there should be no problem about swapping Saturdays and Sundays around. We have also tentatively agreed to eat all together on Sunday evenings. This seems like quite a good plan to me. I was worried about Ads moving backwards and forwards during the school week, and felt he needed some stability; but, I had to reconcile B's need to have half or nearly half of the week with him. Cubs on Friday is B's area, and Saturday she quite often takes him to the cinema. Also she only needs to organise leaving work early two days a week, and one of those days is a club day for Adam. It leaves me in charge for the bulk of the school week and on Wednesdays when we go swimming together. It also clears up some evenings for me to get out and about if I can ever get around to arranging any kind of social life.

By this point Bel – now she had her own house – was spending more time with her long-standing friend who had become more than a friend. Before very long, she was suggesting they might want to live together. Our own relationship had transformed – with barely any discussion or acknowledgement – in the opposite direction, to just very good friends. Here's a short 1998 extract from my diary: 'Adam asks me if I'm jealous. Yes, I'm jealous that she has such a close friend, but I do want the best for her.'

Indeed, I was happy for Bel, in that she was fulfilling herself, with a job she loved, a house of her own (the Brighton house, as with the Aldeburgh one, had been more shared ventures), and a safer, more satisfying relationship than she'd ever had with me. I'd always expected I'd be the one to move away first (after all, I'd tried several times over the years to make a clean break with her), but it was good, very good that Bel moved first. I cared for her too much for this not to be the case. And, as I've said, it would be five years or so before I found any hint of love again in my own life.

But, I was not willing or able to respond positively to Bel's ideas of her co-habiting. More specifically, I was concerned with the idea of Adam spending half of his time living with another man, having a very present step-father in effect. I wouldn't mind, I said if Adam stayed with her and him, for example, every other weekend. This would have been quite a reduction in her wishes and demands (that she have Adam live with her an equal amount of time as with me), and she was definitely not prepared to allow this. I think Bel understood my position, for she accepted it, without a fight or ongoing argument. I don't know if I was right or wrong on this, moral or immoral, to ask as much. Of course, I considered or tried to consider that I might be taking such a stance out of jealousy or some other negative emotion. The way I saw things was that Bel and I had brought Adam up so far in a warm, loving way, with much of the best that a family can give its children. We were still spending time together, the three of us, one evening meal a week, outings, etc. If Bel was living with another man, I would be a stranger in their home, not a family member. I felt strongly that I wanted to maintain the Adam Co-op with the familiarity between us, and a family state of sorts for the Adam Co-op.

As Adam grew older and more independent, he became less interested in spending time with either of us, let alone both of us. Bel and friend bought a large house not far away, and eventually moved in together. By this time, Adam was coming and going when and where he pleased.

Chapter two

THE OFFICE
SUCCESS, FRAUD, FAILURE

Being employed – I surmise now in retrospect – has never suited my personality much. I spent a year working for a pharmaceutical company in New Zealand before packing a rucksack and dusting down my hitchhiking thumb as it were. I spent another year, back in London, with a market research company attempting to forge an office career, but I wasn't able to conform, preferring to step down in favour of 'being a writer'. An existential crisis – a kind of breakdown – eventually led me to journalism, and successive jobs, four year's worth, writing about industry. I buckled down to learn the trade, but no sooner was I making a success of being an employee – at McGraw-Hill – than I broke out of the office environment, yet again, this time in favour of moving to Brazil, to be a freelancer. In London once again, a baby on the way, I had need of employment and financial stability. I found work quickly, at a division of the Financial Times – Financial Times Business Information (FTBI) – wholly concerned with subscription-only business newsletters, many of them covering the energy industries.

I don't believe I had any long-term plan, then, or career path in mind, I was just happy to have a job at FTBI, even if it was in an office. As it turned out, I would stay in that office for five whole years. This was partly because we editors at FTBI had a good deal of autonomy, with management taking a hands-off approach so long as their publications were bringing in profit. But there was another important reason: unexpectedly, I found myself thriving. I started with one failing newsletter and half an assistant. In time, I had three successful newsletters and four full time editors/assistants working for me – very happily I would say.

But, also, I moved on as a journalist/writer – in two very different ways. Firstly, I became more and more enthused about the European Economic Community (EEC) as it was then, and the importance of the policies it was promoting and undertaking. And, secondly, I turned my computer keyboard towards far more challenging writing projects – book length management reports, as would be published by another division of the FT.

During these years, my diary was much preoccupied with writing about my young son (Chapter one) but life as an employee did also provide plenty of fodder for the insatiable pages. As with most other chapters in this memoir, I have, in the writing of this one, relied heavily on entries from my diary. Curiously, though, it seems, at times, I am not only just recording my daily existence, but sometimes I am trying to direct it too.

On returning to London in early 1987, my immediate priority was to find work so that I could support myself, Bel and child. Fortunately, my free-lance activities in Brazil had led to good relationships with a number of editors, not least those working for FTBI. During my two years in Brazil, I'd widened my journalistic scope and had become proficient at finding and writing news on topics not only on the chemical industry (which had been the focus of my work for four years before Brazil), but on mining and metals, airports and aviation, science. Most of my income, though, came from reporting on the country's developing energy industry, oil and gas production, nuclear power, and coal. James Ball, who ran the *International Gas Report* (*IGR*) at FTBI, was one of my early clients. Indeed, on starting out in Rio, it was James who had given me one of my first leads – a potential Algeria-Brazil gas deal about which he knew very little.

This was June 1985, and as a newbie freelancer I was on a fast learning curve. 'I got on the trail', I wrote in my diary, 'and received a full blown account from Julian Chacel, an economist and director at the Getulio Vargas Foundation. I then talked to José Goldemberg, president of Companhia Energética de São Paulo, and wrote a good story for *IGR*.' I asked Paul Maidment at *The Economist* if he wanted the same story. But, when I told James that *The Economist* was thinking of using it too, he went livid. I'd thought he'd be publishing before *The Economist*, but I was wrong. So, I swallowed my pride, and telexed Maidment that I wouldn't be able to send the story until the following week. In the meantime, of course, the story changed dramatically – suddenly an offer by the state-owned Petrobras to supply Sao Paulo with gas more or less pre-empted the Algerian project, and negated my story entirely.

James, unfortunately, was on his way to an international gas conference in Munich with fresh copies of *IGR* under his arm, as it were, and a front page story about the Algerian deal. 'He may never talk to me again,' I speculated in the diary.

Meanwhile, I asked myself, was the story worth sending to Maidment after all? I hated the idea of yet another message to him apologising because circumstances had eclipsed the story. On the other hand, was it morally OK to send a news item I knew to be eclipsed. I reasoned that if there was a story yesterday, there must be a story today too, it was simply a question of writing it clearly. And the fact that Petrobras had agreed to supply Sao Paulo was significant in itself. My relationship with

James survived well, though, even if he tended to take up more of my time on the phone than it took me to write his stories.

Back in London, it would be James who brought me in to the FTBI offices to cover for him as editor when he was away, and this led to Gerard McCloskey employing me now and then to help on his *International Coal Report*, and other editors to do the same. Within a few months, I had been offered a full-time six month contract to edit *European Energy Report* (*EER*), a fortnightly title that had been languishing since its editor, Andy Holmes, had refocused all his considerable expertise on the UK electricity industry into the newly-launched *Power in Europe*.

Andy was a quiet-spoken Scot, a bit of a workaholic with a dry, understated sense of humour. With the Tory programme for privatising the electricity sector under way, his new newsletter would go on to become hugely successful, often featuring well-sourced leaks. Andy died tragically young in 1993 – not yet 40 – from a severe brain tumour. *The Independent's* obituary said he had 'dominated the debate over electricity privatisation in the United Kingdom' and that 'his was a uniquely clear and principled voice in a discussion too often marked by equivocation and muddle'.

Andy had been editing *EER* for some time, and it was only natural that his readers would soon transfer their allegiance to his new title. Thus, to some extent, *EER* was a poisoned chalice: it had lost its acknowledged industry expert editor some months earlier, and since then it had been cobbled together from rather raw material provided by correspondents. Moreover, there was considerable competition from other (and very successful) newsletters within FTBI's energy stable. Apart from *Power in Europe*, *International Gas Report* and *International Coal Report*, there was Chris Cragg's *Energy Economist* and David Tudball's *North Sea Letter*. Clearly *EER's* remit was too wide, too general, how could I give it some industry pizzazz when it promised news from across all the energy sectors, upstream and downstream, and from all over Europe? When I took over as editor, it had a subscription base of 600 or so at the time, and a net profit of £70,000, but both these figures were on the decline.

Here's a slightly edited extract from my diary that gives a good flavour of my work ethic.

> 2 November 1987
> A bit of fun over the BP share sale. As the production week of *EER* progressed unerringly towards the Thursday 5pm deadline, I received no news story worthy of the front page. So, I decided to put the BP story there – not that it was the best rather that it was the most topical. And very topical it turned out to be. The

£7.2bn sale of BP share – government stock and a BP share issue – opened just a few days after the stock market crash. Whereas the BP price had been above the 330p price it dropped back some 30%. Only 250,000 had bought shares by the Wednesday close date, a tiny fraction of those who had registered an interest. The underwriters of the sale looked set to suffer drastic losses and pressurised Nigel Lawson – our heroic Chancellor of the Exchequer – into cancelling the sale. By Wednesday it looked as though the pressure might be sufficient to cause dramatic action. Rowdy Labour MPs took every advantage of the situation in Parliament. Wednesday Lawson said he would make a statement to the Commons on Thursday. Good, I thought, I'll take my radio into work, catch the news, and weave it into the front page story. Unfortunately came the 5pm deadline, Lawson still had not spoken. Complex negotiations with the Bank of England were under way.

There's a regular fortnightly pattern for *EER*: the set of finalised 16-20 pages is collected from our Covent Garden offices at 5pm on Thursday, couriered to our printer in Wetherby, West Yorkshire, with printing midday on a Friday in time for the 4:30pm deadline for delivery to the post office. Thus, copies of the newsletter should be, at the latest, on every UK subscriber's desk first thing Monday morning. [Despite not being a daily newspaper or even a weekly, I strived for *EER* to include as much fresh – if not hot – news as possible.]

A chat with the printer Reg established I could, in fact, send copy on an early morning train Friday – 10:10 to be exact. This would mean I'd have to be at the office well before 8, and the copy would have to leave before 9. But I had a brainwave. I sent down a set of the final pages as usual on Thursday with the headline: *UK declines to cancel BP share sale*. If something radical changes, I reasoned, I could rewrite early on the Friday morning, and send a fresh set of proofs. I took a photocopy with me home, read it on the train, and over dinner (finding a single spelling mistake), and waited for news. Finally, at 10pm Lawson spoke. He said the sale would go ahead but that the Bank of England would buy back the shares at a minimum price of 70p. My story, as it stood, was not wrong, nothing in it could be seriously faulted, and so I felt I could avoid an early Friday morning rush.

But I slept fitfully, and decided to head into the office early, correct the spelling mistake, and add in the extra news that had been announced at 10pm. On arriving, first thing I did was order a motorcycle messenger for 8:45, plenty of time to get the Red Star for Wetherby 10:10 train. I rewrote the story – minus spelling mistake – and had the fresh set of proofs ready in the lobby with minutes to spare. The messenger didn't come until 9:45, and he missed the train! Fortunately, Reg, accommodating Reg, said he could still meet the post office deadline, he'd start printing the back pages, and wait for page one arriving later. Couldn't have done it, though, unless the body of the newsletter had gone down the night before. Saturday morning the issue arrived on my doormat – a beauty.'

On taking over *EER*, I quickly decided on two priorities. The first of these was to improve and extend the existing network of correspondents, not least into the East European countries to provide coverage from places barely considered by the other newsletters. This meant letting some stringers go, because their copy was too wishy-washy or infrequent, and hiring others. After two years of freelancing myself, I knew what I wanted, stringers who were accurate, reliable and efficient. I didn't have a huge budget to pay other than a fairly basic lineage, but good communication, I knew, was the best way to ensure a supply of regular quality copy. I would spend time, enjoyably so, chatting to most of my stringers at the start of the fortnightly cycle, small talk first and then energy talk.

Here's an entry from my diary, some six months into the job: 'I speak to my correspondents. I talk to Sharon in Lisbon about holidays, we almost flirt; I talk to Sara in Cologne about Adam; I natter to Jane in Madrid about illness; David in Rome promises me a handful of smaller stories this week; Michael in Paris prevaricates about anything that involves more than looking in newspapers.'

The second priority was to resuscitate a past feature of *EER*: Country Profiles, free to subscribers. These were 4-16 page supplements on coloured paper that featured summaries of a country's energy sectors (gas, oil, electricity, nuclear, renewables), with stats and charts of production, consumption, trade etc. I developed a schedule to publish new profiles every couple of months, one which could be employed to promote the newsletter, not only to subscribers considering whether to renew their subscription, but for the occasional marketing mail-out to subscribers of the other newsletters. There were additional benefits to the profile programme. It allowed me to travel to cities that I might not otherwise have visited (I still very much enjoyed travelling to new places and would always take extra days on the back of business trips) – Reykjavik, Sofia, Prague, Budapest, Belfast, Helsinki. It also allowed me to offer more substantial work to my better stringers.

The administrative structure of FTBI was sharply horizontal. There was one managing editor at the Covent Garden offices, Dennis, who was in charge of the editorial, marketing and subscription teams. There was also an office manager (Anna) and a receptionist. The editorial side consisted of two dozen or so editors (generally one per title) and a group of Editorial Production Assistants (EPAs). So long as their newsletters were bringing in healthy profits, the editors were largely left to their own devices, only occasionally being hauled into meetings to help guide the marketing direction. Certainly, I felt very much my own boss, and able to work when and how I wanted.

But all of us editors did need help, to type in copy from correspondents (email technology was still in the future), to make corrections, and to lay out the newsletters prior to deadlines. Thus, each editor was assigned an EPA for a set number of days per editorial cycle – some newsletters were weekly, some fortnightly, and some monthly. It was part of Anna's job to decide on who had which EPA and for how long;

and she was also responsible for hiring them on contracts or employing them on a temp basis whenever needed.

I soon found it rather inconvenient and inefficient to have my EPAs changing all the time, and so would often end up doing the newsletter production myself. There's more than a few rants in my diary about the EPA situation. So, on the basis of *EER's* country profiles requiring more EPA time, I lobbied to be assigned a permanent EPA. I was given Kenneth, a shy young man both intelligent and hard-working, who would be based in my office room – this was a significant boon for me, even if he did still spend some of his time working for other editors. I plotted to find ways to have him assigned to me full-time and permanently.

Here is an extract from my diary which finishes with the idea for a project that would come to completely change my working life.

> 20 November 1988
> My mind has been filling with projects at work. I feel it is time to do something new. But what I least need at present is more work. It has to be a project that will enhance *EER*, bring kudos, expand my mini empire at FTBI and satisfy anyone who might criticise my excessive coming and going [I had begun a two-year part-time MSc course at University College, involving me racing off to lectures several times on week days – see Chapter three.]
>
> If I actually sit down just to think of ideas it's amazing how many come. Two Friday afternoons have given rise to these: An energy atlas. This would be an 8 or 16 page booklet of maps that display basic energy stats. One might be borrowed from *Nuclear Engineering International* which pinpoints all the nuclear plants; another might show each country as a measure of the energy efficiency and yet another might use windmills to show the level of renewable use. I do rough costings on this, but worry about how much use it will be.
>
> A reader's research feature. This would be a questionnaire about current topics in the industry. Subscribers would be invited to answer the questions in return for which they would get a copy of the results. The results would either be written up in *EER* more briefly or at a date later than the respondents receive them.
>
> A chronological list of the major events in energy during 1988. I think I'll restrict this to one page and put it on the back page of the first *EER* in the New Year.
>
> A monthly supplement on the EEC. This is the most exciting. It would rely heavily on my correspondent in Brussels, but I could fill it out with graphics from the Eurostat statistics and profiles of member state relationships with the EEC. Each month a different country. This would be given away free with *EER* or sold separately for a £100 or so.'

By this time, and thanks to two stringers in Brussels, Lucy and Brooks, I was already covering news emerging from the European Community's institutions (now being called the EC). I felt these news items were of some importance to the energy industries, but none of the other

FTBI newsletters seemed to be taking much notice. Within a week or two, I'd put together a formal proposal. It was sweet in that I was offering to bring a new newsletter to market with very little cost and consequently very little risk. I attended a couple of meetings with management and marketing in which I stressed the importance of EPA time, specifically for me to be assigned Kenneth full-time. And in return, I said, I'd train him from being an EPA to become my assistant journalist.

The plan worked better and quicker than I'd hoped. Two months later, I wrote this in my diary.

> 3 February 1989
> Last week was hectic. We launched the new newsletter *EC Energy Monthly*. Kenny and I had much work to do, for not only were we expanding the volume of normal editing work from 20 pages to 28 pages but we had to completely design the new publication. [...]
>
> Of course, I undersold the venture, launched the newsletter so quietly that nobody noticed. I said it would be only 8 pages, and it was 12. I originally proposed a paper cover, but we ended up with a card cover. I called it a supplement to begin with, now it's a fully-fledged newly-launched publication. Feedback on Monday, the first day it appeared in the office, was zero. Not a single journalist came in and congratulated me. [...]
>
> The relationship with the Scots lad, Kenny, my EPA, is going well. His work is intelligent, and I feel I can trust him. Since the beginning of the New Year I have him full-time in my office. This is a great benefit, after all it was one of the main reasons for setting up the monthly.

I foresaw demand for EC news growing exponentially – after all, these were the heady days when the European Commission was headed by the effective and headstrong Jacques Delors. I was beginning to imagine myself becoming far more involved in the EC, writing an FT Management Report on EC energy policy, or in time discarding the role of editor and moving to Brussels to work as a stringer for all the FTBI publications. Increasingly, I left Kenny to put *EER* together while I travelled frequently to Brussels, collecting papers, meeting officials in the Directorates-General or DGs as they were known, attending European Parliament committee meetings and so on. There was always much to find out about. It was early days for discussions on a single market for energy across the Community, and for major policy initiatives designed to curb climate change. There were also high value research programmes to mine for information on energy grants, state aid actions likely to affect the declining coal industries, and long-standing cooperation initiatives on nuclear and oil to monitor.

By that autumn, the financial figures for *European Energy Report* were showing it to be in the top three of all the newsletters in the FTBI stable in terms of being over budget on turnover and over budget on net contribution. The subscription levels had shown a remarkable rise, with a 100 extra subs on top of the 70-80 subs we'd attracted just for the *EC Energy Monthly* supplement on its own. 'In high places,' I wrote in my diary, 'this must show that my judgement on investing in *EC Energy Monthly* was sound.'

My 2-4 day trips to Brussels had become rather routine by then. At first, I went by plane from Docklands airport, but later I was a monthly commuter on Eurostar, with blissfully empty carriages in the early days. I did write about my work in the diary, but rather haphazardly. Here's one entry from autumn 1989 in which I again mention some of my correspondents.

16 October 1989

It's good to have Kenny back in the office. Together we really do get through a lot of work when we need to. This week there's *EER* and *EC Energy Monthly*, and most of the latter I must write myself. Much of today spent on the telephone to correspondents. With Sara I discuss how she can best put together a story on West Germany's gas industry. [. . .] Ellen is in London from Rome for a conference on coal; she rings me from a phone box but we get cut off. [. . .] She has a husky voice and a rather American personality. I have no real desire to meet her; sometimes it is easier to maintain telephone relationships at a level which a personal encounter cannot match. [. . .] According to Gerard, just as many of Karen's ace stories from Norway are supposed to have originated in the energy minister's bed, so too Ellen's stories about Enel's coal purchases for McGraw-Hill are rumoured to have come through intimate relations with the buyer. [. . .] I talk to Mike in Paris. I tell him I've already got the Pechiney story covered but I check with him what his angle would have been. [. . .] Lucy in Brussels is bright and cheerful but can offer little in the way of stories. We agree that she will write something on the fact that the energy and environment paper has been pulled from Wednesday's Commission meeting. [. . .] I tell her that the disagreements over this paper are illustrative of the growing tension between the energy and environment DGs and she should play that up in her story. Peter rings from Holland. I have invested three long conversations on trying to get him on board as my Dutch stringer. He is something of an old timer and has worked for the *FT* at times. [. . .] Going back to newsletter writing is something of a come down, but he may need the money, and for an experienced hack we offer good returns; or he may seriously have been affected by my argument that energy and environment (which he writes a lot about) are inextricably linked. He may be somewhat like me in that it makes a great deal of difference to write for someone who values you – thus the investment of long wide-ranging conversations about everything under the sun. Indeed, I've promised to send him a Robertson Davies novel when and if I get his first story on my desk. So he rang, as promised, and offered me one.

Jane's sweet Scottish lilt positively makes her sound attractive. She has written for *EER* [on Spain] for over a year, and now she shatters me by saying she's leaving, going to South America. [. . .] I tell her I'm devastated. She has filed, just on time, her profile of Spain's policy vis-a-vis the EC. It is long and contains good material. I am happy she has not let me down on this. I know how hard she has had to fight to get the information.

I make a call to Nada. She has been trying to reach me in order to file stories for *EER* from Yugoslavia for months. Why I think to ring her this morning, I don't know, but finally we make a connection and she promises to file for the next issue. Lose one stringer, gain another.

Marko [who files Russia stories] calls just to say he doesn't see anything that's worth covering this week. I tell him I've sent the proposal to Management Reports for the East Europe energy profiles book and will contact him as soon as I have a response. Unusually, we don't talk about our children.'

Yes, that autumn, after making an arrangement with Marko to write an energy profile of the Soviet Union, I put forward a proposal to FT Management Reports (a separate part of FTBI) for a single volume containing energy profiles of all the East European countries. Most of these had already been published as supplements to *EER*, but, I'd thought, they could be refreshed, re-edited and combined into a single publication. As with the newsletters, the business model for FTBI Management Reports depended on direct mail (the company had excellent energy lists) and a high price – several hundred pounds per copy. I would get one flat fee for writing the report, and another for doing the production. If the report sold well, I'd also get royalties. The proposal was accepted, and added hugely to my workload the following spring. It came out in early summer, A4 spiral-bound, free of any bells and whistles, as *The New Energy Markets of the Soviet Union and East Europe* – and sold very well.

Around the same time, however, there was an earthquake of sorts in the office. On the back of the sales figures for *EER* and *ECE*, I'd moved into a bigger office so that Kenny and I could have extra EPA help – notably a lovely lady called Miriam. She helped our small operation run smoothly, especially when I was out of the office (at my MSc lectures or travelling to Brussels). But one day, out of the blue, Anna, the office manager, decided she should be sacked. Anna had been manoeuvring for a while by the time I found out, and Dennis, the manager, was on her side. I was outraged, and went on the offensive. The more I tried to uncover Anna's reasons, the more murky her actions seemed, and the more suspicious I became. The stated reasons for dismissing Miriam kept changing every time I successfully argued against the last one. Eventually, Anna fixed on something being wrong with Miriam's work visa (she was American), even though Miriam insisted this was not the case.

It was a horrible, horrible few weeks in which most of the staff seemed to be on Anna's side (she was friendly with everyone) and no one could understand why I was making such a fuss. I did uncover a few rumours about scams Anna had been responsible for – ghost EPAs, expenses forms with unknown items added – but other editors had never taken them very seriously. I was creating quite a hullabaloo around the office. Thanks to my nagging, Dennis, who was about to leave for a two week holiday, decided that nothing should proceed on this question while he was away unless Anna got full agreement from the editors concerned. Nevertheless, Anna saw Dennis's absence as a green light. She was now, effectively, the office boss, and was determined to bring about Miriam's sacking. Dennis did have an assistant, an ineffective one, but when I told him of Miriam's plans, he called me 'paranoid'. What could I do? Miriam was likely to be sacked and gone before Dennis returned.

What I did – and I've been stupidly proud of this simple action ever since – was to write (yet another) memo to Dennis, (even though he was away) setting out in crystal clear language my serious concerns about Anna's unjustifiable and improper actions. I also thanked him for his assurance that nothing should proceed while he was away without full agreement of the editors. Crucially, I copied this memo to Dennis's boss – the so-called 'publisher', John. He was part of the company's senior management but was rarely seen at our premises. Anna knew John better than I did, and was close to getting his approval – why would he doubt her? But, my memo, with Dennis's verbal instruction put into writing, into black and white, caused John to hesitate. He declined to give Anna the authority to press ahead before Dennis returned.

And when Dennis did return, Anna's empire began to crumble very quickly indeed. This was Annagate! I'd amassed more evidence against her by then, and somewhat reluctantly, Dennis launched an internal investigation. This, eventually, led to a police investigation which uncovered a long series of fraudulent actions against FTBI, much of it managed through the temp agency run by her husband: it was billing for temps never used, as well as for longer hours than had been worked. Eventually, they were both jailed, I believe, but I don't know for how long.

But, the question remained, why had Anna been so determined to get rid of my EPA, Miriam? Well, Miriam was in fact dating a young man who had, until recently, been the office boy, Anna's dogsbody. He had got wise to her scams, and, consequently, she had wanted rid of him – and sacked him. But then, someone in the office saw Miriam and the boy together in the street, and the news of their relationship spread through the office. Anna, thus, felt vulnerable to what Miriam might know. Anna had been so powerful around the office, she felt she could hire and fire EPAs with impunity – but not mine! I recorded a dream in my diary: 'Kenny arrives in the office at 8.30. I don't believe it and think the clock says 9.30. I walk along the corridor and pass by Anna who is leaving. I stare her straight in the eye. Not until she has passed me does she say 'You little shit.' I laugh sarcastically, and then add 'You started it.' I derived great satisfaction from this schoolyard exchange.'

There is much in the diary about all this, but here's just one (reduced) entry.

> 7 September 1990
> Ah! the office – what events have unfolded before my very eyes over the last few weeks. I am pleased that I bothered to record the details of my troubles in earlier journal entries. I know that there is ghastly indulgence to much of my diary writing, and I delve too much into the nitty-gritty details of my daily life. Whenever I come to peruse my journals at a later date, it is these interminable passages of explication about the peat of life which will most bore me. The fact that I did bother to explain in some detail the turmoil at my office does, however, illustrate its importance. Had there not been further developments, the episode may well have been left untold. The facts of the matter are that the administrator (did I – do I – give the characters that inhabit my working life names?), to whom I have spoken just once since this whole business began and that was to warn her against pursuing the matter against my assistant Miriam, has now gone forever. A memorandum from Dennis today relayed the news in the most pithy of manners. 'Anna has resigned. She no longer works for this company,' is all it said. This is a great battle won; a far bigger one than I imagined when I first went to war.

Meanwhile, *The New Energy Markets of the Soviet Union and East Europe* was doing very well. The BBC's *Money Programme* (among other press) interviewed me; the US Coal Exporters Association commissioned me to write a 1,500 word piece based on the report; and one of the speakers at a Soviet energy conference this week recognised my name and told me he had found the report very comforting! Most significantly, Dennis asked me to look into setting up an East Europe energy newsletter – which was very exciting because any request from management (i.e. not me doing the asking) implied I'd be able to 'discuss terms'.

I had pioneered a way of launching new newsletters with *EC Energy Monthly*, and told Dennis this would also be the best route for bringing a new East European energy report to market. In the blink of an eye, in but a couple of weeks, I had produced a supplement, largely full of the stories that would otherwise have been in the main body of *EER*. And this we gave free to *EER* subscribers every month, a gimmick maybe, but one that worked well to sell new subscriptions to *EER* and to keep the existing ones renewing.

That same autumn, I started to become life-restless again, and conceived the idea of persuading the FT group to re-locate me to Brussels, partly to be on the spot, as it were, for *EC Energy Monthly*, and partly to service other FTBI newsletters with European Community news. I memo-ed and met both Dennis and John a few times determined to pursue this goal, but they felt that such a move would create too strong a precedent, and they essentially vetoed the idea of a full-time staff member off-site and independent.

Nevertheless, that winter I found myself a small cheap flat in Brussels (next door to another journalist), at my own expense, and began to stay there three or four days every month prior to each *EC Energy Monthly* deadline. A Brussels address was essential for acquiring a European Community press pass, allowing access to all the institutions, press rooms, and libraries.

The following March, I was in a meeting on the future of the proposed East Europe energy supplement, with the marketing department, Dennis and, crucially, John. Here's my diary entry on the meeting.

17 March 1991

In the meeting, John did most of the talking; round and round he went tightening the essential idea that I should put together a PROPER launch document (slight laughter over the idea that he might be suggesting I hadn't done things in a proper fashion in the past – of course he wasn't), that he and Dennis had a very good chance of getting a launch for this project approved even though a freeze is on; and that I could aim at a net loss of perhaps up to £50,000 in the first year.

I maintained a rather stony silence through all this. [...] After the meeting, Judy [marketing manager] quizzed me on my coolness. I told her that I had two reservations: one was that I had no confidence in [the person named to do the marketing] and, secondly, that management could not expect me to develop another newsletter when they had rewarded me not one whit for my past achievements. She said I should talk to John directly; instead I told Dennis (in the corridor because others were in his room).

Half an hour later, he calls me back into his room. Firstly, he tells me I could have Louise from the marketing department. I am told she is considered one of the best. Secondly, about money, he says there are three things he can do: raise my salary but that won't be possible until October or the end of the year; give me a merit award, but there is no money at the moment, I am, however, at the top of the list; pay me editorial costs for running the East Europe newsletter when it is launched.

I respond that it is not good enough. [...] This sends Dennis, poor man, into a bit of a tither and he is about to promise me additional payment for the East Europe supplement instantaneously but before he finishes the sentence he begins to realise he might not be able to deliver on this.

But, I have a solution up my sleeve. I mention the £400 a month I am paying from my own pocket for the Brussels flat so that I can best serve the EC newsletter. Ah ha, Dennis says, well, there's no reason why you can't charge this to the company – put in a monthly claim with documentation, and I'll pass it. These were now good terms, I felt: the promise of an added payment for editing the supplement, a merit award eventually, a salary raise, and my Brussels expenses fully covered. In fact (of course) I, myself, was very keen to move towards a full launch of what became the *East European Energy Report*. It would mean extra resources both in terms of marketing and manpower. By the summer, we had brought in a young qualified journalist – John L. to be my assistant editor for the new newsletter which was launched that October. It now felt like I had a good four-strong team with Kenny, John L., Miriam (soon, in fact, to leave and be replaced by Henry) and myself. We were producing four newsletter issues a month (two monthlies, and one fortnightly) along with country profiles, and annual indexes too.

As if I wasn't busy enough, I offered to write a new volume for FT Management Reports on EC energy policy. Some months earlier, I had begun to write short editorials for *EC Energy Monthly*. Here is the first one I wrote.

'*THE TIME IS RIPE:* EC Energy Monthly *believes it is now time for the Member States to look very carefully at the possibility of giving energy a higher status within the Community and in so doing grant the Commission increased powers to formulate a cohesive approach to the future of Europe's energy industries.*

The benefits of an internal energy market have already been accepted by the European Council, but realising those benefits in one of the most strategic and sensitive areas is proving burdensomely difficult for DGXVII [the energy DG]. Moreover, increasingly, energy policy looks weak next to the competition and environment authorities of the Commission.

Therefore, rather than allowing national energy sector interests to wither under the battering of these environment and competition activities, it is time Member States gave more thought to transferring some of the key responsibilities to Brussels: it is time to consider how supply security can be tackled at the core, rather than in 12 distant centres.'

Writing such a book, I calculated, would have many advantages. It would give me, personally, a wider and richer understanding of the issues emanating from the European Community institutions, leaving me better able to analyse and comment on them. It would raise my profile in Brussels making interviews easier to come by. All of which could only benefit my *EC Energy Monthly* subscribers, and boost sales of the newsletter. The *East European Energy Report* (that was still selling like hot cakes) had not only given me confidence to attempt a more substantial writing project, but had also given the FT Management Reports team confidence in my ability to make a success of it. I was given the go ahead without any preamble, and I gave myself six months to complete a first draft. In fact, I delivered a 50,000 word manuscript before the end of the year. This would be published the following spring (1992) as *EC Energy Policy – A Critical Assessment*.

Over the coming months, I became increasingly involved in EC energy policy issues, and would often return from Brussels with scoops, usually on pending legal proposals from the European Commission for, among other big issues, the liberalisation of the electricity and gas markets, increased Community oil stocks, and the reduction of state aid for coal production. Such proposals – i.e. draft legislation aimed at requiring Member States to implement changes in their national laws – were generally-speaking the most important issues arising at the EC level, though policy papers (Communications in Brussels jargon), setting out future strategy, could also create a lot of heat. That was certainly the case with the 1991 document titled *Communication on a strategy for stabilising CO2 emissions by the year 2000*.

I wrote (in *EC Energy Monthly*) that this paper was important because it detailed how the Community could meet its international commitment for stabilisation and because such a comprehensive, believable strategy was essential if the European Community was to take the lead in international negotiations to ward off global warming. At the time, no details of how this could be done had been made public, but I had a copy of the not-yet-finalised paper, and it included a draft proposal to create a Community-wide energy tax. This was dynamite.

In the same issue of *EC Energy Monthly*, I also had three other scoops: preliminary information on likely proposals for third party access to electric and gas networks (these would go on to dominate the Brussels energy agenda for years to come); a leak from the cabinet of the Energy Commissioner Antonio Cardoso e Cunha (with whom I'd developed a good relationship) on the need for a strategic Community oil stock (similar to that in the US) to be funded by the proceeds of a new energy tax!; and the details of a Community proposal for a convention on global warming (leaked to me by Greenpeace)

A bumper package, and probably the most scoop-heavy, news-laden newsletter issue I ever put together. No surprise then that it generated some press of its own.

30 June 1991
For the first time in my life, I've been in the [daily] newspapers. The *Yorkshire Post* rang me in Brighton and ran a story on Monday based on the energy tax proposal – it quoted me quite extensively but did not state that the proposal had been leaked to *EC Energy Monthly*. On Tuesday, the *Scotsman* ran an even longer item combining both the energy tax and oil stocks story, it did mention *EC Energy Monthly* in the second para and quoted me extensively also. As usual, though, I was miffed that the *FT* newspaper [always very sniffy about its newsletter cousins] didn't take the opportunity to use the material. [A few days later *The Independent* also ran a lengthy story, annoyingly naming and quoting me rather than EC Energy Monthly.]

It took another three months before the European Commission had finalised its *Communication on a strategy to stabilise CO2 emissions by the year 2000*. Looking back more than 30 years, it's hard not to be impressed by both the Commission's foresightedness and ambition. Yet, these proposals never stood a chance thanks to the entrenched and very different energy policies of the Member States – here's an extract from my diary.

> 6 October 1991
> This final document looks and reads much better than the drafts floating around earlier in the year. It is more concise and less detailed (which means it can get into less trouble) except in the area of the tax, for this document has been designed around the need to get Council approval for an energy tax. The Commission justifies the need by saying that all other planned measures will only do half the job to be done by 2000. Yet, I do not believe that the proposed tax – $3/bbl in the first instance and then climbing $1/bbl each year to 2000 – will have the desired effect. Indeed my own view is that the EC will have great difficulty in stabilising its emissions by the end of the century. However, I do believe that all energy saving efforts and indeed the energy tax are justifiable. Energy should be priced at a level where consumers, either directly or through industry/manufacturing, are obliged to count its cost rather than taking it for granted.

As the year closed, I felt reasonably satisfied with my achievements at FTBI: securing finance to focus my journalistic work in Brussels, launching the *East European Energy Report*, writing *EC Energy Policy*, enlarging my team to four, all of us seemingly working hard, efficiently and enjoying our jobs. And I didn't do too shabbily on the financial front, earning close to £40,000 (some £90,000 in today's money). And, this didn't include six-monthly royalty payments for *The New Energy Markets of the Soviet Union and East Europe* which would eventually sum up to £22,000 (15% of the £150,000 turnover). Incidentally, I would, over the coming three years or so, earn more than £18,000 for the *EC Energy Policy* book (i.e. 15% of the £125,000 sales). The two books together grossed £275,000 between them, more than half a million in today's money – and thus are certainly, and by far, the most money I've ever brought in and earned from my writing.

I notice from a diary entry early on in the new year that I was still hankering after being 'a writer' but that the idea of running my own business was starting to appeal.

> 4 January 1992
> Work – I had thought the major choice here was between staying in journalism and leaving to become a full time writer; but I think I have convinced myself that the latter option is unrealistic for the moment. When I try hardest to

project into the future, the life of a writer seems to be rather one-dimensional and impecunious, especially if one remains a moderate writer and never makes it into television or plays; while the life of someone owning their own business seems likely to have more depth and scope for development over a lifetime.

The new year brought troubles for our boss, Dennis. He had made a series of poor management decisions, it seems, not least the whole fraud business with Anna. He'd also blundered badly over bringing in new computers and software, largely by totally underestimating how difficult, costly and time-consuming the process would be. I'd continually counselled him that a full-time computer organiser was needed, someone who could act as a pool of knowledge about the new computers, who could monitor all the equipment and software, act as trainer, trouble-shooter and give design advice when necessary. And when, finally he acknowledged the computer chaos, he heeded my advice but appointed someone 'wholly incapable' (as I reported to my diary). My team seemed to be the most computer literate, and we volunteered to test-drive, as it were, the new hard and software. Subsequently, thus, we were able to help smooth out the teething difficulties experienced by other editors and EPAs.

I was also proactive in the general affairs of FTBI in other ways. I had another newsletter launch proposal up my sleeve – called *The Green House*. These were early days in the development of climate change policies, but I felt there was growing demand for such a specialised publication. I wasn't at FTBI long enough to action this project.

And nor did another of my ideas fly. I'd long since felt frustrated that there was a poor relationship between the *FT* newspaper and the FT newsletters. And this came to a head for me in late 1991. One of the *FT* daily newspaper journalists had asked for my *EC Energy Monthly* scoop on the electricity/gas liberalisation proposals. I faxed him the pages, but he then published an almost identical story in the newspaper without reference to me or my newsletter. I was on friendly terms with the *FT* bureau chief in Brussels, and moaned to him about the situation. He told me directly, 'the page editors just don't like mentioning the FT newsletters'. So, I devised a memo on how we could go about strengthening the editorial relationship between the *FT* newspaper and newsletters. I saw synergies in abundance: much greater and wider exposure for the newsletters (which could surely have a major impact on their circulation figures) and a pool of industry and business expertise for the newspaper. I wrote the memo to Dennis, but I copied it not only to the publisher John (who was not directly involved in the *FT* newspaper) but to HIS boss Will (who was).

The ideas in the memo led nowhere, but it did lead to a first one-on-one meeting with John. We talked about a large range of issues affecting the newsletters division, not least the computer problems, and he asked me if I had any managerial aspirations. As far as I could see, there were no opportunities within FTBI, as the only position above mine was Dennis's, i.e. managing editor. I told John that I was already a managing editor (with responsibility for three newsletters) but without formal recognition. A few weeks later, I heard that Dennis had decided to take early retirement, and although I was not in the habit of listening to, or passing on, rumours (except during Annagate), I couldn't ignore one that suggested I was in line to replace him.

I WAS invited to interview to replace Dennis, and John hinted that I was a favoured candidate.

> 18 July 1992
> Overshadowing the week, has been my interview with John and Will, more so now that it is over than beforehand. I do not feel it went well at all and have thus been involuntarily conducting post-mortems in my head. Although I have thought quite a lot about the job of editor-in-chief, my ideas and ambitions for it, I did not think about bringing these ideas into the interview. Clearly, I did not prepare sufficiently, and I think this must have been because I was under the false impression that my record ought to be speak more obviously for me than anything I might say. I did not feel through the hour (about half of which was taken up answering Will's questions and half answering John's) that I was satisfying them with my answers. On several occasions, I realised that John was repeating a question in a different format because he must have felt I wasn't answering it adequately. [...]
> This morning the idea occurred to me to follow up the interview with a letter detailing some of the initiatives I would want to take. But do I want to fight so hard for this job? I cannot see any joy in working under John; neither can I see any joy in continuing to work in central London with a bunch of frustrated ageing editors. Surely, my best long-term option is to go it alone.'

The rumour-mill would have it that the job would go either to me or someone called Ivo Dawny, a political correspondent for the *FT* newspaper who wanted to get into management. Oddly, I'd met Dawny in Rio de Janeiro, in a lift on the way to a British Consulate cocktail party. In a brief few seconds, he'd managed to get my back up no end, I wrote in my diary, 'public school, self confident, and of the same ilk as Will'. It was all a wild goose chase for me. The appointment went to neither of us but to David, head of computer support at the FT. As far as we could tell, he had no publishing experience to speak of; Dennis even called him a lightweight.

I didn't blink, to be honest, as I was now hot to move on – by starting up my own company. I was in John's office explaining that I wanted to leave and take one or more of my newsletters with me. He asked if I had considered becoming a satellite operation. I knew that a couple of newsletter editors had already started up their own operation, retaining the FT name and its marketing/subscriptions help, but managing everything else, and taking a percentage of net profits rather than a salary. But I wanted all the responsibility, all the risk and all the net profits. I went on to explain how I thought that *EC Energy Monthly* would be worth very little to FTBI without me – after all I researched and wrote every word, and all the contacts were mine. *EER*, I went on, had always been a marginal newsletter, and it was only under my tight control that it had remained profitable. As for the *East European Energy Report*, I had to accept that we were unlikely to agree on a price. John asked for some numbers. I offered £25,000 for *EC Energy Monthly*, something over £100,000 for *EER*, and £50,000 for *East European Energy Report*. I also hinted, heavily, that I would be resigning any way, and would soon not be available to edit my newsletters for FTBI.

I had miscalculated badly; been too much of an optimist (where usually I'm a total realist). John called me to his office on a Monday morning. FTBI is not seeking to sell the newsletters, he said, but everything does have its price. That price is £250,000 for *EC Energy Monthly* and £500,000 for *European Energy Report*.

> 28 September 1992
> After this interview, I was quite in shock, I really couldn't believe [FTBI – actually it was now Financial Times Business Enterprises, FTBE)] would put such a high price on *EC Energy Monthly*. It had only made a net contribution (which is significantly more than net profit) of £40,000 in 1991 and the normal procedure for pricing a newsletter is to look at five years net contribution. But the real shock comes from the company completely failing to take into account the value of me as an editor of these newsletters and pricing them as though I were completely and utterly and instantly replaceable.

> 30 September 1992
> My mind is full of all sorts of possibilities for the future but can I really make the decision to resign when I have such a good post, bringing in, regularly, a high income. [. . .]. I ask myself, why stay at the FT? what for? The only true answer is for the regular income and security that it brings. Well, I've had it for five years and I've got £60,000 in savings, it's time to take some more risks. That's it. Time for a change.'

In my carefully composed resignation letter to John I made a last ditch effort to persuade him to reduce the asking price for *EC Energy Monthly*. Firstly, I emphasised how shocked I'd been at the asking price given that it implied a valuation out of kilter with the title's profits – even with me running it. And, I reminded him that I had devised, designed and launched the title without any management or marketing input, and that

I had written more or less every word of every one of its 45 issues. Furthermore, I argued that it was not a title that fitted well within the energy cluster of FTBI newsletters, partly because of its style, approach and content, and partly because of its need for a journalist to be in Brussels regularly. And I concluded with this rather naive appeal: 'I do honestly (and I have worked honestly and loyally for FTBI for these five years) believe *EC Energy Monthly* will become an immediate liability to the energy cluster without me. [. . .] In the light of my resignation, I would ask you to again look carefully at *EC Energy Monthly* – what type of material is in it, where that material comes from etc. – and reconsider your decision to sell it.'

In early October, I took Kenny, John L. And Henry each for lunch individually, to tell them of my decision to leave, and to discuss their futures. Kenny, I believed, would be made editor of *EER*, and John L, the same for the *East European Energy Report*. Henry, though, I knew, couldn't take over *EC Energy Monthly*, he was still far more EPA than journalist, and needed training yet. With my resignation now a confirmed fact, I continued to hope John would see the sense of off-loading *EC Energy Monthly*.

But that was not to be, and, in my last working weeks, I felt somewhat resentful towards the company. I got into a silly wrangle over my actual leaving date (reduced from three months hence because I was owed holidays), and announced to management that I would not research or edit any material for the December issue of *EC Energy Monthly* (because it fell after my formal leaving date). On the day that I put the November issue of *EC Energy Monthly* to bed, newly-appointed David – all fresh-faced and keen – called me to his office. He said that, legally, the company could oblige me to work instead of taking holiday. So, I was obliged to explain that such strong-arm tactics wouldn't make any difference. I was tired, I said, and I did not intend to go to Brussels for the December issue. So then – and this was rather unexpected – David said he had no choice but to ask me to leave straight away, immediately, that day. He didn't have me frog-marched from the premises (though he was thinking of it) because I argued that I had personal effects to collect, as well as books and papers connected with my (freelance) Management Reports. Having packed my bag as full as I could, I left quickly with barely a word to anyone. It felt like I'd been sacked.

> 9 November 1992
> How high I've flown this year, and how low I've now sunk. Where at one point I thought I might be editor-in-chief of the largest newsletter operation in Europe, and at another that I might buy one or two newsletters and start a significant business, I am now leaving on the worst of terms with the FT, without

even a leaving party, and with nothing in my hands at all – not even my Mac computer in Brussels, which I have to give back.

An ignominious end for the maverick! How could it be otherwise I wonder. In some ways it is such a fitting end, a story book finale, with the successful applicant for the top job dismissing his rival contender within days of taking up his new post.

That was a mistake, leaving so quickly. David had the presence of mind – possibly spurred by Kenny whose loyalty to me had suddenly flipped and become loyalty to FTBI – to check the final page proofs of the November issue sitting in reception waiting for the courier. In fact, I had written a prominent goodbye note to my readers. David ordered Kenny to remove the note and redo the page. If I'd hung on an hour or two, I could have overseen the page proofs leaving for Wetherby. It was only a small thing, in retrospect, but it felt like an emotional sundering of the relationship with my subscribers.

I tried to improve my mood by making a list of what I needed to do in the coming weeks – I had four more of them than I'd expected to have. But, while I was still legally employed – until 1 January – it would be wise do nothing at all by way of formally starting up a competitor to *EC Energy Monthly*. This didn't stop me buying equipment, a new Apple computer, an extra large screen (almost essential for desktop publishing – as it was then called), and other peripherals. A couple of weeks later, half a dozen of the editors, and Dennis, joined me in pub close to the office for leaving drinks, but it was an insipid affair – my FTBI life was well and truly over.

Chapter three

EVOLUTION
IN THRALL TO NATURAL SCIENCE

19 January 1981
Mankind cannot bear too much reality.' [A misquote from T. S. Eliot's Burnt Nor-
ton.] There was a review in the Observer *of a new book called* The Evolution of
Human Consciousness. *It is written by a clever experimental psychologist. I be-*
lieve it comes to the same conclusions as I do. I must see it. The reviewer quotes:
'Total involvement to the exclusion of introspective self-evaluation is the modern
psychologist's recipe for happiness.' And he adds it is amusing to note that this is
a Victorian prescription. Isn't this what I've been saying [to myself] for years. Self
awareness is like a drug, alcohol or opium. It is an addiction and as such endan-
gers mental health. I am a living proof to that theory. This last year and indeed
during other periods of my life I've suffered from an unusual degree of self-aware-
ness. Pain is accepted as abnormal and we do something about it, but about men-
tal turmoil we know nothing. I have adapted to a certain amount of mental tur-
moil, pain, in the same way that people adapt to chronic physical pain. The evo-
lution of human consciousness and all its implications I find utterly compelling.

So began my return, if you like, to an interest or involvement with
science, one that I'd done away with on leaving university. I had spent all
my 20s acquainting myself with the arts, literature, drama, music, self-de-
velopment, cultural worlds which seemed to be full of fun, colour, magic.
And yet, suddenly, I was excited, super-excited by an area of science I'd
barely thought about, having only studied the physical sciences. It can be
no coincidence that this shift in direction of my intellectual curiosity came
soon after my 'existential breakdown' and the discovery in myself of a new-
found determination to do something real – not alternative – with my life.
That year, among many other books, I read Alvin Toffler's Third Wave,
Douglas Hofstader's astonishing Godel Escher Bach *and* The Red Lamp of
Incest *by Robin Fox. But it was* The Evolution of Human Consciousness,
by John H. Crook that was to get inside me most. In October, I quoted from
it in my diary: 'Marx or Maharishi, public or private perfectionisms; neither
can yield an answer, for the psychological naivete of the former is only
matched by the sociological simplicity of the latter.' Science was back in
my life, and became the main line of my curiosity about the world around
me – so much so, in fact, that within 10 years I would undertake an MSc in
biological anthropology. And, a few years after that I would find myself
drawn back to religion, thanks to another scientist, less well known, David

Sloan Wilson – not to spiritual matters, but to an understanding of how religion could have been a mainspring for human cultural evolution.

John H. Crook was an ethologist at Bristol University, and his book was groundbreaking, as much for its scientific content as for its reach into non-scientific areas of trendy personal development. The opening words in his preface had been written directly to me: 'Evolution and enlightenment: is there a connection? What are the biological roots of the higher forms of human consciousness and cognitive ability?' Three quarters of the book followed the conventional style of science publications, but the last quarter veered off at a tangent with chapters on 'Meditation' and 'The Quest for Meaning', concluding with an appeal for Western society to take more instruction from disciplines beyond the realms of science, such as Zen Buddhism. It was fascinating, and I was particularly caught by a paragraph near the end of the book in which Crook wrote: 'My personal concern has been to develop a Western Zen retreat suited to urban Europeans.'

Increasingly, I was using my diary to gauge the state of my own psyche, my own existence alongside the scientific ideas I was reading about. Here's a typical example.

> 29 August 1981
> Do you see all these different levels of consciousness – realising aspects of the universe, the philosophy of this world, the aims of a single life, the daily routine of buying bread? They are all so difficult to correlate, to superimpose, to bear witness to. And the orgasm – that wretched drug – is a complete betrayal of all that is outside of a man. All those levels are diminished to pure irrelevance and the entire soul/body/mind system of a person is concentrated into a pinpoint of sensation that is of complete and utter importance in place and time. So how can man be expected to wake then from his pleasure and cope with a world full of proofs that he is not at its centre, not a king.

The thought of the Western Zen retreat stayed with me for a year or two, until eventually I got round to writing to Crook, care of Bristol University, asking for more information. On 26 December 1983, I wrote this in my diary: 'Dr Crook rang me at work to check if I was really coming to his Western Zen Retreat in the Welsh hills. I told him yes, and then a few days later I received the info on how to get there and what to take – my favourite meditation gown for example. Yelp. What am I doing this for?' It proved to be an experience, though not the one I was looking for. I'll let the diary trace my route to enlightenment.

> 10pm Friday
> This is the first chance I've had to write down something – anything. Although we don't talk it's quite claustrophobic, and I feel I would be doing something

unworthy of a retreat if someone saw me. In the lightless, warmless attic of John Crook's Maenllwyd retreat I write by torchlight whilst others take tea before going to bed. After one day frankly I'm bored. Out of 18 attendees, there are only two or three who are not retreat freaks. And the sad truth is that Crook himself is a Buddhist freak. I have just attended what can only be described as a church service – we prayed for all those that suffer in the world! The rest of the day has been split up between walks over the hills (alone) and meditating. We do not talk except to help in some task or other. This evening, though not during the day, for I've kept a very open mind, I have wanted to leave. I feel an unwilling victim of religiousness. More about Zazen, Kundalini and the black sheep fight tomorrow.

6pm Saturday
Ah, we've progressed to Koans. 'Who am I?'. Now there's a dumb question to ask me. I love talking to myself – I mean about myself. Communication sessions they're called. We team up in pairs and for five minutes at a time, we listen to each other. My answers are glib. [. . .] Had my little talk with guru Crook who told me to concentrate on spaciousness and not worry too much about the Buddhism. I'm being a good boy, but the meditations seem increasingly purposeless for me. [. . .] There's a guy who's higher in the hierarchy to enlightenment because his koan is 'What is my true nature?' He talked about not expecting the flash of enlightenment, just waiting patiently till it comes.

Lunchtime Sunday
The CX sessions have taken over. There are a million and one ways of defining who I am, but old Crook will say it is not a definition we want but an experience. In those counselling sessions, I find myself trying to tailor my answers to the person who sits before me. Mike is the ostentatious buddha, the one who asks for more meditation instead of rest. With him I found myself talking in metaphors because I thought he'd like them. Then after Mike I had the orange one, who talked about love.

6pm Sunday
Now my head begins to ache. I feel very weary and next is Bhagwan's dynamic meditation. That's much more exertion again. The spontaneous ah-ha experiences, as Crook puts them, have begun, but as I expected they are between confirmed ah-ha experiencers. It's so similar to the conversion experience. The teacher/mentor/missionary inspires complete confidence that something will happen which paves the way for it to happen. And the mantra – om – it never struck me before how similar the chanted 'om' is to the sung 'amen' in Christian prayers. I've begun to see contradictions in Crook's [ideas as] to where we should be heading in our communication exercises. Until now it has been important to concentrate wholly on the koans – who am I?

2pm Monday
The end is in sight. Yesterday was a miserable day. The clouds came over and brought snow and darkness and my head tensed in response. Today, it is lighter and airier. Yesterday went on forever and the question 'Who am I?' rang religiously through my bloodstream. Today I am easier and I can no longer answer the question. This morning I had a second interview with Crook. He asked me who I was. God/buddha! Does nobody in this world have any other question. I told him it was a secret. This was an ah-ha experience I

had this morning during the Tibetan humming. [. . .] Then he asked me if I really knew who I was. I said yes.

4pm Monday
What is quite clear from these five days is that I know distinctly who I am, and did so with clarity before I came. Here, however, I've looked at the question from dozens of different angles, and lost sight of the clarity – endless metaphors come to mind from the countryside – rivers I can't cross, streams I can't find the source of, footprints in the snow – oh do go on. The last evening and I've sat out of the action yoga. Thank god for that – all that pumping of the lungs. And Ralph has sat out too – we have made friends and sit like small boys, playing truant, whispering in the dormitory.

Wednesday 11 January
The metamorphosis from Paul the monk to Paul the chemicals reporter has not been difficult. Leaving Maenllwyd I was quite stoned with a deep directional consciousness rather than a braced superficial one needed for doing. But after a while it wore off. I have not found myself resisting the temptation to tell colleagues/friends the details. In one sense it is amusing. Now, here in the office, I don't feel anything strong from the week. I say to people it was worth doing, it was different and Crook was a lovely man. I know that it is easy to dress oneself in a cloak of saintliness, but it is much less easy to retain mastery and to make oneself vulnerable as well. He kept remarkable control and direction through the five days, never for a moment appearing to be anywhere but with the group. Crook came through with a heavily religious message in the end, [. . .] It is obvious that the religious aspect of Buddhism keeps him going – the will to make the world a better place, to at least use one's power and influence in that direction.
    Black sheep. I saw two black sheep having a fight. Facing each other head on they took a couple of steps back and then a couple of steps forward, paused and then locked heads for a few seconds. They repeated this ritual several times. I never knew sheep to be so intelligent. Who am I? A sheep trying not to be a sheep.

All of which is to emphasise how disappointed I was in the retreat, in Crook. I had thought – naively perhaps – that after a bit of Zen teaching, I'd get to sit around a log fire with Crook and others, night after night, debating all kinds of issues connected with human consciousness. I'd already done with religion long since (*Why Ever* – Chapter six), and had no need of a refresher course. If I'd had any lingering, sub-conscious, hankering after alternative secrets to life, then this was the moment I let them all go, and focused instead on the rational, the scientific reasons for my own and for human aliveness.

Fanning my interest was Stephen Jay Gould, a genius at ferreting out examples from the history of the natural sciences to illustrate and develop modern themes on evolution. He was also, for me, on the right side of a die-hard debate with the likes of Richard Dawkins over evolutionary mechanisms. Gould advocated that evolution played out over multiple levels, not only genes but individuals, and even groups. Dawkins insisted that natural selection was best understood as competition among genes, and that selection at the level of groups (group selection) was effectively irrelevant. I read several of Dawkins' books, and was always left utterly unconvinced by his 'selfish gene' model, as well as bemused by the popularity of his ideas.

The mid-1980s saw me settled in Rio de Janeiro, freelance journalist at large. In the early months, alongside my reasonably successful efforts to write and sell a wide range of business stories (*Why Ever* – Chapter fourteen), I was also determined to turn myself into a science writer. I'd noticed how the daily newspapers often ran stories about the country's science and R&D achievements, exuding a national pride, of a kind that I'd never experienced in British papers about British science. I established links with *The Economist's* science editor, Matt Ridley, the BBC's *Farming World* Programme, and the *New Scientist's* American editor Christopher Joyce, all of whom encouraged me to file. One early success came with an article about nitrogen fixation in sugar cane. I sold a half hour interview to *Farming World* (the only radio journalism I've done), and an article to *The Economist*. Matt Ridley was so encouraging, telling me it was just the kind of story he wanted, and suggesting that I must have 'a flare for that sort of writing'.

The New Scientist thought differently. However hard I tried – and I did work hard to find the right kind stories and to write them in the right way – I couldn't land a single line. This was very disappointing, and galling considering I'd been partly guided by Christopher Joyce, the US editor, who had become a friend and stayed in my Rio apartment a couple of times. As it turned out the *New Scientist* had not only been my main but my only chance to transform myself into a science rather than a business journalist – I never sold another radio piece to the BBC, and I felt fortunate if I sold one science piece to the *Economist* each quarter. On returning to London, having accumulated too little in the way of experience, my strenuous efforts to find a job in science journalism came to naught (Chapter two).

Nevertheless, my interest in the sciences, as opposed to the arts, which had been whetted not dulled in Brazil, needed satisfying. I'd taken night classes in various subjects during my 20s, but my motives had been largely social – meeting people, or personal development. I'd certainly never considered any return to university or the idea of studying something intellectually serious. But I was in my mid-30s by now, and much of my life was on an even keel. I soon settled down as an editor at Financial Times Newsletters, and one-year old Adam, Bel and I – a part-time family – were spending every second weekend at our little cottage in

Aldeburgh. I no longer felt in need of widening my social world or of personal development but, rather, I had a deep yearning to understand more about human life, evolution and the workings of the human brain. It was as though the interest I had when younger in the workings of my own psyche had developed into a broader curiosity about man. I continued to read widely around the subject of evolution, trying to slake my thirst, but this only left me wanting more knowledge, more understanding, yet without any obvious route to acquire it.

During the summer of 1988, my Bulgarian cousin Martin (then Goldsmith, now Zaimov) was living with me in Aldershot Road, and it was he that suggested I do a Masters degree. I thought the idea completely unfeasible, for all sorts of reasons. I was not prepared to leave work to study full-time, and there was no chance of there being any part-time courses I actually wanted to do; moreover, any formal course in evolution would surely require a background in biology studies, of which I had none. Nevertheless, I went to the library to look at prospectuses, and discovered that University College (geographically en route, more or less, between my house and the FT offices) offered a fantastic-sounding Masters in a discipline called Biological Anthropology. It was a bingo moment. I'd never known such a subject – defined basically as the study of the evolution and ecology of humans and other primates – even existed. A closer inspection of the prospectus promised a course that ticked every box for me, yet this immediate excitement was soon dampened by glancing at the course requirements which did indeed include biology A-Level. Days later, a visit to University College confirmed that my lack of biology might be a hindrance. Nevertheless, I filled out an application form, and was invited to an interview.

13 October 1988
My heart flutters for I must go to an interview at University College on Monday concerning my biological anthropology degree. I am afraid – because I cannot fully comprehend the amount of work I will have to do. The course will last two years and take up more or less all my spare time and more. But yet it has no real relevance to my future. It is one of my dreams. I seem to be a master at fulfilling my dreams. I can identify several: Going round the world; Working in the theatre (especially with the Phantom Captain); Becoming a journalist; Working in Brazil; Having a cottage in the country. And now: Studying evolution.

22 October 1988
I went for an interview with the tutors on Monday and was very nervous about it. I suppose I feared some quizzing of my knowledge, instead they were only interested in my motivation. By the end of 20 minutes they were positively assuring me I would have no problem with the course content, rather my problems would be time. Indeed time looks as though it will be a major hurdle (one that I shall have to leap over every day, press days on my newsletter included).

I shall be forever running back and forth between Gower St. and Southampton St. more than once on some days.

The time requirement aside, I came away from the interview with unexpected doubts: a couple of topics on the prospectus had been dropped ('it transpires that the prospectus is a load of hogwash', I wrote in the diary) and the tutors I'd met seemed to 'lack enthusiasm'. One of them, Robin Dunbar, I already knew as the author of *Primate Social Systems*, a book I had been struggling through in readiness for the interview, though I hadn't known he worked at University College. As I weighed up the pros and cons of making such a commitment, I discovered that University College – miraculously – had a creche for the infants of students and staff. It could, I thought, be perfect for Adam. On visiting, Bel and I both liked the ambience, much preferring it to the idea of a nanny or childminder, which we had been considering. Adam, too, loved it, and most importantly there was space for him to attend two full days a week.

Thereafter, for the best part of two years, I juggled a full-time job and a part-time Masters, relying heavily on my assistant editors at the FT to cover my absences (though I worked early or late hours to make up the time). It's worth noting that this crazy whizzing around was only possible because I rode a bicycle, meaning it was only a matter of minutes to get from being in my office to being present for a lecture, and vice versa. During the first of the two years, I was also often transporting Adam by bike to and from the creche. By the start of the second academic year Adam and Bel had moved to Brighton, relieving my weekday schedule a little.

Mostly, I found the taught modules – in human genetics, demography, palaeo-anthropology, human ecology – fascinating. Without a background of studying human biology, the genetics was most challenging but also most useful, though it was the module on demography that was surprisingly the most interesting, fascinating in fact, uncovering the historical sources for demographic information and how they lead to explanations for variations in population growth over time. For every module I took there were essays to be written, requiring a style of academic rigorousness very different from the journalistic writing I'd become used to churning out day after day. On the other hand, it's possible, my academic essays benefited from the lightness of a hack's need to communicate well.

And then there were exams in every subject too. I would have paid good money to avoid these. I had no desire, no wish to spend many hours 'revising' or 'cramming' information to prove that I'd stored it in my memory, nor did I relish the idea of spending several hours for each exam having to handwrite. By this point in time, I was only using a pen when on holiday, writing in journals. My handwriting had always been poor (especially when scrawling under time pressure). It wasn't just a matter of my script's physical appearance, though, but of the mental process – in typing I wrote more fluidly, more accurately, than when handwriting. The exams were a trial to be undergone in my quest for a deeper learning, understanding of science, and undergo them I did. Dismay at my own performance is well documented in this diary entry.

29 May 1989

The first exam, last Monday (from 10 to 1), was on human evolution and primate social behaviour. The amount of material we had studied during the year for this exam far exceeded that for the others. The human evolution course especially seemed to cover two or three times as much material as any of the other courses. I was so nervous beforehand but taking Adam into the nursery at least meant I was occupied. I met up with Nilofer [another MSc student] in our study room before walking over to the examination hall, we were both as nervous as hell. My hands were sweating, so that once in my seat and given the signal to start I couldn't write a thing for minutes.

I must say, this was not a pleasant experience. Having identified the position of my desk from the noticeboard outside the hall, I snaked my way through others already in place. Sitting down at the desk, I realise that the paper is already visible, I dare not look at it. I avert my eyes. Only when we are told to start do I glance at it. Yes, there is the 'Out of Africa' question (which I had expected), but I am disturbed by the lack of any other question in that section that I feel ready to answer clearly – my revision has not directed me to any one in particular. In the other section I see a question on the reasons why primates live in groups and another on monogamy, so I know I am reasonably safe there.

I look around at the hundred or so other students, they are mostly sitting a psychology exam. They all seem to be writing away, and the handwriting of those nearby seems so legible. Oh Dear. I must start, and I do so with the 'Out of Africa' essay. I spend a few moments trying to decide how to approach it, but there is no time for thought. I just begin to write, and what I write is so poorly composed, so badly expressed. I am forever making crossings out and wishing I had organised the material in a different way. I am barely half way through my hurried and untidy attempt to answer the question when I realise that my time is already up: there is just 45 minutes for each question. I keep on writing, I have to, until well past the hour. This leaves me barely half an hour each for the other questions. I am writing so poorly no one will ever read my writing. I am probably leaving out key words and mis-spelling others. I know for a fact that I miss out a mass of information that I do have, I just lack the time to retrieve it accurately from my mental store. This is such an absurd way to test people. For me it is even worse. I am an editor, for god's sake. My life's work is making written material readable and legible and presenting it in an attractive, intelligent and digestible form. In these exams I am forced to create utter chaos with words, chaos in the structure, chaos in the presentation and chaos in the ideas. It is painful. Moreover, for the last six years I have done most of my writing on a word processor, I do not need to spell a word right first time, I do not need to express the word order in a sentence right the first time; I am addicted to word processing; I no longer write, I word process.

Two weeks later, I dreamt that the exam results have come through. I have 35-40%, i.e. a fail. Nilofer has 95%. In fact, I got As or high Bs for my essays, and, despite the dream, I passed all the necessary exams (with marks over 50%). Next, I had to turn my mind to a subject for a thesis. This would not only take up most of my time for the second year of the course but the marks for it would be the most significant factor in my final grade. I sweated for months over what to do. Initially, I was attracted to a project on the paleoecology of Java during the time of *Homo erectus*, simply because it was all ready to go – some data for this had been collected by a PhD student who had died. Moreover, my supervisor would be the very well-established Dr Peter Andrews, head of anthropology at the Natural History Museum. I'd read many of his papers, and they had always seemed extremely well argued and clearly written.

On the other hand, I found myself unwilling to devote much time for a project that would be, largely, an exercise in research techniques and statistics. I was increasingly determined to find a topic through which I might try to shed light on an aspect of human evolution that I, personally, found interesting rather than banal. Through the summer and into autumn, I turned more towards Robin Dunbar, who was very much the live wire of the biological anthropology teaching team, and who, I discovered (astonishingly), had studied under John Crook! He was also the author of several articles I'd cut from the *New Scientist* over the years, and which I was browsing in search of inspiration. At first, he thought I might like to massage behavioural data on macaques or some other old world monkey, thus undertaking the same sort of analysis he had done on baboons. But I couldn't get very excited about monkeys. I was leaning more towards human sociobiology, I told him, and he offered several very interesting ideas, using the bible and/or other religious texts as a source of sociobiological information, or even folk songs (for mentions of cuckoldry, for example). One of my own ideas was to look at history from the point of view of wars and conquests, looking for patterns in the social structure of defeated nations; particularly in terms of male/female roles.

It was Nilofer I have to thank for leading me out of what had become, for me, a quagmire of indecision, my head full of half-baked ideas. Through her help I came across a book called *Primate Paternalism* by David Milton Taub. This was a collection of papers describing and attempting to explain the behaviour of adult male primates towards infants. A wide range of such behaviours had been observed and recorded during the previous 20 or so years, but no consensus had yet emerged on the sociobiological mechanisms. Indeed, any analysis of the subject – variously called male parental care, primate paternalism, paternal care

– brought the two major paradigms of sociobiology, kin selection and sexual selection theory, into opposition.

At one end of the explanatory scale was the idea that males invested time and energy into their infants to improve their evolutionary fitness (i.e. that their kin would go on to reproduce successfully). With this theory (kin selection), it was reasoned that adult males should invest in offspring to the extent of confidence in their own paternity of the infant. At the other end, by way of sexual selection theory, it was argued that males invested in their offspring basically as a way of attracting/keeping a mate. A long chat with Dunbar led to three potential routes forward with data collection focused on a) marmoset observations at the zoo; b) human questionnaires; c) utilisation of an ethnographic atlas. 'I must be very sure,' I told my diary, 'before I discard Peter Andrews. I really should be in the library, these days, studying primate paternalism.'

It was November, before I settled on what I would I do.

8 November 1989
I have been struggling away at the idea of analysing paternal investment [PI] in primates without apparently getting anywhere; but this morning [...] my ideas crystallised rapidly. I think it might have helped being in the company of the academics yesterday and being struck once again how very little data is often used to take theories a long way. All the PI information I have found seems so bitty and diverse; of course it is, if it weren't then somebody would have done what I want to do a long time ago. The idea is simple: I want to construct a PI index for different primate species using the available data, and compare this index with several variables. In order to give the study an extra dimension I will construct indices based on different premises. The main index for example will draw on all PI info, but another one might exclude info from captive populations, yet another might look at PI only after a certain age. Whether construction of such an index will show anything useful at all remains to be seen, I'm hoping Robin will be able to advise me.

Here, at last, I had a research objective that felt not exactly important but worthwhile, in the grander scheme of things – no such index existed in the literature. It also felt personal since I was by now investing significantly in raising my own infant! Why was I doing this? Perhaps I would find out.

For the best part of a year, I studied 80 or more papers on the behaviour of prosimians, new world monkeys, old world monkeys, and apes and man. For all the species, I collated parameters such as weight, sex ratio, group size and group structure. I also gave each species a ranking of 1 to 4 based on the observations of paternal care recorded in the papers. This quantitative approach then allowed me to plot variables against each other, and to develop conclusions on the links between them. In addition, I was able to use an existing scientific paper that listed carnivore species with paternal investment observations and sexual dimorphism data to look for correlations that could confirm the validity of my scientific approach.

By way of conclusions, I hypothesised that it may well have been competition for mates that led primate species down the evolutionary path of paternal care, but that the high levels of paternal care seen today among some species is not due to such breeding competition but rather because the behaviour is genetically 'useful' as a mechanism for helping infants to maturity. I extrapolated in my discussion.

'I would like to take this hypothesising just one step further and really down an avenue of pure speculation, but one which arose out of the reading and thinking connected with this study. Given the fundamental existence of differing mating strategies in males and females and the ongoing evolutionary adjustments that take place between the sexes, I found myself asking whether there is any evidence for a connection between this possible 'quality' factor and a gender component. Firstly, there is ever increasing evidence of the connections between human and non-human primate social behaviour. Secondly, Harlow's classic deprivation experiments showed the importance of parental care in successful primate rearing; and, thirdly, it has become increasingly apparent, over recent years, that in our Western society, at least, the quality of not only maternal but paternal care can and does affect children's development.

In conclusion I would simply like to suggest a question: Does the battle of the sexes rage not only at the level of mating strategies but also at the infant rearing level and could paternal care have been utilised, on the evolutionary path towards man, as a vital male response to successful female rearing strategists?'

I had brought the whole shebang – my two year scientific foray into human evolution – round neatly, I might say, to my own developing personal preoccupation – being a father. I'd not had the best of experiences with my own fathers, all two of them, and I was consciously and, I suppose, unconsciously acutely aware of wanting and needing to do better. Now, I had given this wanting and needing a rational scientific explanation.

Here's my diary entry dated one week after completing the MSc.

8 October 1990

People keep asking me what will I do with it. What will I do with what? The knowledge? The degree? Who knows. Taking the course has certainly cured me of wanting to give up work and study human evolution/psychology/ artificial intelligence/brain sciences or whatever full time. And that is probably a very good thing. But as far as advancing my career prospects or even my social life, or even my leisure interests it is hard to answer the question in any positive way. All I can say is that it adds another string to my bow. Unfortunately, I am already vastly overloaded with sideways knowledge and the world only respects/pays for/rewards vertical knowledge. I already have so many strings to my bow and make a very fine instrument but neither I nor anything or anyone I know can play such a complex me.

I may not have had a concrete purpose in undertaking the MSc, and nor did I find myself with any post-MSc ambitions. Nevertheless, on reflection, I believe it led me to a more rigorous, intellectual approach not only to my reading and thinking about such subjects (there are many flights of wayward scientific theorising in my earlier diaries) but in my writing also. There is a challenge to the writing of scientific subjects with efficiency, clarity and logic not required in literary works. My daily work as a journalist had given me a head start, perhaps, in meeting this challenge, but the essays and thesis I had to write for the MSc were a step up in terms of accuracy and of needing to source every piece of information. I liked it, this collating of relating information and forging rational argument – but also I knew that I didn't have the patience to a be (or to have been – given my high maths/physics degree) a scientist. On the other hand, I believe the whole MSc experience did play some part in the way my journalistic career veered sharply towards me working within the policy and legal institutions of Brussels (Chapter two).

The geographical travels in my 20s had left me connected to all the places I'd visited so much so that I've always been more interested in news from them than from other countries. Similarly, the MSc left me always on the alert for news on the human evolution front (constantly changing with new fossil and genetic discoveries).

In terms of more general evolution, I continued to read and enjoy Stephen Jay Gould's collections of fascinating essays, published every year or two, while at the same time growling at the apparent popularity of Dawkins. In 1998, I took the opportunity to attend one of his lectures, in Guildford. Here's my rather disparaging review of the event.

24 October 1998

It was a pleasant enough evening last night [. . .]. Dawkins was a real failure. He simply confirmed all my prejudices about him. During the question session, I asked him if, scientifically speaking, he was still happy with the selfish gene theory and whether he was happy with the way the term had entered the common currency. He didn't give me much of an answer. He said yes, he did feel the selfish gene theory held up, it didn't explain everything, but nevertheless it was still a good explanation. He didn't answer the second part of my question. I can hardly remember much of his talk, so ephemeral was it, other than that he was asking for better links between science and poetry, and that science deserved more awe from the general public than it generally got. He suggested we should go out on a moonless night, lie on the grass, and look up at the stars, in order to experience the wonder of nature (yawn, yawn, yawn).

Earlier in the year I had made the mistake of buying his latest book, *Climbing Mount Improbable*: 'It is simply a book that tries to explain how evolution has given rise to some of the more difficult-to-explain features of animals – such as flying. Mount Improbable is a metaphor: if you look up the vertical craggy rocks, of course it looks impossible to climb, but if you look round the back of the mountain, you can find a gentle slope to walk up to the peak. Stunning! Why did I buy the book, I don't know, I thought I ought to read it if only to criticise it.'

Evolution was and is a fascinating topic to study and read about, but with the MSc over I was drawn back to the question of how specifically human consciousness had evolved and how it functioned, not least in my own brain. This seemed to me the 'final frontier' of science rather than, say, macro or micro models describing the physics of universes and atoms. Back in 1986, before the MSc, I'd been stretched by a heavy tome *Neurophilosophy* by Patricia Churchland. 'The sustaining conviction of this book,' she writes at the beginning, 'is that top-down strategies (as characteristic of philosophy, cognitive psychology, and artificial intelligence) and bottom-up strategies (as characteristic of neurosciences) for solving the mysteries of mind-brain function should not be pursued in icy isolation from one another. What is envisaged instead is a rich inter-animation between the two, which can be expected to provoke a fruitful co-evolution of theories, models and methods, where each informs, corrects, and inspires the other.' Right on lady, right on, I wrote in my diary, this is where I want to be – in the middle.

The MSc put my reading about mind on hold. A year after completing it, I was back, riveted by a new book *Language and Species* by a scientist I'd never heard of, David Bickerton. In it, he argued that the possession of language alone may be sufficient to account for both our unique minds and our unparalleled success as a species. And through it, I came to see how the study of languages and their evolution provides an intriguing route into understanding human evolution more generally, and how our brains work today.

> 28 April 1991
> Bickerton's book is fascinating. [. . .] His prose is clear and precise; his ideas, though complex, are patiently delivered across to the reader. For years I have wondered, or half-suspected, that language holds a major key to the workings of the mind. Bickerton has unlocked this possibility and taken my understanding to a new level. [. . .] In my library this book deserves to sit next to Crook's *The Evolution of Human Consciousness*.

And in 1994, Stephen Pinker stepped into the limelight for the first time with his groundbreaking *The Language Instinct*. 'This is quite a remarkable book,' I wrote, 'for being so readable and accessible, almost overwhelmed with anecdotes and examples. His main thesis is that there must be a genetic component underlying human language capability. He argues persuasively from every corner of relevant science, not just linguistics, and slowly builds up a mountain of evidence. [. . .] Certainly, he has persuaded me, I think, that there may well be more to language than education, but what is that 'more' – a language gene?' His next book, as it happens, would be entitled *How the Mind Works* (1997), a hugely interesting work, for bringing the power of evolutionary psychology perspectives to a wide range of human behaviours, and doing so in such a readable way. Which is not to say I didn't find him veering too close to Dawkins for my liking and taking the Neo-Darwinist approach too far at times.

In 1998, I read *Figments of Reality* by Ian Stewart and Jack Cohen. The authors endeared me with this critique of Dawkins' *The Selfish Gene*: 'superb, well worth reading, but don't believe it'. I liked the fact that they wrote at length about there being no language with which to discuss how the mind and consciousness work, for I have been saying the same things (albeit only to myself, for who else can I talk to about these things) for years. But, most importantly, the authors, I felt, had made a brave attempt to link up the relevant science to an individual's personal subjective experience of what thinking, and consciousness are. One of the key points they made, and demonstrated, is that many of the decisions made by individuals are only consciously acknowledged after the action. Thus we do not decide to pick up a cup of tea and drink, we simply do it and then our conscious self, milliseconds behind, registers the action. Every driver has surely experienced that weird feeling of minutes having passed by without her/him having actually been conscious of them. I wrote in my diary that this book 'has got closer than anyone to nailing down consciousness'.

Since then, there has been a flourishing of progress on the brain and how it functions, with contributions from many different disciplines apart from evolutionary psychology, i.e. neuroscience, cognitive behaviour, psychology, genetics, artificial intelligence, and so on. If the 20th century saw spectacular advances in each individual science, it's in the 21st century that researchers have found a much greater understanding through drawing together and unifying these bottom-up and top-down advances. Where once I longed for a science book that would bridge neuroscience with psychology, genetics with behavioural studies, and give me the answers to life (!), I find now, well into the 21st century, they're almost two a penny.

I am tempted – though I shall desist largely – to make a few lists of the many other important and fascinating 20th and 21st century science books that I've read and been impressed by, whether on evolution, the human brain, language and social development or whatever. However, how could I not mention, for example: Jared Diamond's *Guns, Germs and Steel*; *Evolution and Healing* by Randolph M. Nesse and George C. Williams; and Antonio Damasio's *The Feeling of What Happens*?

Finally, though, I do want to mention *Darwin's Cathedral* by David Sloan Wilson first published in 2003, partly because it vindicated my long-held views that Dawkins et al were wrong in rejecting group selection so wholeheartedly, and partly because Wilson's arguments in favour of group selection come from a very unexpected quarter: religion. The wholesale rejection of group selection, he says, was a wrong turn from which the field is only starting to recover. It had always seemed to me, I wrote in my diary, that the idea of natural selection is too powerful to be confined to one biological level, and that it must surely work at lots of different levels (from gene to culture) at the same time, to varying degrees of success.

I had been through my own religious period as a teenager and university student, before experiencing a dramatic revelation that of course god doesn't exist (*Why Ever* – Chapter six). Thereafter, for a while in my 20s, whenever I met anyone religious, I would try, energetically, to undermine their faith. However, it wasn't long before I mellowed in this regard, accepting by degrees the importance of religion – psychologically, culturally, philosophically, or politically – for many people, and many societies. By the time Richard Dawkins – not Dawkins again! – published his book *The God Delusion*, destined to be another best seller like *The Selfish Gene*, I was definitely in sympathy with his critics, some of whom described his confrontational stance toward religion as narrow and embarrassing, while considering him as fundamentalist as the believers he attacks. One atheist philosopher, John Gray, denounced Dawkins as an 'anti-religious missionary' (as I felt I'd been for a few years in my 20s), and suggests that he is 'transfixed in wonderment at the workings of his own mind' and thus 'misses much that is of importance in human beings'.

For me science and religion are like water and oil, distinct and separate fundamentals of life, but not to be mixed, and won't make sense if mixed however hard you try. Except that the disciplines of science, it seems, can be brought to the study of religion, not to the understanding of religious belief or faith itself but to the reasons why religion exists for mankind – as opposed to all other life as far as we know. Thus, Wilson argues that religious groups can function as adaptive units; that many resources can be achieved only through coordinated action of individuals; and that human groups are able to function as adaptive units because they have moral systems, expressed through religious imagery and symbolism, which regulate behaviour. In conclusion, Wilson develops a general theory of unifying systems, arguing that religion is just one of many such systems in society and that he could have brought a similar analysis to sports teams, or political and military organisations, institutions that could regulate and coordinate individual behaviour for group advantages.

By way of conclusion to this foray into the realms of science, here are several paragraphs from the concluding chapter of Darwin's Cathedral. I wrote them into my diary at the time because they chimed so well with my own thinking just as passages in Crook's book had done more than 20 years earlier. Crook tempted me intellectually back towards religious comfort; Wilson offered me intellectual understanding of how/why that comfort had ever come to exist.

7 October 2003

[From *Darwin's Cathedral*]: 'Those who regard themselves as non-religious often scorn the other-worldliness of religion as a form of mental weakness. How could anyone be so stupid as to believe in all that hocus-pocus in the face of such contrary evidence? This stance can itself be criticised for misconstruing and cheapening a set of issues that deserves our most serious attention as scientists.

In the first place, much religious belief is not detached from reality if the central thesis of this book is correct. Rather, it is intimately connected to reality by motivating behaviours that are adaptive in the real world – an awesome achievement when we appreciate the complexity that is required to become connected in this practical sense. It is true that many religious beliefs are false as literal descriptions of the real world, but this merely forces us to recognise two forms of realism: a factual realism based on literal correspondence and a practical realism based on behavioural adaptedness. An atheist historian who understood the real life of Jesus but whose life was a mess as a result of his beliefs would be factually attached to and practically detached from reality.

In the second place, much religious belief does not represent a form of mental weakness but rather the healthy functioning of the biologically and culturally well-adapted against which all other forms of thought are to be judged. Adaptation is the gold standard against which rationality must be judged, along with all other forms of thought. Evolutionary biologists should be especially quick to grasp this point because they appreciate that the well-adapted mind is ultimately an organ of survival and reproduction. If there is a trade-off between the two forms of realism, such that our beliefs can become more adaptive only by becoming factually less true, then factual realism will be the loser every time. To paraphrase evolutionary psychologists, factual realists detached from practical reality were not among our ancestors. It is the person who elevates factual truth above practical truth who must be accused of mental weakness from an evolutionary perspective.

In the third place, disparaging the otherworldly nature of religion presumes that non-religious belief systems are more factually realistic. It is true that non-religious belief systems manage without gods, but they might still distort the facts of the real world as thoroughly as the Four Gospels of the New Testament. We know this is the case for patriotic versions of history, which are as silly and weak-minded for people of other nations as a given religion for people of other faiths. Many intellectual traditions and scientific theories of past decades have a similar silly and purpose-driven quality, once their cloak of factual plausibility has been yanked away by the hand of time. If believing something for its desired consequences is a crime, then let those who are without guilt cast the first stone.'

Chapter four

EC Inform
A business of my own

Writing, writing, writing – it was the want to write combined with the need to earn a living that had brought me here, from my Corsican sojourn a decade or so earlier, to setting up and running my own business. It had never been a dream of mine to do this, to run or own a business. My step father, Sasha, started up Innovative Marketing International 50 years ago, and my brother Julian worked there for many years before taking over when Sasha died unexpectedly. There were many ups and downs over the years, I've learned at family meets, as the company expanded and diminished with the trading tides. A friend of mine had a vintage emporium for years, and a lucrative car park on land rented from British Rail; and another set up, with colleagues, a firm supplying computer services to the water industry. I wasn't trying to emulate any of these entrepreneurs, nor was I motived by lucre. I simply arrived at a place in time where I could see no alternative route forward for my working self.

It felt like I had made the FT group a lot of money, and – to be frank – I resented that. And even though we editors at FTBI had plenty of freedom to run our newsletters the way we wanted to, I still felt constrained. I'd always been something of a free spirit – right back to when I failed to fit into a proper job, at the market research company, MORI. I tried again in New Zealand with the medical rep position, but I always knew that was a temporary affair, and besides mostly I was a thousand kilometres from my bosses. And then at FTBI, to have the managing editor position dangled in front of me – that's what it felt like – before it had been whipped away and given to a whippersnapper, felt like a kick in the teeth. I'd accumulated plenty of experience in running business newsletters by this time. I understood the model, the marketing, the financials, and I was pretty sure I could turn a profit – and make more money than the FTBI had been paying me. I would also be free to focus exclusively on European Union affairs – international cooperation (and disputes) on policies, laws, funding programmes – rather than on the nuts and bolts of industry, trade business. I'd had a good five-year run at FTBI, but it was time to go it alone.

Initially, I'd planned to run my new business from a small room in Sasha's office near Baker Street station but within days of my parting ways with FTBI, Sasha and Julian had changed their minds about allowing me the space, so I set up office in my Aldershot Road house, in a small spare room at the back. There were no complications arising from the flat in Brussels as I'd rented this personally not through the company (as a result of the compromise I'd reached with Dennis over my trips), and I was able to switch my EC press pass (requiring a Brussels address) from FTBI to EC INFORM. Yes, after much word juggling, I'd decided on EC INFORM as the company name, and EC INFORM-Energy as the title of my first newsletter (with INFORM always in small caps). It wasn't a name that tripped off the tongue, but I decided that it was more important to communicate – quickly, easily – the services my new small company was offering than to be stuck with a slick name that was functionless.

Once the decision was made, what did I need to do? Not hang about! I wanted to produce and market a first issue of EC INFORM-Energy in January. To be able to do this I required:

> – computer and communication equipment (hardware, text and production software, desktop printer, telephone, fax etc);
> – business communication and banking services;
> – a finalised layout and design for the newsletter (i.e. I didn't want to start chopping and changing the design in months to come, very unprofessional);
> – marketing materials and marketing lists;
> – a printing company ready and willing to print and mail the newsletters and marketing letters (with very short turnaround times);
> – a trip to Brussels to collect news for the first edition.

All of which made for a busy December, while I was still officially on the FT payroll, too busy for me to record any of the details in my diary, other than pithy summaries.

31 December 1992
Everything is now in place for the start of my business and I can go ahead on schedule with my first issue next week. One thousand lucky punters will get the January edition for free, but how many will buy – I need 1% to keep my morale up. 1993 here I come.

I experienced two significant hurdles in this very early phase of my new venture that required a cool head, and a modicum of business tact. It was clear to me that I would need the facility to take payment for subscriptions by credit card. In early December I opened a business account with the Midland Bank (because I'd been a personal customer since student days), and asked how I could go about taking credit card payments. The branch manager explained that another division of the bank dealt with so-called 'merchant services', but he would call a contact there. He then advised me that because my business was based at home, the bank was unable to offer me merchant services, at least not until I'd been trading for 12 months. I spent a couple of days in panic, phoning around for advice on how merchant services operate, only to discover all banks had prohibitive conditions of one kind or another. I did, however, learn that within the Midland group there was a discretionary element, allowing branch managers to recommend clients for merchant services. I resorted to seeking Sasha's help. He also banked at Midland, and he put me in touch with Jim, his branch manager. I telephoned Jim, explained my problem, and within a couple of hours I'd had a call from a lady at Midland merchant services. A few days later I met with the lady, she handed over a bunch of stuff – a physical card reader, credit card forms etc. – and talked me through the process. Over the years, the vast majority of subscriptions were paid by credit cards (so the effort had been worthwhile).

The other hurdle was more of a launch crisis. Although I solicited quotes from various London printers, very few were able to handle this kind of business. Firstly, I needed the newsletters to be printed and posted – every month – in less than 24 hours after receiving the copy. However, it was not just the subscription newsletters that needed to be printed and posted (which in the early days would only be a few dozen copies), but much larger print runs for marketing purposes. Almost all the marketing of such newsletters is done by direct mail, and as I felt there was no substitute for providing punters with the product itself, I needed a company able to print and mail, for example, a thousand copies of a 20-page A4 newsletter together plus promotional letter. And, I wanted my printer to be able to turn these bigger jobs around very quickly – as soon as the proofs were ready. You can't sell a NEWSletter with old news, was my feeling.

No surprise then that the only printer I could find willing and able to provide this magic service at a price I could afford was Artigraf, the very company who served FTBI's newsletters (not least the three I had been editing). I already had an excellent relationship with its staff, especially the printer Frank, so it proved straightforward, in the end, to negotiate on timings and costs. Unfortunately, it all went horribly wrong with the first print run and mailing. Of course, my own address was on the mailing list (labels provided to the printer before each mail out), and when the post arrived, I opened up – excitedly – the envelope. I was aghast to find my brand new publication WITHOUT any accompanying letter! I imagined execs everywhere, across the UK, Europe, the world indeed (though postage costs made foreign promotional targets significantly more expensive) would be handling the new light blue-paper EC INFORM-Energy without any explanation as to what it was, or why it had arrived on their desks.

I was somewhat panic-stricken. EC INFORM had only just been launched, and, it seemed, I'd spent thousands of pounds on a dud mail shot.

Fortunately, Artigraf immediately accepted fault, though what else could Frank do? The only acceptable remedy, I decided, was to re-print and re-send the very same newsletter with the promotion letter to every one of the same address labels I'd provided. This would incur, for Artigraf, a huge loss on the job, not only having to repeat the printing but to cover the doubled postage costs as well. In fact, I, personally, had little more to do than reprint the labels and courier them to Artigraf. All the effort was not in vain, the first orders soon arrived – often signalled by the whirring into life of the fax machine.

> 23 Jan 1993
> It is two weeks since my first mailing went out. I have a total of about 14 orders and possibly two more. However, only eight are paid and I anxiously await payment in response to my first invoices. Last week was not a pleasant time; during the previous week there was a certain amount of fun associated with the waiting and hoping for orders, but during this last week the reality of needing orders for the business has struck home more forcibly. Only on Wednesday was I reasonably buoyant as I got three orders in the post and two on the fax machine making five in all. One more day like that I could rest fairly satisfied.

This is the first of many, many diary entries over the coming years in which I obsessed about mailings, orders, renewals. The bottom line, the number that meant the most, was always my total number of subscriptions, and I was aiming for a 100 by the end of my first trading year. With a subscription costing £300, that would bring in £30,000. With 200, an income of £60,000 would see me doing nicely, thank you. My early hopes, however, were for double that. (For comparison, the FTBI newsletters, including mine, generally had circulations at 400 or higher, each one grossing over one hundred grand.)

I made an early decision to introduce a second title into the EC INFORM stable.

> 13 March 1993
> Write up my diary, huh! there is no diary any more. This is my first entry in March. I have neither anything to write about nor time to write it. I have just published issue three of *EC INFORM-Energy*. Each issue so far has contained 20 pages and about 13,000 words, every sweet one of them written by yours truly. It's not surprising therefore that I don't find much enthusiasm to write down the banalities of this life. Between the moment I go to Brussels – which is two

weeks before publishing day – and publishing I barely think or breathe anything other than stories for *EC INFORM-Energy*. Once the issue is out of the way, though, I tend to relax for a week or so. After issues one and two, I've had a fair amount of admin to sort out – cash books, subscriptions that sort of thing. This time I could truly have relaxed but for my decision to launch a supplement in April – *EC INFORM-Energy Review*. This needs a new marketing approach, a new marketing letter, a subscription form, a design for the front cover and inside, and, of course, some content. This supplement, a modest 8-page quarterly, is aimed at associations who will buy a number of copies for distribution among their members. I have no idea at all whether it will work but, at the very least, it is a marketing bonus for the main newsletter and also justifies my use of the slogan 'Independent Quality Newsletters'.

EC INFORM-Energy Review proved a burdensome way of justifying the use of the plural in my company slogan. I'm unlikely to mention it again in this memoir, so this short paragraph will have to serve as its only memorial. While the monthly, *EC INFORM-Energy* was published on light blue paper which, I thought, would give it identity, I decided to publish the quarterly review on darker blue paper – so distinctive it was difficult to read! I think I wanted to discourage photocopying, and encourage companies to hold multiple subscriptions (at £90) time. I also used the quarterly as a vehicle to promote the idea of a bespoke service whereby EC INFORM could provide companies with a similar publication but with news tailored specifically to their requirements. The whole concept was a failure, I sold no subscriptions, and no companies ever called to discuss a bespoke service. Nevertheless, I kept publishing the quarterly for years – my thinking being that it provided a valuable bonus for my monthly subscribers. I could not forget, of course, that *EC INFORM-Energy* had a very direct competitor – *EC Energy Monthly*, the very newsletter that I'd set up for FTBI and which now had a young editor keen to prove her journalistic credentials.

18 September 1993
How is the business doing? I am now three-quarters of the way through my first trading year. I have around 85 subscribers; and, bearing in mind that subscriptions are paid in advance, I have made a slight profit of income over expenditure. But then I have kept my costs to an absolute minimum and taken no risks [other than the modest Quarterly]. It would be fair to assume now that I shall make my arbitrary target of 100 by the end of the year. Although I might have hoped for a larger migration from the FT's *EC Energy Monthly* by now, I cannot be too disheartened. I have not had a single cancellation or complaint; and every invoice has turned into a cheque; indeed almost every enquiry has turned into an order.

That autumn, I made a fresh marketing move. Rather than mailing out sample copies of the newsletters, which was so expensive (but which brought in roughly 1% subscriptions), I decided to create an eight page A5 brochure and mail this out to a whopping 5,000 potential subscribers (but expecting no more than a 0.1% conversion rate). Apart from new subscriptions, I felt the brochure would help bolster the overall image of EC INFORM, its credibility, give the company more depth, more status. It was with this same rationale that I'd launched the second newsletter, offered credit card facilities, enlisted for VAT (though this wasn't legally necessary at first), and registered for ISSN numbers. I confessed to my diary that designing and proofing the eight page A5 brochure was one mammoth task and organising the labels was another.

I don't have a record of how well or not the brochure achieved its aim, but by year's end I had achieved around 110 paid subscriptions, just exceeding my original target. EC INFORM was viable, yet it was a long way from being a runaway success (as had been the two newsletters I'd launched for FTBI). As soon as January came round, my focus turned to renewals. It is a marketing truism that it's much more cost-effective to keep an existing customer than find a new one. Well, this is super-true for the newsletter business. If less than 75% of my subscribers renewed, my business was unlikely to succeed. A renewal rate of over 90% would indicate the newsletter's editorial and financial value.

The maths is simple. It might cost, say, £200 in marketing to win a new subscriber. When all other expenses are taken into account there's barely a profit from a £300 subscription – until that is one includes renewals in the sum. By way of illustration, a subscriber who renewed year on year for a decade would bring in £3,000 – not bad for the original £200 outlay.

> 19 January 1994
> A day without orders is like a night without sleep – exhausting and unsatisfying. I wait anxiously for the results of the mini-subscription mailing and the January renewals.

Another route to promoting EC INFORM, and by extension its newsletters, was to put myself about. I was fairly well known in the corridors of DGXVII (the European Commissions's Directorate-General for Energy), by some of the members of the Council's energy working group, and by a few MEPs that sat on the European Parliament's energy, research and technology committee (CERT). I also had good relations with the energy/environment lobby groups and think tanks in Brussels. Occasionally, I was asked to do a bit of public speaking. My knee-jerk reaction was always to say 'no way José' since I had such a fear of being in the spotlight (*Why Ever* – Chapter ten) but I simply had to rally myself and hope the benefits outweighed my anxieties. One invitation, from

Professor Thomas Wälde at Dundee University's Centre for Energy, Petroleum and Mineral Law and Policy came early on. This was to sponsor and speak at an EC energy policy seminar in St. Andrews. It was somewhat disappointing, however, to find the keynote speaker, Harald Norvik, president of Statoil, had cancelled and that only 20 people were attending. It was a long travel to St Andrews, further than to Brussels.

Another speech I gave to a Scandinavian electricity seminar. It was the last of the day, and I felt little enthusiasm left in the audience for my presentation. Yet one of the electricity lobby groups liked it well enough to re-publish it in an internal publication, and to offer me – gratis – a mailing list of 700 names. Gold dust. I was always on the look out for mailing lists, and conferences were great opportunities to collect them. Occasionally, I swapped lists/promotions with other publications, such as when the editor of *Coal Voice* (published by the US National Coal Association and mailed to 15,000 names!) offered me an advertisement in exchange for some European mailing names.

One trip, a couple of years later, to Thessaloniki in Greece proved particularly sweet, though it started out sour. I was invited by a consultancy in Athens to a conference on energy connections in the Balkans. It was largely funded by DGXVII (though its Synergy Programme), and the consultants were anxious to grace it with some international press coverage – I was the only foreign journalist. I had to endure a five-hour journey, a debilitating virus, and a hotel room that faced on to a six-lane race track of a road. Nevertheless, I was very glad to meet up with Costis, a friendly guy who had been my Greek stringer while at FTBI. I explained to him I'd been having some trouble with Greece's Public Power Corporation (a state-owned monopoly) which owed me almost £500 for subs and had failed to answer repeated invoice reminders. Costis said he wasn't surprised, but he introduced me to the company's PR manager who promised to look into the matter. The debt was paid within days.

Secondly, I met an Englishman who worked as a liaison between the Romanian government and the Synergy Programme. He expressed an interest in buying the Romanian rights to distribute my EC energy policy book. In the days to come, he agreed to pay £1,000 for the rights to translate it into Romanian and distribute up to 50 copies. I dreamed of similar deals across the Balkans, but no similar (lucrative) deals ever came my way.

Yes, by this time, I'd written and published a new and better version of the management report I'd compiled for FTBI. I had conceived of the idea in early 1994. I reasoned that I would only need to sell about 100 to make as much money as I did with the original FT one, but more importantly, I felt, it would attract publicity, and it would consolidate EC

INFORM's prime position in the market for information on EC energy affairs. The thought of writing another book did seem rather daunting, especially as this time I'd have to do all the marketing as well as the writing, editing, and proof-reading – and without the Financial Times group name to back me up.

Six months of hard work later, in September 1994, EC INFORM published *Energy Policies of the European Union*. The book had been trailed in the newsletter with subscribers offered a significant saving, and I'd put together a first mailing to 3,000 prospective buyers. Foolishly, I'd allowed my expectations to get out of hand, and thus was sorely disappointed by the trickle of orders that came in during the first few weeks. I'd hoped for a minimum of 100 by the end of the year, but had only half that by early December; and, as my diary shows, I was worrying constantly. Nevertheless, I concluded 1994 with book sales up to 77.

Early in 1995, a stunning review of my book appeared in the highly respected British trade magazine *Electrical Review*.

'This impressive volume is a positive encyclopaedia of information. It is all here. In 12 chapters, each dealing with discreet aspects of EC policy, former Financial Times journalist Paul Lyons takes the reader succinctly through each of the issues now affecting European policy-makers.

There is no confusion between the rhetoric and the reality. Lyons has worked the EC energy patch for a decade or more. He knows where the power lies, where the bodies are buried. He provides that information without fear or favour, even when his conclusions may offend powerful interests.

This is a positive tour de force, prepared by someone who not only knows his subject well, but can communicate that knowledge. A five-star recommendation.'

I knew the reviewer – Andrew Warren, a lobbyist for the energy conservation industry. I mentioned him in my diary, 'a sweetheart' I called him, 'I don't know what I've done to deserve his attentions, but I will ensure he gets his next subscription free'.

And here is another review which I cannot resist including in full (at length, in fact), this time by John V. Mitchell at Chatham House, and published in the academic *Journal of Energy Literature* – I'm particularly fond of Mitchell's last sentence.

'This is a timely report by an author whose insights and knowledge have illuminated the scruffy caravan of European energy policy for some years. Newcomers to any particular topic – or to the broader cross-cutting themes – could not find a better introduction to the current state and status of particular issues and the processes by which they are handled by the warring institutions in Brussels.

This study was published in September 1994 – ahead of the Euro-pean Commission's 'Green Paper' on energy policy but after the post-Maas-tricht depression had reached Brussels. The Green Paper has not broken new ground since: it has fulfilled Paul Lyons' prediction of 'a confusion of issues, a mix-up between structure and objectives'.

Lyons' book ends with a proposal for a Chapter on Energy to be added to the Treaties by the 1996 Intergovernmental Conference. The Chapter he proposes would provide a legal basis for Union level action on energy security (which currently has no specific basis); energy efficiency and renewables (which currently spin-off from environmental and re-search policies), and would provide a remit for DGXVII – The Energy Direc-torate – to bring together periodically in a single document a 'policy framework' which for each energy industry would include the single mar-ket, competition, security and environmental dimensions.

These proposals are for procedure, rather than substance, because of the author's analysis of what went wrong with the attempts to develop EU energy policy between 1989 and 1993 when many of DGXVII's pro-posals for directives on the internal market and security of supply failed to get support intra-structure projects in Southern Europe and Ireland, and to projects improving energy transport links between EU members. Of these the 'Trans- European Networks' have, in Lyons' words, 'rocketed into favour': these are projects so large that they are approved at ministerial or even head of government level without much coherence of purpose or process.

Lyons' chapters on enlargement and on relations with the former Soviet Union, discuss the Phare and Tacis programmes, led by DGI, which are supposed to provide technical assistance in the respective energy sec-tors of these regions. Substantial, and controversial EU support for nuclear safety projects flows slowly through these programmes. Lyons relates their difficult histories with his usual attention to the institutional problems.

This study is rich in detail, and the nature of the topics is such that the connections between the details of different subject headings are often tenuous. Because of this, and despite its being written in clear, non-tech-nical language, it is not an easy read for a non-specialist reader. But the book's great merit is that on each topic the connections with other policies are clearly drawn, and the politicking between the Energy and other Di-rectorates, and between the Commission, the Council and the Parliament is crisply narrated. The study is thus not just of energy policy, but of how the 'Brussels' processes worked and are working over energy and related matters. It is far more useful than any Commission document on energy policy, or than commentaries which are limited to the substance of policy without attention to the policy process.'

My turnover in 1994 reached £60,000 with a net profit – in effect, my earnings – of £28,000. 1995 saw turnover of £70,000 and net income of £45,000. I certainly wasn't earning a fortune, and I'd never expected to, yet these figures were hugely important to me, not only because, clearly, I needed an income, but also because they were a real world measure of my journalistic worth, and my skill and ability to run a business.

From the start, my ambition had been to launch a series of newsletters focusing on different sectors of business which were increasingly coming under the aegis of a European politic. Transport was the obvious first addition to my newsletter group given the important commercial and political links that exist between transport and energy.

However, if I was ever going to move out of London then I needed to do this before enlarging my operation. And so, much of 1995 was given over to finding and buying a place (which proved to be a detached house in Elstead, a village in Surrey), and transferring the business. I now had a good-sized, pleasant office on the ground floor with views out to an extensive garden (and I was no longer having to operate from a small cramped back room).

In the spring of 1996, I made the decision to go online. Today, it takes little more than a phone call to get connected to the internet, but back then it took more work.

> 30 May 1996
> About two weeks ago, I got hooked up onto the internet. There were some complications, but I made it in the end. It cost me about £150, including a year's subscription to the service provider – Demon Internet. I can now send and receive e-mail, 'lurk' with newsgroups, and browse the world wide web. The main business justification for this expense, and for the time in getting it all going, is so as to offer my subscribers an e-mail address for communications about EC INFORM-Energy. I can see no business purpose for the web or newsgroups yet. I have accessed the web pages of a firm called CMS, which sells a wide range of newsletters, including those of the FT, but I'm not convinced that CMS wins much new custom through those web pages. I have also looked for a news group connected with energy politics, but without any success.

Finally in autumn, more than three years since I'd started EC INFORM, I could tarry no longer.

> Thursday 19 September 1996
> I am petrified – not frightened as such, but turned to stone, unable to make a move, frightened of doing the wrong thing, or the thing not good enough. I am silent and inactive with indecision. I do not know what to do. My little, titchy, minuscule, electron-sized, insignificant company is at the biggest turning point it will ever have. And I am afraid to even arrive at the cross-roads, let alone to take the turn.

Ever since I started out alone, nearly four years ago, I have planned to set up a second newsletter, probably on transport. But I have not done it. During the first year, I was preoccupied with getting *EC INFORM-Energy* up and running, and then I wrote a new management report which kept me busy through to the autumn of the second year. And then I decided it would be foolish to employ someone before I had moved, so moving became a priority and that took up the third year. Then, I made myself extra busy by writing a second report early in the fourth year – this was completed at Easter. Since then, I have known, that I must get on with it. But in the six months since the report was finished, I've dallied and dallied; preferring to sink my time into various short-term projects, like getting linked up to the internet, like buying the new computers, and doing work on the house and in the garden.

However, finally, I did get down to some action. I went to visit a couple of associations in Brussels and I am collecting all the material I can on transport issues. But then I decided that I really couldn't proceed without finding some-one to work for me, so I advertised in the *Guardian*. I have received about 150 replies. [. . .] I found it quite frustrating sorting through them every couple of days. I was not really hopeful for any of them but I wrote back to ten applicants, a few with no experience and a few with some, with a copy of my newsletter and a fairly detailed letter about the kind of work they would have to do. [. . .]

But my problem lies in trying to visualise the day-to-day working situa-tion and relationship. [. . .] I worry a lot about how I would have enough work to keep them busy without giving them week-loads of database work, but most of all I worry about them being bored or fed up.

Here's my ad: 'Journalist with interest in EU affairs. Busi-ness/technical writing or editing skills necessary. Small company seeks self-motivated person who values independence and a challenge. In-volvement in newsletter launch and all aspects of production – work/re-wards to expand with ability. Home working possible (although 2-4 days in Brussels and 4-8 days at Godalming office required each month). French an advantage. Please reply with short cv and informative letter to PO Box 145, Godalming, Surrey GU8 6YW.'

I calculated my chances of finding someone suitable at 50% or less. Indeed, dissatisfied with the 150 replies from the first ad, I found it necessary to place a second advertisement. I whittled down the applica-tions, interviewed six candidates, and invited two of them to work with me for a day – choosing, I admitted to my diary, potential intelligence and likeability over and above experience. Only one of them came (the other having been offered another job) – Theo. With fluent French, a first class honours degree in English, a competence with technical subjects, he also lived nearby (a huge plus) and said he was happy to remain in the (rural) area. I promised to pay him cash for a trial period, and there-after a salary that we agreed. After one week, I was able to report to my-self, 'He worked well and hard, and remains keen. He is sharp and took instructions all week. I am sure he will do well.' And he did, excellently, staying nearly three years. Today, he is (and has been for many years) an international business reporter with the BBC, often compiling TV and radio reports on transport issues.

Theo and I worked hard on the format, style, content and schedule for *EC INFORM-Transport*. I took him to Brussels, showed him around, introduced him to key people, and apologised for the rather down-at-heel accommodation – i.e. the small flat I'd first rented back in my FTBI days. The title was launched in January 1997. The first copy arrived in the mail, a day late (as the printer had failed to meet the agreed schedule) and looked good. I was very pleased with it – until I looked inside and saw that some of the pages had been bound upside down! I was furious, especially recalling what had happened with the launch of *EC INFORM-Energy*. As before, the printing company agreed to reprint the whole job at no cost to me, but it still meant I, myself, had to reprint all the labels, and that my prospective subscribers would be getting slightly stale news. Within a week of *EC INFORM-Transport* landing on punters' desks, though, we had seven orders, which promised well. And by the end of the year, my annual turnover figure (sales of books and newsletters) had risen to £100,000 – though my own net income had gone down to £30,000 because I was now paying Theo's salary.

We – Theo and I – established an efficient four-week work cycle, alternating between research (trips to Brussels), writing, editing, and database inputting. It all became quite routine, increasingly hectic towards the end of each work cycle, with a relaxed few days after. I only published 11 issues a year, so August was holiday period (as it was in Brussels). In addition to the two monthly newsletters, there was the rather superfluous *EC INFORM-Energy Quarterly* to put together every three months, and in January there were annual indexes (free to subscribers). Otherwise, there were always names and addresses to input into our databases, and marketing campaigns to organise. I, personally, also had the subscriptions to manage, invoices, reminders, accounts etc. And there were the books. I was usually working on a new edition of my energy policies management report, and once *EC INFORM-Transport* was well established, I put Theo to work on compiling chapters for a similar transport book.

By this time, it had become (abundantly) clear to me that I would never earn enough from these niche EC policy newsletters and books to grow my company to the point of being able to pay for, let's say, a subscriptions manager, a marketing person, an accountant or a production assistant. They simply weren't that commercial. The information I was providing, at a high cost, didn't impact day-to-day commercial decisions, but only provided a steer on the way future policies, albeit important, might impact the energy or transport industries in the medium or long term. And there was limited demand for such information. It just so happened that I much preferred writing about the nuances of policy and law-making than I did about the nitty gritty of market prices or new construction contracts.

There was another significant reason why EC INFORM was not going to make me rich. Despite my very best efforts, I was never going to be able to compete with the FT name. I knew, when I started my company, I'd have an uphill struggle to establish EC INFORM's name, but I believed – naively – that the market would recognise quality in time, and that I'd be able to aim at the kind of subscription numbers I'd achieved at FTBI. I was never in any doubt that *EC INFORM-Energy* was providing much richer, fuller, and more consistently insightful news than FTBI's *EC Energy Monthly*. Yet, no matter how much marketing I did, my EC INFORM title never topped 150 subscribers, whereas I'd had over 400 for the FTBI title when I was still the editor – the FT brand, I worked out, was providing a three-to-four fold marketing advantage. 250 extra subscriptions would have netted me a whopping extra £100,000 a year – and then I could have grown my business for sure.

In June 1998, I published a revised version of my energy book, calling it *EU Energy Policies towards the 21st Century*, and charging £425. It was a mammoth tome (including listings of documents, websites, abbreviations and Decisions/Directives) and was surely the most comprehensive such document available anywhere.

So much of this chapter has been about the mechanics of running EC INFORM and not the issues I was concerned with on a daily basis that I've decided to include the first page of the introduction to this latter book I authored – by way of offering a brief glimpse into the issues I was writing about on a daily basis.

'The last decade of the 20th century has seen radical changes in government attitudes towards energy policy. These changes have evolved because of a weak market in energy, a growing scientific and public concern over environmental damage, and wider pressures for improved conditions of competitivity. The Member States of the European Community, with their very different energy supply structures and policies, have responded to these changes in an equally varied way, some focusing on environmental concerns, others racing ahead with market liberalisation, and still others with continuing concerns over security of supply or bringing economic development to certain regions. However, these radical changes have also been the very focus of a growing attention to energy-related issues within the framework of the European Community. Negotiations on electricity liberalisation and a climate change strategy, for example, have required a deeper understanding of the objectives underlying energy

policy, and have also provoked some governments to rethink the direction of their energy strategies.

With the 1990s drawing to a close, and the opportunities of the 21st century beckoning, it is a good moment to step back and take a detailed look at the extent of Community activities concerning energy.

The EU's influence over the shape and direction of the energy industries themselves, and over the way other industries and consumers use energy, is escalating rapidly. Even if the Member States continue to refuse the transfer of any significant broad-based energy policy responsibilities to Brussels, the power of the Treaty provisions on environmental and Single Market rules is such that the EU is already controlling the way energy is produced, transformed and consumed. At a national level, however, citizens may never be fully aware quite how much of the policy framework is being fixed at the Community level. This is because of the particular legislative mechanism – the Directive – used by the EU for important rules and regulations. Such Directives, many of which are now agreed by the Council of Ministers in conjunction with the European Parliament, require transposition into national laws. Thus, when new laws are introduced into national parliamentary procedures, they may well be the subject of a public debate without any reference to the EU framework which has already been agreed. The obvious exception to this is where politicians wish to blame Brussels for an unpopular measure. When the measure has some public appeal, of course, politicians are unlikely to pass on the praise to Brussels.

Thus, the rationale behind this report is twofold. Firstly, it aims to provide a comprehensive survey of the many and varied actions undertaken at the Community level with an impact on energy, in one way or another. Not even the European Commission provides such a service. This is partly because the Commission itself is only one of the relevant institutions, and the Council of Ministers, and increasingly the European Parliament, are the actual legislators. But it is also because energy issues are dealt with by so many different parts of the Commission and one Directorate-General (DG) does not always know what another one is up to, and they may even hold very different views on the same subject. It is worth noting that, under President Jacques Santer the divisions within the Commission (and those involving energy policy) appear to be less dramatic than they were under the previous President Jacques Delors, and are fading. But then, this current Commission is a softer giant, intent on compromise, building bridges, and steady progress, rather than on the leaps of vision that were more evident in the early 1990s.

Secondly, this report aims to provide a much-needed commentary on the process of policy-making at the EU level. There is no shortage of analysis and criticism of individual policies and how they will affect *relevant parties. One aspect of this is focused through the lobby groups in Brussels, such as Europia, for the oil industry, or Eurelectric, for the electricity industry. At the national level, too, topical issues flare up into publicity when one particular group is adversely affected. But, unlike the unceasing analysis in national media of the way national governments operate, there is almost no analysis and criticism, beyond the very big issues (such as monetary union or enlargement) of the way the EU institutions are conducting their business. Thus, each chapter in this report concludes with a personal assessment of some of the issues covered in the chapter. These assessments are largely aimed at commenting on the process of policy-making, rather than on the policies themselves.'*

In the hope of sparking some media attention, I included, in conclusion to the nuclear chapter, one particularly controversial comment. But – truth to be told – it sparked no attention whatsoever, media or otherwise. Much as I would like to write in more detail about many of the issues included in the book – from liberalisation to climate change (there so much effort happening 25 years ago) to enlargement – I shall limit myself to this (nuclear) one.

The EU was born out of a first treaty covering coal and steel in 1951. This expired in 2002, its activities being fully absorbed into the modern treaties. In 1957 came the Euratom Treaty, aimed at creating a specialist market for nuclear power in Europe. This treaty has no expiry date, and has remained largely unamended ever since – all of the EU's nuclear affairs continue to be conducted under its umbrella. Article 1 of the Treaty states: 'It shall be the task of the Community to contribute to the raising of the standard of living in the Member States and to the development of relations with other countries by creating the conditions necessary for the speedy establishment and growth of nuclear industries.'

'One could put forward a quasi-legal argument,' I wrote, 'that the Treaty has already expired. Because 14 of the 15 Member States have now come to reject any growth in nuclear power, the Article 1 objective can no longer be considered valid. Alternatively, one could say, as the Commission does in its latest [strategy document], that the nuclear industry in Europe is a mature industry. By that argument, the objective in Article 1 is also more than outdated, it is invalid – there is no need to create the conditions for it to grow, if it is already mature. The consequence of this line of reasoning is straightforward. Whichever way Article 1 is viewed, it is invalid. Therefore, if the Treaty's objective has been removed, the Treaty itself cannot be considered valid. It must be considered defunct.' In reality, of course, nuclear issues have been and continue to be so sensitive that the Member States consistently avoid going anywhere near the (anachronistic) Treaty, let alone trying to bring it up-to-date.

By and large, I was very cautious in business matters, and stayed clear of engaging in any risky ventures. But I got burnt three times, I would say, in 1998-2000, coincidentally or not in the period marking the zenith of EC INFORM's trajectory.

In spring of 1998, I invested £2,000 in printing 13,000 mini-editions of *EC INFORM-Transport*. These mini editions were cute. An exact replica of the newsletter itself, only in A5 format, not A4. Cheaper to print, and much cheaper to post. The plan was to pay a consultant working for the Chartered Institute of Transport £1,500 to insert a mini-copy of EC INFORM-Transport in 13,000 mailings to the Institute's members. I expected scores of enquiries if not subscriptions, yet, in the following week, nothing came in, not by mail, not by fax, not by phone. It was as though the mailing had never happened. This was unprecedented in my experience for such a large promotion.

I contacted the consultant. He had no explanation and sent me the postage dockets to prove the mailing had gone out. When I examined these dockets carefully, I discovered that a) the mailing was for 9,000 not 13,000; and b) the weight of each item was far below what I would have expected for the Institute's own magazine plus my insert. So, I refused to pay the insert fee – none of it – and found myself in a dispute with the consultant and then with the Institute itself. Sleepless nights followed as I feared legal action. It never came, but as I'd spent so much money on the print run, I felt frustrated at the failure. I think, eventually, the promotion brought in one solitary order.

More serious, though, were the consequences of my deciding to launch a third monthly newsletter – *EC INFORM-Health* – and employ a second trainee journalist. Theo had already fulfilled his commitment to stay with me for two years, and was likely to leave before the end of his third year. Employing a new assistant made sense as a way of covering myself for his leaving, and, meanwhile, to be working towards expanding the business with another title. I advertised first in late 1998, but it wasn't until the following May that I made the decision to employ a young woman called Krysia. In interviews, she had shown an immense keenness for what EC INFORM was doing, and a background that gave me hope she could be a second Theo. On the down side, she was going to have to move to Surrey from the North, find a flat and car (no public transport to Elstead). 'I have no idea whether Krysia will make it or not,' I wrote in my diary. 'I have made the best choice I can, but I don't know if she'll be able to hack the density of the work. Only time will tell. [. . .] I think she is the biggest risk I have yet taken.'

Within days of her starting work, I had serious doubts; and after 10 days I was worrying about her constantly. There's a fair bit in my diary about her, but here's the final summary.

5 July 1999

Krysia, yes, I must get her off my chest, so to speak, and out of my journal. She was a big mistake. I thought about her constantly for near on a week I suppose. I had to sort out why she was not meeting my expectations, whether I was being unfairly judgmental, impatient, and over-demanding; and how best to deal with the situation. By her second week I was already beginning to doubt I could turn the situation around, but I didn't believe I should be able to make a decision so quickly. I bounced my thoughts off Theo once or twice, and he was fairly supportive of my opinion – that she was slow, and unable to use her initiative – but was not willing to commit himself to agreeing that I should get rid off her. By the end of the week, I was thinking I might talk to her seriously and suggest I give her another two weeks. However, she went up to the City Business Library with Theo on Thursday (to research health issues, lobby groups, marketing ideas) and brought back some reasonable stuff on Friday, so I decided to leave my decision until Monday. Theo came in on Saturday. I quizzed him about the day with Krysia, and he confirmed my worst suspicions that she had only come back with reasonable material because Theo had actually helped her hugely. This time, when I suggested I would have to let her go, he agreed. And so my mind was made up.

The only problem then was how to actually broach the subject. Unfortunately, however many times one tries to predict a future conversation in one's mind, one can never get much further than the first part. I did go over it all, trying to find both the full justification for the decision, in case she challenged me in detail, and a soft gentle way of explaining it all to her. Monday morning came, by which time I was actually quite calm (I had told Theo to keep his head down). As soon as she arrived I sat her down in the kitchen and told her I felt it wasn't working and that I thought we had both made a big mistake. I explained that I felt it would take me much longer than I had expected to train her and that – quite simply – I couldn't afford it. [. . .] When she said it was a big dent to her confidence, I suggested that perhaps she needed that dent, that she had taken on something too big, something out of her depth. There was no hint of an apology on her part, no sorrow that she had let me down. And I took a goodly proportion of the blame for the situation, allowing her to slink off, an half hour later. What a relief, but what an expensive mistake (two weeks wages). At least I can be thankful that I didn't keep her on longer. She sounded so plausible and yet had a completely disproportionate belief in herself.

Krysia may have had her confidence dented, but mine was broken, in that I was now certain EC INFORM would never flourish. For just two weeks, it had been a three-person business; within a few months Theo would be gone, and it would, again, be just a one-man band.

Before leaving, in autumn 1999, Theo had drafted most of the chapters for the transport book, yet there was still a huge amount of work to prepare it for publication, and this kept me busy through 1999. Indeed, I would only finalise the proofs and put them in the mail (to a printer in Suffolk) late afternoon on 31 December, with just hours to go before the Millennium Bug was due to bring the world as we knew it to an end – or not.

As I indicated above, there was a third major disturbance to the equanimity of my business life. In 2000, I took on a commission from Eurelectric, the association representing the common interests of the electricity industry at a pan-European level. It was one of the most active energy lobby groups in Brussels. I had always had a very good relationship with its staff, and occasionally been invited on free press trips, such as one to Paris which included attending a World Cup match at the Stade de France. Later that year, Eurelectric was planning a series of events to mark the 75th anniversary of cooperation within the industry, and it wanted a publication to celebrate the event and to distribute to its many members. It contracted with a third party, a company called Atalink, to produce, promote and distribute the book, and I was asked to write the text – 50,000 words for a fee of £20,000.

Despite the sizeable fee, I was reluctant and initially rejected Atalink's offer. After a first meeting with Eurelectric staff, I felt they were reliant on Atalink to magically produce the book, and showed little willingness to cooperate in terms of providing information, contacts, pictures, etc. I explained this to Atalink's managing director who then talked to Eurelectric staff before subsequently convincing me that I would get all the help I needed. I didn't, no assistance was ever forthcoming. The staff repeatedly told me they had no time allocated to the project.

Nevertheless, I worked very hard to structure and write an informative and lively text, combining an historical panorama of cooperation in the industry alongside the association's modern day activities and priorities. I kept Eurelectric and Atalink informed of my schedule, submitted drafts regularly, and delivered a final copy of my text on time. Atalink produced a smart, glossy document, and this was launched in December 2000 at a big anniversary bash in Brussels. I got back to my flat a little merry, and took a first close look at the document. It didn't take long to notice that my name was missing from the front cover, and nor could it be found below the title on the title page. In fact, my name appeared in only two very insignificant places inside: once in tiny print next to a copyright symbol, and once as 'the author' at the foot of a page with several other acknowledgements.

I was livid to say the least, and remained so for a couple of weeks. Firstly, I composed a letter to the Eurelectric chief, detailing my resentment. Despite not having benefitted from any cooperation from you, I wrote, I produced a high quality text on time, and now, clearly, you are trying to usurp my authorship. Initially, I was in doubt about how and why this had happened, but as emails went back and forth, I became more convinced that a particular individual at Eurelectric had conspired to minimise acknowledgement of my contribution.

Eurelectric was slow to respond, and I thought it not impossible that neither Eurelectric nor Atalink would care two hoots about my fury. Fortunately, I found a loophole in their joint corporate might. Part of Atalink's business model relied on guaranteeing those companies that had paid handsomely for advertising inside the anniversary publication, a website with further advertising. I checked the website and found that this made no mention of me – the author – none at all. I scoured my contract and could not find any mention of my text being made available on the web. So, I wrote to Atalink insisting that no extra use be made of my text over and above that which was initially agreed. This excluded, I emphasised, any further print runs, and any use of the text in any other form, whether it be electronically, on the web, or as part of any other publication.

I wrote in my diary: 'It's hard to know if I'm making too much out of this – and I probably would be, if there was a genuine mistake in there, but every time I think I might be making a mistake, I remind myself that R__, either with the chief's knowledge or without it, deliberately chose to leave my name off the book's cover. This was such a mean-spirited, dishonourable kind of action that I am spurred on to do my worst.'

Several further letters flew out to both Eurelectric and Atalink. Fairly swiftly, I would say, the website was taken down. And not long after, the boss of Atalink called me, generously and humbly asking how the matter could be sorted out in my favour so that he could get his promotional website for Eurelectric and the book back up and running. And a letter from the Eurelectric's chief also arrived apologising for the situation.

I'd hit a commercial nerve, but, as it happens, I also had a simple solution up my sleeve. The website could easily be adjusted to ensure that my authorship of the book was properly acknowledged. And, as for the thousands of copies of the book waiting to mailed out to electricity industry firms and associations across Europe, I asked if it would be possible to print 'by Paul K Lyons' on transparent labels and affix them to each and every one of the front covers. Yes, of course, Atalink's boss responded. And it was done. The text of my name was in the same font as the title, and positioned exactly where you'd expect to find an author's name.

I had been tense throughout the dispute, and I certainly had not enjoyed it, but I did relish having got into a fight – through no fault of my own – and won it.

But I have a postscript to this story. Among my old business papers, I found – while writing this chapter – the original Atalink contract. It is written on one A4 page and has nine provisions, content, payment, deadlines etc. The last provision reads: '9) Credits. The author will be credited within the publication.' WITHIN! I don't believe I'd bothered to check the contract when first so startled and angry about the absence of my name on the cover. If I had, I might not have raised the matter at all, let alone gone at it like an enraged bull.

By early 2001, I'd been back to running EC INFORM on my own for over a year, researching, writing, producing the two monthlies, the quarterly, the website summaries etc., not to mention all the admin. It was gruelling, and lonely. I was already of a mind that I would have to shut up shop sometime in the future, but when and how? Subscriptions, by their very nature, are paid upfront, which means that publishers are always in debt to their customers. If I did not want to repay subscribers then I would, at a minimum, have to print and distribute a full year's set of 11 issues without taking any new subscriptions. Alternatively – and this is what I chose to do – I could issue renewal invoices, not for a year but for steadily decreasing portions of the year. Evidently, there would be no marketing spend, so the largest costs would be my time, and printing/posting the newsletters.

There are a number of entries in my diary during the second half of the year in which I write of my concern for the future. Here's one: 'Will I just go into freefall depression and end up a postman or barman? If I think I'm getting bad enough already – in terms of my isolation and lack of social intercourse – what will I be like when all structure is removed from my life? A jelly?'

After much soul-searching and consideration of practical realities, I made the decision to definitively close down EC INFORM at the end of 2002. But it was also clear to me that I would need to stay put in Elstead for a while, at least until 2005, when Adam, by then a fairly independent teenager, had finished at the nearby sixth form college.

Meanwhile, I was still travelling back and forth to Brussels, to find stories to fill my monthly newsletters, but increasingly I was finding access to officials more difficult. The Directorates-General for Energy and Transport had been merged into one – DG Tren – which should have made my life easier. Yet, at the same time, there had been a crackdown on security, and I was unable to enter commission buildings unchecked, and waltz from office to office looking for off-the-record chats as I'd done for more than a decade. Energy and transport liberalisation had faded as priorities, and the internet was being used to distribute information more widely and quickly, often leaving the news in my printed newsletters less than topical.

I'd long since stopped bothering to write in my diary about the issues in Brussels, after all I was recording enough about them for the newsletters. But every now and then, I did feel the need to outpour, as it were, as with the Atalink affair. In 2001, there's a long entry on my views about climate change ('The Bush administration has cut the Kyoto Protocol into shreds . . .' – see also Chapter ten.) And there's another about corruption in the Commission. I'd once uncovered some murky details about a Commission official directing grant energy project money to his wife's company. But my newsletters were hardly the place for such journalism. With the help of a colleague, we brought the matter to the attention of an MEP, who then asked a parliamentary question, a very pointed one (which, months later, would be published in the official records).

A juicy morsel came my way in 2001, again not one for publication. Francois Lamoureux, the Director General in charge of DG Tren, was not much liked. He had decided that a small grant (Eur10m/yr) programme for international projects outside the EU (Synergy) should only accept larger projects so as to minimise the number of projects and associated admin. The Member States did not agree, but Lamoureux persisted, pressuring them. The Danish government's chief negotiator in Brussels told his energy official (a good source of mine who relayed the story to me) that Lamoureux had offered to intervene on behalf of Denmark in a state aid dispute if only he would support the Commission's plan for Synergy. When I asked my source if this kind of horse-trading was a common occurrence, he said absolutely not, he'd never come across it before. The Danish, I felt, must have been pretty cross about this to have tittle-tattled to a journalist. I had a good enough relationship with the Commission spokesperson on energy to tell him the story. He flustered a bit, I wrote in my diary, while supportive of Lamoureux's sense of purpose on Synergy, he wouldn't say anything about my allegations, claiming they were unfounded and he didn't believe them (with a little tongue in his cheek).

In October 2001, I met up with Vladimir Putin – via video-link! (I only mention this spurious fact because, as I write, the man is in the news every day, having ordered Russia to invade Ukraine some three months ago.) Here's my diary entry for the occasion.

3 October 2001
Vladimir Putin was in Brussels today (and yesterday) for a Russia-EU summit. I watched him (on a screen video link) answer questions from the press. He looks so young to be in charge of such a huge country with so many problems.

Early on his microphone wasn't working, and the person next to him leaned over to press a button. Putin stretched out an arm to pat the person on the back. 'Prodi's in charge of who talks', he joked, only it was Javier Solana next to him not Prodi. Energy remains a key component of the partnership, and I have a working paper describing the state of the talks. Usefully, because I'm short of energy stories, this should provide a feature. Interestingly, Putin also seemed to soften his stance against the expansion of Nato.

In December, I published the 99th edition of *EC INFORM-Energy*. In the diary: 'The next issue will be a landmark 100th issue, and mark nine years of running my own business; three years of working alone, three with Theo, and three again alone. It must be time to call it a day. It must be time to call it a day. But I have doubts all the time.' On 1 January, I noted that that 'the big news of the new year is the cold-blooded murder of twelve currencies.'

My renewal invoices – in Pounds Sterling – went out to subscribers with a letter explaining about the reduced subscription period: 10 months, 9 months . . . By mid-year, I was starting to explore whether I could sell EC INFORM or one or other of the newsletters. I advertised in my own titles and in one mainstream weekly newspaper; I even contacted a sales agent but he was too expensive.

By October, I'd provided details to half a dozen prospective buyers of which two seemed serious, with talk of a £60,000-80,000 price. But time was getting a bit tight: if there was going to be any continuance beyond December, renewal invoices would need mailing in November. Neither prospective buyer was proactive, and only seemed to react when I emailed them with deadlines for various possible decisions.

I took my last trip to Brussels and cleared out the flat. I wrote and prepared the last editions of the newsletters, including indexes, still without knowing whether they would exist in January.

Late in November, I was called to a meeting with a guy from The Waterfront Partnership. He was a recent subscriber to *EC INFORM-Transport*, and had been immensely complimentary about the title, saying 'it doesn't get much better than this'. But at the meeting, I realised he and his colleagues had little idea about the economics of the newsletter business, and after the meeting I wrote in my diary 'these guys would never get their heads round taking on *EC INFORM-Transport*, they didn't really have the first idea of how to run a newsletter and they weren't about to start now.'

The other prospective buyer, Newzeye, which already published not dissimilar newsletters, was only interested in *EC INFORM-Energy*, and by the time we sat down, in early December (one day before publication of my last issue of *EC INFORM-Energy*), to finalise a deal, I still didn't know how they wanted to handle the transition. I made it clear, though, that I needed a signed contract and a cheque for some of the money BEFORE I went to press with the last issue in mid-December (so that I could advise readers as to what was happening). And how much was it worth, *EC INFORM-Energy*? The figure had come down a long way from my initial hopes (well, no, to be exact, I never expected to be able to sell either newsletter) – £80,000, then £50,000, and finally £24,000 to be paid in tranches. I did some soul-searching over this figure. I felt a strong temptation to forego any money in exchange for being completely unfettered within days. It wasn't a fortune, but for me it was still a lot of money – half my net return for one of EC INFORM's better years.

At the meeting, we agreed there was no need for legal wrappings, and we signed a Heads of Agreement. For the agreed price, Newzeye would receive subscription lists, marketing databases, editorial files, back issues of the newsletter, and a list of lapsed subscribers. It would also receive from me editorial assistance for the first four issues in 2003 (requiring me to be at its offices in west London), marketing advice and contacts, and assistance with the transition.

I'd prepared a letter for my *EC INFORM-Energy* subscribers – a last editorial but a good-bye also – to be inserted into the last issue IF Newzeye had failed to finalise its purchase. I wrote in my diary instead.

'What do I feel,' I asked my diary, 'as I come to the end of EC INFORM? A great sense of relief (tempered somewhat by the thought of having to continue part-time for four months); no regrets at all that I can touch; no fear at all about the future. [. . .] On the whole, I feel certain I've made the right decision, and that I've managed the closure in an orderly fashion.'

I'd started a business from scratch, debt free, run it for 10 years making a decent living, and now I was closing it down, smoothly, efficiently, and for a decent price.

Suddenly – well, by April at least – I was a free man. And what was I to do next? I'd been a journalist, on the Brussels beat for the best part of 15 years, and now I was not a journalist any longer, nor did I have any beat. However, I'd already – a year earlier – started work on *Kip Fenn – Reflections*, a novel of ambitious proportions. I relished the prospect of being able to work on it full-time.

Chapter five

ADAM
THE JOYS AND PRIVILEGES OF FATHERHOOD

I have written about how Bel and I came to the biggest decision of our lives, to have a child together (Why Ever – Chapter fifteen), and how our lives dovetailed to become what I've called the Adam Co-op and then how our lives diverged (Chapter one). In this latter chapter I wrote about the complexities and tensions of parenting in such a way. But in this chapter I want to focus on Adam himself, to show, if I can, how it was such a privilege to be his father, and to recall – with help from my diaries – how much joy he brought. Along the way, there were challenges, and while I intend Adam to remain the hero throughout, I will bring heavy judgement on my own failings. I am no wimp in this regard, I believe strongly in parental responsibility, and thus this will serve as my confessional. Evidently, if Adam were not today a stable, happy and fulfilled individual, I might have decided against divulging such matters. You will have to wait for his own biographical writings to be published (he has a huge hoard of diary material, digitalised and safely archived already) for his opinion on if and how those failings caused him any untoward strife in his adult life.

I've covered Adam's early years already in the context of the relationship between Bel and I, our times in Aldeburgh and in Brighton (Chapter one). Here's a typical entry from my diary from when he was around 18 months old: 'After supper it is bath time and then we spend a pleasant 30-45 minutes in the lounge as usual. He is always (of late at least) very good humoured at this hour and we play a lot. He climbs up and down the sofa, and on to the table, he throws himself across me and dives into the cushions. We laugh together over the slightest game – this evening it was just putting hands in front of eyes.' In late April 1990, he and I took our first holiday (other than Aldeburgh) – to the Peak District. Another snapshot.

29 April 1989
We wash up a bit, and then go out for a walk along the river. The house nests at the end of a terrace right below a small cable car operation to the Heights of Abraham. I point out the cable cars and tell Adam we are to go in one of them tomorrow or Saturday. The cable car will prove to be the highlight of this short holiday for the young man. When it starts to rain we make a beeline for a bandstand situated on the river path. There we perch on the floor and eat a picnic. I

suggest Adam tell his mother that we had 'a picnic in the rain in Matlock Bath'. Quite a mouthful but he manages.

This is such a pleasure: sitting with my son, sharing each bit of the picnic, talking about the food, about the river, about the rain. Here we are Adam and I alone, enjoying our first trip together; the first of many, many such trips. We wipe our hands on the grass and walk on a little more. The rain, however, gets heavier and we are forced to return to the B&B. I read Adam some new books I have bought. One of them – 'Kimi and the Watermelon' from New Zealand – he asks me to read again as soon as I've finished. He has never asked me to re-read a book. I oblige.'

And also in 1990, we went to France, Adam and I, to stay with my good friend Raoul and children at a farmhouse owned by friends of his – it was an unusually social time for us. Adam blended in immediately, loving the space and the excitement of the place; just being with other children made him so happy. The first day we spent by and in a glorious river, and another day I took all the children for a walk. On the way, I awarded imaginary red stars for special finds, hedgerow flowers, snails. When I asked them to listen to the distant church bells, Jack (Raoul's oldest) said that's special and won another red star.

There were other moments of magic on that walk. Having both armed themselves with sticks, Adam and Jack together started singing a mantra – 'knock all the dangers down'. From then on, the two marched along the overgrown pathways swiping at the brambles with their sticks, singing the mantra with every swipe. When we were buried deep in a forest, I suggested we should all scream as loud as we could – the forest being a good place to let off steam, make noise. The screaming developed into animal noises, a booming amalgamation of pig oinks, cow moos, horse neighs.

During that holiday, I made up a series of stories for Adam, about a bicycle called Henry and a boy called Robert. After the initial story, I'd ask Adam for key words to include in the next one, to give each sequel a focus. Occasionally, I'd run out of steam, and Adam would become upset, 'Daddy, you're not talking, you're not talking.' I think I must have discovered my tale-telling self on this holiday for on at least three occasions I found myself able to enchant the small group of children with make-believe. 'Throughout the three days I barely got a minute to myself,' I wrote in the diary. 'I didn't mind since I so enjoyed the positive interaction with the children; but in my talks with adults it became apparent that they somehow expected to have time to themselves, like it was their right.'

I would find this time and time again throughout Adam's childhood, i.e. that whereas it was normal for parents to need time free of their children, to socialise with friends, to indulge in adult past-times (not least drinking), it was time with Adam that I found most fulfilling, most rewarding. Bel and I, for example, never fought to have more time free of parenting duties – but the reverse was definitely true.

In January 1992, a letter arrived for one proud dad in Kilburn. It contained Adam's first ever story, complete with a picture of a pig. 'THE PIG FELL INTO THE MUD AND FOUND SOMETHING HARD AND HE THOUGHT IT WAS A DIAMOND. HE FOUND HIS OWN SHOE THAT HE LOST IN THE MUD BECAUSE WHEN HE FELL OVER IT SANK DOWN.'

In March, Adam started school at St Bartholomew's in the centre of Brighton. He loved his first days, trying to offer his new teacher an old penny he had in his pocket, and hiding from me in the classroom because he didn't want to come home. It wasn't long before I discovered that he had developed – already, so soon – a secret life during his school days. From the beginning, we would pepper him with banal questions which he couldn't or wouldn't answer. One time, I stopped in the middle of reading him a story, and unexpectedly asked him something about his school day. He said he was a bit sad. A BIT SAD. We had assumed all had been hunky dory since the first, so this was a shock. I quizzed him intently and decided that he himself didn't know why he was sad. Yet, a little while later, he let slip that he was sad because Darran had pulled his hat off several times despite pleas for him to stop. I wrote in the diary: 'It was truly painful experiencing that playground loneliness, that playground humiliation on the basis of the few bits of information gleaned.' After talking to Bel, and mulling things over, I decided it would be best to leave Adam to his own devices, to let him navigate his own way out of trouble. The most important thing, I concluded, was to find ways to encourage him to communicate.

His very first school report: 'Adam demonstrates a very wide vocabulary and an acquisitive interest in language. Adam has made a good start with reading . . . Adam counts reads and writes numbers to 10 very reliably. . . Adam enjoys involvement with experimental activities and can discuss possibilities of outcome. Adam shows a clear ability to hypothesis and can demonstrate his understanding through language' and so on. But it would be remiss of me to leave out a comment by the RE teacher: 'He does not always accept his responsibilities as a member of the class at tidying up times.'

In January 1993, Bel and Adam moved to live with me in Kilburn, temporarily, and Adam started at a newly-built school – St Mary's – only a few minutes away. Bel and I were so pleased, not only at it being so nearby but because it had such excellent (spanking new) facilities. Unfortunately, Adam soon came home asking why everyone at school was so rough, and he reverted to chewing his shirt or hoody cuffs, a behaviour he had exhibited when younger, when stressed at nursery or school.

He reported several incidents, like playing a game of horses with lots of different boys sitting on him. On arriving home it would take him several hours before he'd relaxed enough to smile and laugh. Sometimes, I would observe him with blank eyes staring into space.

An interview with his teacher convinced me that there was a serious problem with discipline in the school, the culture, and no short-term solutions were likely to be forthcoming. By April we had moved him to Emmanuel School in West Hampstead, much smaller (with a playground the size of a postage stamp), much less well-resourced, and significantly further away (i.e. not in easy walking distance). But, crucially, it was well run by an old-fashioned teacher (Miss Goddard), rather elderly and Victorian in outlook, but Adam was transformed almost overnight back to his cheery smiling self. And for the next two years, he thrived and thrived, to the point where he was in a class a year ahead of his age, despite being an August child and thus the youngest in his natural year cohort.

One of his teachers, a Miss Oliver told me that Adam was one of the cleverest children she had ever taught! And another, a young man called Mr Page, was particularly inspiring in the way he encouraged Adam into a love of writing stories.

The school had a small parent-teacher association, effective enough but yet a closed shop. Its chairman was in cahoots with the head. Two of the teachers, liked by both Adam and myself, wanted him replaced, and I was tempted to become involved. But when the parents re-elected him chairman, I decided to focus instead on the school's forthcoming 150th anniversary celebrations in spring 1995, for which a sub-committee had been organised. The primary role I created for myself was to produce an anniversary newspaper/magazine to be given away to every pupil. This proved to be a time-consuming but very enjoyable project: researching the school's long history and creating a time-line, interviewing Miss Goddard, liaising with the local church and Father Peter (Emmanuel being a Church of England school), taking photographs, commissioning pictures and poems from the pupils, and selling advertisements to local businesses (I was determined the magazine would pay for itself). My own research led to several items for the magazine. One concerned the school's 100th anniversary in 1945, the details of which I'd found in the church parish magazine; another was a compilation of the school's current stats and finances. I also compiled a full list of heads complete with short commentaries on their legacy (again taken from the church magazine), and a chart of pupil numbers throughout the 150 years.

I employed my company's business printer whom I'd persuaded to do the job at cost, and we sold quite a few extra (over and above those given out free) during the festivities at £2 per copy. A few years later, when I'd developed a personal website, I created a pdf of the magazine and made it available online – it's still available today as I write, just search for Emmanuel School "Souvenir Programme".

Bel had returned to full-time work in 1994, which, since I now worked from home, left me mostly responsible for Adam during weekdays, taking him to school, collecting him and looking after him until Bel came home from work around 6:30. I found Adam astonishingly self-sufficient, able to amuse himself for long periods. We'd usually spend half an hour on fun reading or maths, and then he'd watch a TV programme or two.

Though I was keen to be teaching my young boy, I didn't necessarily get it right.

> 19 January 1994
> [Adam] demonstrates a really superb temperament – he never loses his temper, or even gets remotely cross – he puts up with everything I make him do, and, most of the time, perseveres with the tasks I have given him. However, he will take any opportunity to turn anything into a joke or fun. I suffer greatly from not knowing how much to expect of him. I am hugely anxious not to expect too much, but it is astonishing how easy I can get caught into a belief that he should know something. This leads occasionally, more often in the last few days, to me getting cross when he fails to meet those expectations.

> 12 April 1995
> I lay awake for some time in the night worrying about my behaviour towards Adam. I felt very vulnerable and sorry. I really shouldn't get cross and shout, I shouldn't be explaining so much all the time. We need more silences, more ordinary spaces between us. Today we have a no-telling off day. In fact, I don't find this difficult, having taken the conscious effort not to get cross. I just keep a cool temper and ask him to do whatever needs doing instead of getting cross that he hasn't done it.

By way of balance, here's one of my very favourite memories from Adam's childhood.

> 26 January 1994
> While I was preparing supper this evening, Adam climbed up on his small chair, that sits by the sink so he can wash his hands, and asked if he could have a climb. Yesterday or the day before he'd climbed on to my shoulders. I had stood very still so that, eventually, he climbed down out of shear boredom. This time, however, I saw a twinkle in his eye, 'Don't look in my pocket,' he cried, trying hard not to turn his smile into a laugh. When I turned round, he said 'Oh darn it' or something like that it (he's full of good value old fashioned expressions such as Yippee, and Yummee). Then I saw that he had a mini-book in his trouser pocket. Adam had assumed I had sussed him out directly but it took me more than a few seconds to work out the joke. His plan, quite simply, was to take a book up the mountain so that he wouldn't get bored while at the top.

We moved to Elstead in Surrey in the autumn of 1995, which meant another move of school for Adam, this one more traumatic for he was leaving behind good friends he'd made at Emmanuel School. We would stay in Elstead for the next ten years, until Adam left to go to university in fact. It's a large village, is Elstead, with a handful of shops, not least a post office (which was extremely useful for my small business), no more than 200 yards from Russet House, and a school even nearer (Chapter one). Nor were they the only benefits that we hadn't known about before moving. Yes, we had to drive most places – for a supermarket, train station, the leisure complex – but we were surrounded on all sides by the most beautiful countryside, made up of large tracts of open heath land, peat bogs and deciduous forests, with a multitude of good tracks, river walks, and even wild swimming ponds. Some of the land was, very occasionally, employed by the armed services for training purposes (there were notices to this effect), and though caterpillar tracks could be seen in the mud in the winter, I never actually came across any such manoeuvres. Which is not to say we didn't see Chinooks hovering above the heathland now and then.

Over the next years, Adam and I would spend much of our free time – summer and winter – on bikes, riding free and fun-filled through the largely unspoilt landscapes. We imagined a fantasy world, in which we gave names to characterful trees and told stories about the Moss-heads and the Stickwigs. At the centre of this world was Dragonfly Island, a dry patch in the middle of bogland, accessed by boardwalks, with an encyclopaedic information board on dragonflies – thanks to the Thursley Nature Reserve. We would sail a model boat (coloured red and yellow, first sailed on the ornamental pond by the Aldeburgh seafront) in different locations. There was one largish pond called The Moat which had the advantage of having accessible edges all the way round. Another, though smaller pond had shrubs on one side (very near where we once found a feeder stream with giant fresh water mussel shells), and rescuing the boat with long sticks became part of the game. Half way along the track from Elstead to Tilford, the very one that monks would have trod centuries earlier from Waverley Abbey to their little outpost church in Elstead, we'd park up the bikes, strip off down to our trunks, and swing backwards and forwards from a high rope before plunging 10ft into the deep part of the river run. In the summer, we'd never miss the Tilford fete, a lively affair that was held on the triangle green at the village centre, the same triangle that was used for Tilford's home cricket matches, despite the unnatural shape and a very significant slope!

Mushrooms became a thing for us in the autumns, with many varieties springing up among the beautiful birch trees, and along the fields.

I bought identification picture books, but there seemed more fun in finding poisonous red-spotted toadstools than in frying up the ordinary field mushrooms just for eating. Besides, I never developed enough certain knowledge, and we never found a reliable source for edible mushrooms – though the lady in the post office told me it was the Poles who knew all the best places. Apparently, there had been a camp of Polish refugees nearby, on Hankley Common, during the war. Many of them had stayed in Britain, and passed on their top secret mushroom knowledge to subsequent generations.

There were also trips at night or slightly further afield than a bicycle would take us: such as to the annual Chiddingfold bonfire night, for example, a sparkling Guy Fawkes event; or to press day at the Farnbourgh Air Show where Adam once got to sit in a Eurofighter. And for these – from 1996 on, until 2002 – I often preferred to use Kiwi (rather than the car), a Kawasaki GPZ 500S motorbike. I'd learned to drive a bike in Brazil, and I'd passed my British motorbike test on returning to Kilburn. But it wasn't until Elstead, where I had a garage, that I bought a bike. And it was significantly more powerful than the 175 trail bike I'd had in Rio. It felt swell to be out and about on two motorised wheels again, though I missed being helmet-less (as had been my way in Rio). Adam did get used to the means of transport, but I don't believe he ever much liked it; there was a never a wow factor from him, not even when I rocked up on Kiwi to collect him from school.

At home and at school, all seemed to be going well with Adam. Here is an abbreviated entry in my diary from early on in our Elstead time.

9 May 1996
IN PRAISE OF ADAM
Yesterday Adam and I rode out to the common, I wanted to have a look at the marshy area near Dragonfly Island, to see if any insect or plant life was beginning to flourish, but all we found were a few water skimmers and the water fast filling with algae. Adam asked me about evolution. His questions were so intelligent. He wanted to know what might happen to a fish which was left in a pond with no food for several million years, whether it would survive. I sensed a real inquisitiveness behind his rather awkward question and so tried to explain the principle of the survival of the fittest in this way. [. . .]

This evening we play a game of Scrabble. I explain how important blanks are and the letter 's' and that they should not be wasted. Once a week, he stays after school for a scrabble club. And once a week, like today, he stays to play chess, but the teacher who looks after the club doesn't know how to play very well. [. . .] When he's at home, he's always practising with the football, and the rackets. What sets Adam apart, I think, is his wonderful loveable personality.

What else can I record about him, while I'm on the subject. Over the long bank holiday weekend, he wrote a magnificent story for homework. He was asked to write a diary of someone going to the North Pole. Encouraged by the purchase of a fountain pen, he spent a long time writing a first draft. It was really well constructed, well written, good handwriting, and it had a beginning, a middle and an end. I was really very impressed. His mental arithmetic is excellent. I think he's in the top groups in all his subjects at school.

And when he's at home, he's never bored. He will dig in the garden, or read, or prepare a magic show, or play games on his computer, or watch television, practice bouncing a ball on his racket; or he'll come to the supermarket, go for a bike ride or a walk on the common, or he'll do something for Bel or I. Always enjoying it and rarely complaining about anything, unless it's going to bed.

The year 1997 had more than its fair share of difficulties for us. After the death of Diana, I asked Adam if he was sad. He said – simply and clearly – he wasn't, he didn't know her, so why should he be sad. He was, however, very interested in the news, which he listened to on his radio every day. One morning, he came bounding down the stairs to tell me that it looked like the seven paparazzi were going to be charged with manslaughter. (Incidentally, he had also taken great pleasure in calling Theo and I 'paparazzi', or 'pratz' for short.)

But two deaths did affect Adam that year. First, in the summer, our friend Rosy died tragically young, after a short sharp cancer. A couple of years earlier, Adam had got to know her and her husband, Andy, while staying at their house in the Sierra Nevada. I took him to the funeral in East Sheen cemetery. A vicar, Andy and Rosy had known since Dublin, conducted the service, a friend played the guitar, several friends spoke. After the service we followed the coffin through the cemetery to the grave. The 100 or so people crowded round as the coffin was lowered. Andy read a poem, Loreena McKennitt sang an ode, and a piper played music in the background.

And all the while that year, Bel's mother, Adam's grandmother, was getting iller and iller. It was a rather slow, difficult dying, much of which, obviously, Bel kept from Adam. She died in November. Bel, Adam and I had just finished our Halloween supper by pumpkin candlelight. The telephone rang with the news, Bel got into all a tizz and raced off almost immediately. Adam, with such feeling, said 'so much for Halloween'. At first I thought he meant he was cross that his Halloween evening had been ruined, but then I realised he was angry with Halloween for, in some way, being implicated in the death of the grandmother that he loved. He was so upset, and he cried off and on until he went to bed. We sat on the sofa and I held him tight as I read him short stories of Scandinavian/Dutch origin. I hadn't looked at that book for ages, and picked out a story simply because it was short. It proved an amazing coincidence though, for it was about an old couple, who lived an insular life, and about how the husband grew so ill that he really wanted to die. Of course I could have stopped reading, but it seemed just right, and the couple seemed so similar to Adam's grandparents. On the evening of the funeral we were talking after dinner, and Bel really just wanted to go home and cry – she'd been bottling it all up for ages. I was trying to cheer her up and said something like, you know she was ready to die. And Adam chirped in with this: 'Yes but we weren't ready for her to die.' Bel's father survived the death of his lifelong partner for a few years, finding new friendships, but eventually succumbed to illness. Adam – by now a teenager and surprisingly smart on the day – gave a reading at his funeral.

Adam's last six months at primary school happened that same year, 1997, and did not go smoothly; he was bored witless. In his school report, Adam was criticised for lack of concentration, fiddling, disturbing other children, and poor presentation – nothing at all about his academic achievements. He had a lousy form teacher, who left under mysterious circumstances, and a head teacher who was not up the job. At home, Adam's behaviour deteriorated sharply, he became lazy, forgetful, rude. And then one day when I was telling him off, I noticed his tie had been cut. He proceeded to make up some excuses for this, and as I tried to get to the truth, his easy lies multiplied. I soon discovered other clothes (and shoes) had been cut, so I piled on the punishments. He'd got hold of a razor blade, I eventually uncovered, and wanted 'to see how sharp it was'!

Children get into all sorts of scrapes, and as the adults around them – whether at school or at home – react, so children learn to fend off the worst of the anger or punishment responses. I soon realised that often what this teaches them is to lie and how to lie more and more effectively. The only way to help avoid this happening is to keep to one of two paths: one is to avoid confrontation that gives a child the need or opportunity to lie; and, the other is only to confront a child with misbehaviour when one has a clear and strong understanding of what has happened. Nevertheless, I think most teenagers learn to deceive their parents effectively, mostly perhaps by omission, but also with imaginative excuses. And thank goodness they do. As an adult, Adam has recounted to me some of his teenage antics. I've listened aghast at what I didn't know, but what on earth would I have done if I had known. Unfortunately, I was a confrontational parent, liberal often, yes, but also determined to hold certain boundaries. I have more to say about this, but, for the moment, let me move on to see Adam, in September 1998, finally progress to secondary school, at Rodborough in Godalming.

The new school was a five mile journey but luckily there was a free bus which stopped at the end of our road, making for easy logistics.

I only had to collect Adam in the car on days he stayed behind for a club, or when we went together straight after school to the leisure centre to swim. Once at secondary school, he very quickly re-established a much-improved norm. He was interested in the lessons, worked hard, joined a few clubs. As before, he would usually spend Sunday-Wednesday nights at my house, returning home from school on Thursday night to Bel's house. He would also be at Bel's house during my monthly trips to Brussels; but the weekends were freer, and I'd see him often, and Bel too. After all, her house was but 200 metres away. The system wasn't ideal – Adam had trouble keeping track of his clothes and stuff for his school bag – but it was the best we could manage, given a) that we both wanted to be as much a part of Adam's life as possible, and b) I was best placed (working from home) to provide the practical base for most of his school week.

Very soon after moving to Elstead, I had volunteered myself to join a small group of villagers organising an annual paper boat race – held on the largish nearby pond called The Moat. These were no ordinary paper boats, though, because they had to carry at least one person, and be rowed around a circuit for 15 minutes – or longer than any other boat stayed afloat. Strict rules were applied to the type of glues and paper permitted in the construction (i.e. to avoid anything remotely plastic). There were trophies to be won, not least for the best-looking boat. In times past, the event had been held annually, but then it had lapsed for lack of interest. Now it was being revived. Unfortunately, this first paper boat race in ten years proved a bit of a wash out, thanks to rain and wind, and only four boats turning up. Nevertheless, I thought it such an original, lively and colourful event that I wanted to help keep it going. I joined the small committee made up of the local dentist (who was very handy with boats), a lady-of-the-manor type (who organised us and hosted meetings in her manor), and an old timer who had run the event in the past and knew all there was to know about building water-tight paper craft. He also ran the events on the day through a hefty tannoy system. I looked after press and publicity, producing posters and pasting them up around the village, issuing press releases, and inviting local press to attend. We didn't raise a whole lot of money – from entrance fees, volunteers rattling cans in the crowds on the day, cake and drinks sales, and local sponsors – but what we did raise all went to local causes, like the school.

In subsequent years, the paper boat race became a highlight of village life, with many varieties of boats, some more pond worthy than others, taking to the waters. Every race would end with water fights, flour bomb throwing and – in theory – boat sinkings. As organisers, we were a little disappointed to find that a couple of winning boat-makers extracted their craft out of the water quickly, before they could be sunk, in order to store and bring them back the following year. That was not in the spirit of the event!

Adam with a friend, James, made two boats (with parental help). The first was a patriotic effort, in 1998, named 'England-for-the-Cup'. Here's a flavour of the day.

> 21 June 1998
> What a day yesterday. The Elstead Paper Boat Race 1998. We've worked all week on the boat, gluing scraps of cardboard together, gluing the joints over with newspaper, priming it, and painting it. [...] On Saturday morning, Ads and I were still doing the final decorations, red crosses for the England flag, putting some black spots on the two mock footballs made of paper, and pasting the printed nameplates on the sides.
>
> There was a magnificent turnout, with a dozen or so boats for the junior race and almost as many for the adult race. [...] The first boats started arriving at about 2pm – I couldn't believe how neat and tidy and big they all were; some looked like perfect boats; they had no ragged edges, and the inside was as sealed and perfect as the outside. They were all painted as though by an interior decorator. Later, a few less perfect ones did arrive; on the whole, though, there was a fantastic range of styles and names, and themes. [...] There was a huge hubbub around the boat area before the first race, for the under 14s, got off.
>
> We carried HMS 'England-for-the-Cup' to the water's edge, Adam launched off on his own [we'd decided at the last moment it wouldn't hold two boys]. He had three painted cardboard paddles, but these soon let him down and he was left stranded mid-Moat before even completing one lap with only his hands to propel him along. We waited for him to come near and then pushed a bona fide paddle out to him. As soon as he got used to it, he made good time but others were too far ahead and he didn't win one of the two little cups for the junior race. There were lots of flour bombs being lobbed around from shore to boats and from boat to boat, and some boats did sink. I'm pleased to report, though, that HMS 'England-for-the-Cup' survived the full 15 minutes and lots of messing around with both children on board. Eventually, the kids broke it up and we filled four refuse sacks with the wet remains.'

The second boat we made – in 1999 – was based on several large sheets of bright yellow cardboard I found at the back of a Homebase store. It looked great, and we named her 'Yellow Shark Machine'. But, she didn't float very well, especially with two sizeable teens inside. She sank in the best possible way, slowly and steadily, disintegrating entirely after 12 of the 15 minutes had elapsed. But Adam and James won the most coveted prize – for best design. Pleasingly, a photo of them both and 'Yellow Shark Machine' was featured in the local newspapers turning them into celebrities at their schools for a minute or two.

Adam also took part a couple of times in another local event – the Elstead Marathon. He ran the three mile race for the first time in 1999, and was furious with himself for letting himself be beaten. I wrote in the diary: 'All the time, Ads couldn't get over his disappointment at not having done better, so I was able to keep congratulating him. And, in the end, he was quite pleased with his medal for second place.' But he was more determined in 2000 – and won.

> 8 July 2000
>
> [Adam] practised several times a week for about three weeks beforehand (mostly at my prompting). He also did well in the District Sports recently, coming second in the 1500 metres. According to Ads, he ran with a boy called Richard, new to Rodborough and new to Elstead, but also good at long-distance running, all the way until just before sight of the winning line. Then Richard broke first, but Ads managed to beat him on the sprint. The Elstead marathon is no minor event. They had some 200 entries all told, in the junior, women's and men's races, and a lot of people were congregated on the green for burgers, raffles and so on. There was a tug-of-war afterwards. Ads was well manic after his win, and milled around with his friends rather than with us. At one point, I couldn't find him at all, and it transpired that he was at The Golden Fleece pub, where Richard lives. Later, he went, uninvited, to a disco in the village hall!

There were plenty of other riches in our life. Would it be too banal to list some of them? After all, memoirists – published ones – do usually prefer to supply the hurt-felt, the heart-felt for their readers. But hang around, because there are some of those to come as well.

We had a fair share of culture, did Adam and I. Not as much as we'd had in London, but enough. The Yvonne Arnaud Theatre in Guildford regularly hosted Shared Experience (*Why Ever* – Chapter ten) – Evelyn Waugh's *A Handful of Dust* and Bertol Brecht's *Mother Courage and her Children* – and other top quality touring productions. And every now and then, we visited the National Theatre on the South Bank – *Guys and Dolls* and Simon Russell Beale in *The Humble Boy*. There was a cute little backstreet theatre in Aldershot – the West End Centre – where we went to see folk, jazz and blues.

Paul Lamb and the King Snakes was one highlight, particularly because Lamb himself was a virtuoso harmonica player – and Adam was patiently teaching himself to play the blues harp. We also went to see Larry Adler – in Basingstoke – world famous for his harmonica playing. It must have been one his last foreign tours. I wasn't expecting much from the gig, but was surprisingly engaged. Between a well-honed patter of jokes and anecdotes, he played many tunes from from *Porgy and Bess*. I reminded Adam that I'd taken his mother to see a fabulous production of the Gershwin musical (with an American cast) in Rio de Janeiro – when and where Adam was conceived.

And of course, there were holidays. I have already mentioned the regular holidays we took with Bel in Britain, the West Country, the Peak

District, Wales, but Adam and I also went abroad. The 'knock all the dangers down' trip to France was the first, but then when Adam was not yet five, we flew to Faro, hired a car and spent a glorious week touring the golden beaches and towns of the Algarve. I was happy to be back speaking Portuguese, though I felt *saudades* for the lyrical music of the Brazilian language against the dry, formal tongue of Portugal. We drove to the very west of the region, to Ponta da Piedade, a headland near Lagos. I thought it the most spectacular place on the coast, with fabulous sea- and weather-carved rock formations – arches, stacks, caverns, tunnels, natural bridges, narrow walkways. We found a flight of steps, built into the rock and intimidatingly steep, that led down to a tiny viewing platform at the water's edge. There, the water swelled and ebbed against the myriad rock forms – quite eerie and majestic, I wrote at the time – and close by was a spectacular blow hole. I mention this place specifically because Adam and I joked for ages about who had got splashed the most – and we're still arguing about this 30 years later. I think it was on this holiday that I first tried to teach my son that his smile was a passport of sorts – it had managed to gain us entry into an ancient Roman site that was, in fact, closed at the time.

The following year, we visited my old friends Peter the Girl, German-born, and her English husband Tony in the Black Forest, where they lived, and Tony painted, in a picture-book village. Our forest walks gave me the opportunity to tell more stories about the Mossheads and Stickwigs; and there was one picnic which Adam insisted we ate on a rock, high above a plain, from which we could see farmhouses, people and cars far below – ever since known as the 'funny willy picnic' for obvious reasons. In late 1993, I took Adam (and Bel) to Budapest, on the back of one of my work conferences. We swam in both the public Szechenyi open air baths and at the fancy Gellert Spa, the former being so much more fun. And for New Year 1994/1995, Adam and I went for the first of three trips to the Granada region in Spain, staying at Rosy and Andy's house in the tiny white-washed village of Acequias. On this first visit, Rosy, Andy and two children were there too, and so we had quite a social time of it, with many friends of theirs popping in or meeting us for meals. We had plenty of time for exploring, the Alhambra of course, the High Alpujarras, the Moorish castle ruins in Lanjaron, the beaches down on the coast, and so on. And when I had a few minutes peace, I devoured *South from Granada* by Gerald Brenan, which brings the history and culture of Sierra Nevada to life, veritably as well Lawrence Durrell did for Corfu say.

Easter is the best time to be in the Granada region for the Easter parades and processions – seemingly put on by every town and village – are simply wonderful to watch, the fields are full of bright red poppies, and the climate is usually a perfect combo of sunny days and cool nights. But it also suited us because, with luck, the ski field above Granada might still be operating.

In 1997, in February, I noticed I had a free week in my work cycle that coincided with Adam's half term. On a whim, I visited a travel agent, and found a bargain chalet holiday at the French ski resort Les Deux Alpes – half price. It was only so cheap because it was imminent – we'd have to leave in two days. I moved into overdrive, and before we knew it Adam and I were on a plane to Geneva. It didn't turn out to be our best holiday, though the chalet was superb (and had its own chef). I set Adam up with ski lessons in the mornings but grew increasingly cross at his failure to take them seriously. Things did improve, but I sprained a knee, and there were always long queues for the lifts. Nevertheless, over the next few years, Adam and I skied at least three more times (Adam was able to negotiate black ski runs by the last): for a couple of days on two separate holidays in Granada during the Easter vacations, once for a week at Morzine, and then a few days in the Pyrenees, when we managed to meet up for a day with Roser also. Much as I loved skiing for a day or two at a time (when one is filled with a sort of wow factor), I've never really bought into ski culture, the expense of it, time taken to get to snow, all that specialist clothing, having little else to do at ski resorts, the vagaries of the weather/snow conditions, the crowds, etc.

We had much better, richer times, I believe, on our hiking holidays. One to Snowdonia stands out. Of course, we climbed the highest peak in England/Wales, we camped by mountain lakes, drank the river water, and, one day, we cycled to the coast and back. But surpassing all that was, what we christened the 'Poolathon'. Some days earlier, on our route down from Snowdon, we had discovered that the river cascading the mountain's southern slopes – Afon Cwm Llan – was replete with crystal clear pools, large and small, deep and shallow, some with mini-waterfalls, others with trees overhanging making for very attractive photos. So, we decided to revisit Afon Cwm Llan simply to swim in the pools, as many as possible.

27 August 2000

'We had discussed at some length a sophisticated points system by which we would compete in the Poolathon; it was subsequently adapted several times. Basically, we got one point for a full single swimming stroke across the pool; a second point for four full strokes; a third point for three strokes swimming under water; a fourth point for a surface dive, i.e. from standing in the water; and a fifth point for diving from a rock i.e. with one's feet out of the water. There were also bonus points to be had: Ads got one for a somersault for example. We both achieved full points on the first pool... It is hard for me to do justice to the joy of this experience with words here in the journal. It was a glorious day, with the sun masterful in a cloudless sky. The water in the river was as clear as I have ever seen water in a river – there was no mud or moss or sand or slime to make it murky. Although it was mid-summer, the river was full with a good strong current and plenty of water to fill the pools and swell the cascades. But the river was not so strong or wide that we couldn't walk through it, and along it, and up it. Indeed, rather than having to return to the path, we managed the challenging climb and scramble up through the main cascades. [. . .] Above, we found lots of bigger and better pools all in a row, often with cascades or little waterfalls between them. [. . .] We lunched and read a chapter of Evelyn Waugh's 'Scoop', which we are both finding very funny. Eventually, with the sun heading behind the hills and threatening to throw us into shade, we decided this glorious day had to come to an end.'

In August 2001, not long after Adam's 14th birthday, we joined a two-week organised tour of Kenya and Tanzania – our most adventurous and expensive holiday to date. The previous year, I had taken a similar tour to Egypt. I'd been fearful of trapping myself (so to speak) with a group of strangers for 10 days, and of being obliged to follow an itinerary and sightseeing schedule set by someone other than myself. There was an element in my psyche, I suppose, that I was abandoning my independent travelling days, my free self. However, I'd surprised myself, in that I had enjoyed the holiday hugely, and had been able to profit, not be constrained by, the social elements. Plus, I had seen and experienced much more than if I'd had to plan and organise each day myself. Thus it was that I asked Adam if he'd like to go on safari in Kenya and Tanzania! I'd never travelled in sub-Saharan Africa, and nor had I been on any kind of safari, so there was plenty for both of us to look forward to.

18 Jan 2001
I told Adam I'd booked for the Africa trip – he must have dived at me with his arms outstretched half a dozen times since then and given me a huge hug while saying 'you're a lovely dad'. These days, these months, these couple of years – maybe one or two to come, and one or two just gone – with Adam I feel I'm being treated to a bonus reward for being a hands-on father. I've always said, I've always felt that my fatherhood has been a responsibility which is a reward in itself, without ever expecting or wanting anything in return in the future. I have enjoyed and loved him from day one, and that has been my fullest reward. But these days – with Adam so intelligent, so funny, so warm, so loving – are a bonus I never really expected. I imagine we could be such good friends for the rest of my life (although I hold out no expectations or illusions) but he will never again (after the next year or two) spend anywhere near as much time with me (or Bel), he will have his life, his friends, his lovers – I will be background, not foreground.

It's tempting to revisit, through my diary, those two weeks in tourist detail, but this chapter on Adam's development and the relationship between us has already drifted too often into holiday mode. I'll confine myself to a few highlights. The animals, of course, were amazing – more so for Adam than I since I've never been a great naturalist. On several safaris, taking up most of the first week, we feasted on elephants, lions, buffalos, warthogs, giraffes, hippos, rhinos, ostriches, impala, flamingos . . . A week of them was enough, I wrote in my diary. The most exciting moment came when one night, while we were camping by a river, a small herd of elephants thumped through our camp in the night – no one was hurt fortunately. In the second week, we travelled a bit by train, and drove into the Usambara Mountains where we stayed, near Lushoto a busy market town, in a very clean, cool convent. We flew in a light aircraft, Adam taking the co-pilot seat, to Pemba – fabulous views of the islands and Tanzanian coast. We opted not to pay extra for a tour of the island but to find bikes to hire, which we did, and using them we tracked down a detailed map to guide our day's activities, a fish market, a couple of beaches for swimming, papayas, bananas, and coconuts for sustenance. And all the while the sweet and spicy aroma of cloves filling the air everywhere. There was barely a house or hut we passed that didn't have a mat or three out front covered in cloves, drying in the sun – fresh ones with green yellow and some red in them, and dried ones, darker like the cloves we use at home.

And finally to Zanzibar, such an exotic sounding location, but I summed it up as having decrepit buildings, a few nice doors, and brilliant beaches on the east coast. Again I eschewed the extra cost of a sub-tour to those beaches, opting instead for Adam and I to hitchhike. We confidently set off early in the morning, heading for Paje beach, walking out of Zanzibar town. But I became rather dismayed at how few cars we were seeing, and those that were passing were tour operators. Eventually, though, a lorry stopped, and we were signalled to climb in the open back with three other men standing on a thin layer of rubble. Here's my diary – for in-the-moment excitement.

2 September 2001
Ads had a large smile on, and when I asked him why, he said it was because it was a good feeling to get a lift. We talked a bit about the joys and pitfalls of hitchhiking. The truck fairly whizzed along, but I wasn't exactly sure where it was going. One of the men got off, and one of the others moved closer and started asking Adam a lot of questions. The truck stopped again in the middle of nowhere, and a conversation started up between the driver and a cyclist on the other side of the road. The cyclist then hurried to leave his bike somewhere in the bushes further back along the road from us. Meanwhile, I asked the inquisitive guy where we were going. He didn't seem to know, so I prompted him by saying the name of the town we needed to pass on our route. He pointed in the direction from which we had already come! That started me worrying. I became more anxious a few moments later when I saw the cyclist, now without

his bike, running down the road towards the truck waving a MACHETE! I signalled for Ads to get off the truck immediately, mumbled goodbye and jumped off too. We were alone again walking on the side of the deserted road.

But then our fortunes changed. A smart car pulled up with a big fat man in the passenger seat. He told us to get in the back, which had us feeling a bit locked in. Nevertheless, I felt safe because there were several different types of people in the car. The fat man introduced himself as the Police High Commissioner. He told us he wasn't going far but that he would find us a lift. [...] At the next police point on the road, he said he'd just have a word with his staff, and they would get us a lift to Paje. We got out and stood by the police post for no more than five minutes when a guard stopped a van and told the driver to take us to Paje. I couldn't understand the Swahili, but I got the gist. Rather stupidly, I mentioned money (I suppose I didn't want to be hit with a 4,000 bill at Paje) but I realised immediately I opened my mouth that this would have been a free trip – under the order of the Police High Commissioner. The guy inside the van said 4,000, and when I said no, he asked, what do you want pay. 1,000 each I said, and he accepted snappily. The van took us very quickly to Paje, the driver telling us all the while how famous he was, and that he could get us anything we wanted in Bwejuu. He gave us his address and asked for mine. Adam was shocked when he saw me writing out an address, until he realised it was a false one.

And here, by way of light entertainment, are three Kikuyu proverbs from Kenya: Women and the sky cannot be understood; An old goat never sneezes for nothing; He who asks for mashed food has someone to mash it.

If Kenya was the zenith of our holiday times together. Two years later, a week in Portugal, in the north, would be the nadir. I seemed interminably cross with my son, most noticeably at what I saw as his non-stop resentment at being stuck with me, and his failure to input any initiative into our daily activities. I pressed him over and over again to consult the *Rough Guide*, and tell me where he'd like to go next, what he'd like to do, largely without result. Except that, a couple of weeks later, when I'd had my camera film processed and photographs printed, I found among them a close-up photo of the *Rough Guide*. He was on the cusp of 16 by then, and the father-son relationship had been somewhat challenging for a while.

I was too harsh, too often, rarely without cause, I would say, but, crucially, so often without GOOD cause or even adequate cause. I expected too much, in many different ways, from his young and developing self. Occasionally I physically knocked him. It's not a confession I make lightly. I didn't do so to hurt, but rather to shock – in much the same way I had slapped his hand when he was two, say, as a shortcut to righting behaviour that might have harmed him. He was also subjected to many a lecture, as if my droning words would change anything either. But in no way – none at all – were many of my actions acceptable, warranted or effective. It was just my good fortune that Adam was such a stable even-spirited boy. I do have an explanation, or several, for how and why we got into such a pickle for several years. I don't offer them as justification, rather only as a means to understanding.

First of all, Adam was a teenager, and it's common knowledge that teenagers can be tricky. They are establishing their independence, and to do that they develop a high degree of self-centredness which often causes friction with parents, especially those much involved in their children's lives, though I'm generalising, of course, as innate characteristics mitigate or exacerbate individual routes through adolescence. All so obvious, perhaps. By the time they are teenagers, children have spent much time with their parents; they have learned their foibles and vulnerabilities. Thus, when attacked (as their psyches might feel it) they've an armoury of well-honed defences. As a parent, I was determined to hold fast to certain behavioural boundaries, perhaps too many, but where Adam was unable or unwilling to meet the standards I was hoping to set, he would inevitably fall back on some tried and tested means – argumentative techniques among others – of, as I say in the diary entry below, lighting my touch paper.

But there was a peculiarity about our situation which I believe made our situation worse – a distinct negative consequence of the Adam Co-op. For his primary school years, Bel and I had maintained a reasonably united front, coming together for meals, outings, games, in and out of each other's houses. But as Adam moved through his secondary school years becoming more independent (and as Bel was spending more time with her partner), he was subjected to two very different environments, a fairly relaxed one at Bel's, and a more disciplined one at my house. Though I tried to ensure Bel and I followed a similar pattern of rules (on tidiness, helping out in the kitchen, homework standards, caring for his clothes at school, not being rude, communicating adequately, etc.), it always felt like Adam disregarded them when not at my house. And when he was at my house, I had to work all the harder to re-establish them. He was only with me for three or four days at time, and half that time I had to be serious, hard, in re-setting the rules I wanted him/us to live by.

I tried sometimes to diary document the breakdown – which happened on a fairly regular basis – in our daily communications. But I was too involved, and often too cross to bother. But here's a couple of entries.

20 January 2000
Adam is on the cusp of teenagerhood. [. . .] He has started to care about his appearance a bit – particularly his hair. He takes special care over combing it, and, by using gel, creates a strong central parting. It does suit him, but I

tease him about using gel. (At present his hair is far too long, and hangs down in his eyes. It makes him look older.) He is taking more responsibility for his belongings, so that he doesn't come home every day missing his coat, or with his trousers torn; and, generally speaking, he is in control of his school books, remembering the right ones each day. [. . .] At home, he does regularly do a couple of jobs (clearing the draining board, putting away clean clothes that I leave on the stairs), but despite my best efforts, he still won't automatically do any jobs without being told, I mean he won't think 'Oh that needs doing' and then do it – sweeping the kitchen, cleaning the bathroom, tidying and hoovering his room.

He has a deep and broad sense of humour, which can be both adult and very childish. He remains obsessed with comedy programmes and has been developing a database of information about them. (I recall that when he was younger he would read joke books over and over again.) Our conversation is full of teases and jokes, and when I'm not shouting at or lecturing him, I am usually making him laugh, or he me. He can really stun me sometimes with his teases, which only recently have developed an almost adult subtlety. [. . .]

But why else do I think he is on the cusp of teenagerhood. I suppose, it is a fast-evolving sense of stubbornness that is starting to fill his head. It is this stubbornness that provokes my anger usually (rather than the initial fault) and his wayward attempts to bolster unacceptable behaviour or lousy work. I suspect this will only get worse and that, although I still ensure that I 'win' every escalated argument, as I said above, I wonder whether it wouldn't be wiser to refuse to go down these emotionally tiring roads.

He is the sun and the stars of my life, and is and will continue to be the most important person/thing/event of my entire life. What a burden for the poor boy.

2 January 2002

I want to record that I shouted at Adam again on Tuesday. He has learnt to light my touch paper so well now – and I blame him for it, but I shouldn't. I never just fly off the handle, it's much more complicated than that. We start talking or quarrelling about something, and I patiently explain this or that, or try and draw him back from some stupid comment, or irrelevant jibe, and patiently explain something again, but this time a bit more insistently, and he jibes back with something more stupid than the first time, or a repetition of a red herring that I thought I'd dealt with, and then I repeat myself again, louder this time, more insistently, somehow imagining if I say it again, he'll understand or take it in this time. And he doesn't, and he says something ever more stupid, ever more illogical, or he refers to something he said or did which indicates that he has said or done what I'm trying to argue in favour of; and I try and point out that yes, he may have done so once, but that's not what I'm talking about, I'm talking about something more general; and so on and on and on; and then as I realise I am beating my head against a brick wall, I decide I must bang it harder to get him to understand, and I start shouting and screaming – and for why? And once I've started shouting, I can't just revert to being nice and normal again – it takes me a day or more, or an absence. And it's not as if I've got anywhere or made him understand anything any better – because I've probably done the reverse. Moreover, he is so used to me shouting now, that he doesn't take it seriously – it never upsets him that I've been shouting. It's too normal.

5 May 2002

In line with teenagers everywhere (I suppose), Adam is always trying to establish his independence and control over the world around him. He constantly accuses me of being patronising (when I'm trying to explain something to him, or telling him off for a little thing), even though I'm not really being patronising, or, if I am, then I behave like that all the time and he doesn't mind or notice then. He's very quick to anger now (more so than at any time in his life beforehand, I think), and he's multi-armoured when it comes to deflecting my accusations or attacking back. One of my main problems with him is separating out the roles between friend and parent, between talking to him (arguing) about some subject or other, and telling him what he should be doing or how he should be behaving. Often I want to stay serious, whether about his behaviour (not washing his hands, not tidying his room, throwing his clean clothes on the floor) or about issues (a film, politics, sexuality), but he flicks the conversation into comedy mode with a facial expression, an action or a comment, and I find it hard to keep a straight face. I can often be heard to say 'Adam, you're not listening to the words I'm saying – I may be smiling, but I'm getting cross'; or 'ADAM, I'm serious', or 'ADAM do what I say BEFORE I get cross'.

But despite this, Adam remains a beautiful child. He is funny, warm, an attentive companion, helpful, generous, honest, clever. He has so many grand attributes, I cannot believe he isn't going to make more of his life than I have.

And so to something lighter by way of ending this chapter (which already has gone on too long but is yet not nearly long enough) – The Day of the Thousand Handshakes.

As the end of the year 1999 approached, I was keen to imagine some novel way of marking New Millennium Day – especially to Adam. Over Christmas, I hit on the idea of trying to shake hands with a 1,000 people, one for every day of the millennium (the new one or the old one, it didn't really matter), I even envisaged inviting every one of the 1,000 people (via a sticker or note we gave them) to meet for a summer picnic in Hyde Park. It would be an antidote to the internet – a real physical meeting of people who had nothing else in common except that we had shaken hands with them on New Millennium Day. We tried to think of what signal would be appropriate for this brotherhood, so that everyone would recognise each other: a straw hat, an orange bag, white shoes.

I was extraordinarily busy in the final days of the year, not only finalising issues of my two newsletters and their annual indexes, but preparing to send the final proofs of a 250-page management report on EU transport issues to the printers. Once I'd despatched the pages on New Year's Eve, Adam and I set about printing at home 50 sheets of 21 labels of small sticky labels, numbered from 1-1,000, each one saying 'THE DAY OF THE THOUSAND HAND SHAKES: On the first day of the new Millennium. Our quest to shake hands with one person for every year of the old Millennium. Have a happy one! Paul and Adam. AdsLyons@hotmail.com'. We'd created the email especially for the labels. By then it was

7:30pm. I stuffed sleeping bags and blankets in the back of the car, and we left for London and Shepherd's Bush for a party at Andy's house (his first since the death of his wife, Rosy).

We started on the hand shaking at the party, around 1:30am, and then drove into the centre, to near the Royal Albert Hall. We found hoards and hoards of people which is what we wanted. But people were streaming along the road, they were too rushed, we couldn't engage with them sufficiently to give them a label. Also, because it was dark, they couldn't see the label, and that made some of them suspicious. The throngs only seemed to get denser around the tube station entrances, where no strangers were in a mood to engage in our private game. We gravitated towards only shaking hands with those people sitting down on steps or walls.

It all seemed so petty. Didn't all these people realise how lucky they were – to be alive, first and foremost, to be alive as one millennium seamlessly transposed into another (civilised mankind has only witnessed four or five millennium in its entire history, and we were living through the change in one of them); to be in a place with peace all around; and to be fortunate enough to have such mild and clement weather. To all these hoards, the millennium was just one more spectacle, just one more entertainment, and now they were on their way home. It was a very disappointing feeling. I became suddenly tired, and unwilling to carry on. We drove back to Andy's, but I realised we wouldn't be able to sleep there if only because of the sheer noise. So, defeated (we'd shaken less than 200 hands between us), I drove us home, back to Surrey, Ads slept almost all the way, dear of him. He was such good company, taking this challenge all the way with me, not questioning my decisions, and throwing himself into it with characteristic energy.

The next morning was such a glorious day, with sun blazing down on a fresh year/decade/century/millennium that I was all determined again to complete our challenge. I had a vision of strolling along the Thames wishing hundreds of people Happy New Year and enjoying the glorious sunshine and views. After an initial hesitation, Ads joined in with my enthusiasm. We collected supplies quickly, fruit and biscuits, and raced off to the station by about 10:30. The gods were still not with us, as the trains were badly delayed – one had hit a cat and the driver was trying to clean up his wheels! That was it. I was hungry, I was dying for a pee and I had no idea what we were actually going to do when we arrived in London. I'd had enough waiting. Darling Ads went along with my decision. We drove home and had lunch.

In the early afternoon, I began to feel restless. I was very unhappy that we had failed miserably to meet our challenge. Even at three a minute, assuming we could keep up such rate, it would still take us over four hours to do another 800 I calculated. But still I wouldn't let the idea go – I particularly didn't want Ads remembering for the rest of his life that on New Millennium Day we had tried to shake a thousand people's hands, and failed. I called to find out the times of the trains, and started thinking about it more carefully. Then I had a brainwave – the Tube. I talked to Ads who was a little reluctant this time, but I won him over, and we soon hotfooted it back to the station, and trained to Waterloo. From there, we walked over towards the spectacular and not-working London Eye. There were many people milling around there, so we set to, shaking hands with them all. I particularly went for the family groups with children. Having read our sticker, one woman called out after us – 'Good luck Paul and Adam'. That was great.

Even though there were crowds walking slowly along the river, stopping groups in their tracks to shake hands with them did not work very well; partly because it tended to block the passage of other people, and partly because the gesture and reaction were all a bit sudden and staccato, if I can explain it that way. By contrast, shaking hands with seated passengers on the tube proved to be as simple as shaking hands with a friend. Adam and I soon developed a technique: we would start at one end of a tube train, get on the first carriage, immediately go up to whoever was sitting at one end, a hand outstretched, say, firmly, with a big smile, 'Happy New Year', and give them a sticker. We would then work through the carriage, separately, until we reached the other end. At the next stop, we would move to the next carriage and do the same thing. Once we had completed a full train, we simply waited for the next train.

The dynamics between Ads and I inside the train were amazingly smooth. I always started and then he would work around me, sometimes going on ahead to deal with a different group of people sometimes shaking hands with the person next to the one I was talking to. If possible, I chose to put the label on a person's sleeve, the right way up, so they could read it; otherwise I put it on their lapel, or on a bag, or on the seat next to them. Sometimes Ads would place a label while I was shaking hands, and sometimes we gave out stickers before we shook hands. No one really had a chance to read the text until we had moved on, which was a shame. If we encountered some slight hesitations, we would quickly explain our purpose – that we were trying to shake hands with a thousand people.

Over 90% of all the people we shook hands with gave us a positive or nearly positive response, gauged through their facial expression or the tone of their words – 'That's great' or 'What a great idea'.

We did get off the Circle Line once to have a look at the Monument, because Ads wanted to see it, and once to try out Trafalgar Square. But I simply didn't like shaking hands with people outside in the dark. We walked past Downing Street, took a peek at Big Ben and the Houses of Parliament, before a last blitz on the circle line to finish off the 999 – the 1,000th I had promised for Bel. We just had time to walk along the river, past County Hall, to Waterloo and catch the 7:30 train home – well, well tired.

Most of the above is taken from my diary entry which finishes as follows: 'I am so pleased we did it – and so proud of Ads that he was so easy going and positive about the whole thing, and about how well he managed the business of shaking hands with strangers. There was never a moment of complaint from him or a whinge about being tired or hungry or cold – and certainly no question of 'What the hell are we doing this for Dad?', which any sane child might have had the right to ask.'

Where should I end this chapter? My intention was never to write a biography of my son's life, but to reflect on and celebrate the father-son relationship we had as he was growing up. By the time he went to Sixth Form College, he was very largely grown up, independent, and we were spending much less time together. (One beach/cycling holiday on Skiathos, two years after the frustrations of the Oporto trip, went some way towards restoring a happy modus vivendi between us.) I continued to try to influence him on bigger issues where I felt it necessary, what to study at A-Level, which university to choose, and which course to take. It was difficult for us all to decide on where he should be living, at Bel's in Guildford or at Russet House, during the week. One summer, I was disgruntled enough with him for not trying to find a job that he spent most of it at Bel's. I believe he spent two productive years at Sixth Form College, finding new friends, and coming away with five A-Levels, more than enough to see him accepted by Sussex University to study politics and economics. He moved to Brighton in September 2005, leaving me alone in Russet House, and more alone than I'd ever been. Within six months, I, myself, had sold up, and moved to Brighton, to start a new life. Adam would not stop ragging me for having followed him. I hadn't, of course, I hadn't. In fact, I'd lobbied long and hard for him to choose a different university, not Sussex, and I would have still moved to Brighton. It was the obvious place for me to start the difficult process of, what felt like, reintegrating myself back into society: while the joys and privileges of parenthood had extinguished much of the angst of my youth, the passing of so much time had left me wrung, dried out and wrinkled.

Chapter six

MUSIC
WHERE LIFE IS BETTER

I cannot say that music has played a significant role in my life, as it would have done had I been involved in the music business, or if I had ever played an instrument, or sung in a choir. I would not even describe listening to music as an active hobby of mine, even though I probably have music playing several hours every day – switching from folk to jazz to classical depending on my mood or current activity. Indeed, I've spent so much time listening to music – sometimes in a captivated or focused way but mostly as an accompaniment to many other activities – that I want to try, at least, to reflect on a lifetime's relationship to music. I say 'to try' because music is a foreign language for me, one I've never been able to speak or understand. Moreover, I cannot even sing, remember or recognise any notes. This is going to be a challenge.

One of the first issues I have to face is to understand why I feel this need to write about music rather than, say, visual art. I mean music and art are conjoined in some ways, for they are both major realms that impact on human culture and brains and yet are beyond textual language. So, why a chapter on music in my memoir, but not one on art? Thinking about how visual art may have impacted on my life, I can't see that it has in any particular way. I've visited a lot of art galleries in my time, and seen many an exhibition, but to what end? What has ever changed in my life because of art? Yes, favoured artists (whether classical or local) figure on our walls for decoration, but decoration can't be said to have had any impact. Can music?

It was a question that found me turning – as so often when employing words to explain oddities of the human condition – to analogy. Whereas art can be likened to an acquaintance I've had through my life, music is more akin to a very good friend, a lifelong friend. She's been there so often when needed, in so many different circumstances, when I was youthful and joy-filled, lonely and angst-ridden, ill and bed-ridden, bored and dull-ridden, happy and laughter-filled, love-sick and love-well. What emotions has art invoked or assuaged? To what highs or lows has art accompanied me? None. It's a formal relationship I have with art, she gives me thoughts on occasion, and annoys me on others, but it's all in the head, and rather lightly so. But music, oh she's a lover, one that's ever present, asks nothing for her favours, rich in variety, ready to take many forms to suit the gamut of my moods. And surely, it is music that takes one away so readily to a rhythmic melodic place where life is better, without conflict, washing up, traffic jams, uncollected rubbish bins, tiredness, ill health ... As such, I feel not only that she deserves a chapter of my life, but that I want to write that chapter, explain her presence in my life, her friendship.

One way of approaching this subject is to consider the hardware I've accumulated over a lifetime, I mean what art do I have on my walls, what music is there in my record collection? There are pictures all over the walls in the house (which I share with my wife, Hattie), many of them framed prints of my own photographs, of Hattie's paintings, of illustrations by her mother (a well-known illustrator), and drawings by our children. There are framed pictures that we've bought at auction or local studios simply because we like them, not because we've ever heard of the artists, and of course family photographs. In terms of non-2D art works, we have a few ceramics and other knick-knacks, and I have a collection of (mostly wooden) carved figures all around 2ft tall. With less than a handful of exceptions – a couple of small Turner prints, a Ravilious – we don't have copies of any famous art. Yes, we have many art books, with reproductions by world-class, and lesser known, artists of different genres, but most are never touched by me unless to be dusted, and but a few are consulted rarely. The art around me on a daily basis, I can conclude, is little more than decoration – it barely arouses emotion.

By contrast, virtually ALL my music is by well-known, famous musicians, and almost ALL of it has been actively listened to very often over the years. I bought LPs when a teenager, cassettes in my 20s, and, from the 1980s, CDs – a format I still buy. Early on, I learned to borrow LPs and cassettes from libraries and copy them onto my own cassettes. In the 1990s, Sony brought out a new playing/recording technology – MiniDiscs – which gave me the opportunity to transfer and thus store all the music I'd acquired digitally, on small square discs – each one holding the equivalent of three or four LPs or cassettes. This allowed me, by the early 2000s, to finally dispose of my (fairly small) collection of LPs. However, it's worth noting, that each digital recording of my old LPs carries with it the hisses and scratches acquired over the years, so that listening to them is somehow a more authentically nostalgic experience than listening to a pure recording of the same music.

Having transferred every bit of my music (as well as a few EP recordings of children's stories I'd kept since my childhood) onto MiniDiscs, it was simple enough, in time, to import the digital files onto a computer. And so, today, amazingly, I have access to a lifetime's worth of my music wherever and whenever I want, through a multitude of appliances, playable via bluetooth through the house, or on an iPad, or in the car.

During the period I was drafting this chapter, I discovered something genuinely peculiar about myself. I can't bring any music to mind, I can't summon up any at will – other than a few very basic and very short snippets. I know how to sing *Happy Birthday*, *Frère Jacques*, and a few of my own made-up mantra-like tunes. Similarly, I can half-sing snippets of a few favourite songs if I know the words. But ask me to hum a few bars of any jazz or classical music, no matter how many times I've listened to it, and I'm at a loss. The da da da dum motif from Beethoven's Fifth, just those four notes, is literally the only one from classical music I know.

Human brains, I believe, not only start off from birth with very different capabilities, but they then develop and can be nurtured through childhood to varying degrees, with capabilities often languishing and ultimately fading. Music and language and mathematic abilities are among the skills that some people have naturally, while others have to work much harder to develop them. Maths came easy to me, but neither music nor languages did. Maybe I had latent abilities in both areas – I doubt it – but even if I did my schooling/upbringing never got close to uncovering them.

So, throughout my life, it seems, I've enjoyed plenty of music but none of it is in my head in a way that I can access. Astonishingly – and this is by way of a linked aside – not long after discovering this about my mental world, I found out that my conscious brain has no pictures either, no music and no pictures. When I close my eyes, all I see is grey (occasionally with light driven patterns). When I read books, I see nothing the authors are describing. When I describe images to friends, I'm not actually seeing them in my head. When I talk about places I've been, I'm not seeing them in my mind's eye, because I don't have a mind's eye.

Until I came to be writing this chapter, I had no inkling about either this music or visual blankness of mine. The visual condition, I soon uncovered, has a name, aphantasia, and affects about 2% of the population. Although I see nothing in my imagination with my eyes closed, I do have knowledge (doesn't quite seem the right word, but I have no better one) about what I might want to imagine. Also, I have detailed dreams, which I record in my diary – how is that possible without seeing pictures? Well, it seems, I just 'know' the information. I can imagine a banana, and 'know' if it is green, or with black patches. I can describe a familiar beach, and imagine people swimming or building sandcastles –

but it's not 'seeing' in pictures. My brain gives me the information that might be in the pictures but without a visual aspect.

In *Why Ever*, I wrote about how poor my memory has been, and still is, and about how few actual memories I have from the early part of my life. Well, now I have an explanation: very recent studies have begun to show how those who have aphantasia often have less vivid autobiographical memories.

There was no music in my early life, not as far as I can recall; the earliest memories I have and diary entries with any link to the music world come from my teenage years. There were music lessons at school, in which we learned about the components of an orchestra, and occasionally practiced singing – *Shenandoah*, *O Susannah*, songs from *The Mikado*, and rounds (which I thought were great fun, according to diary entries). There were carols at Christmas, and hymns at church on Sundays.

There was also my transistor radio which after lights out – starting in my pre-teen years – I would listen to secretly in the hope of hearing my favourite band, The Dave Clark Five. I championed The Dave Clark Five as a better band than The Beatles for all my school years. I believe this (ridiculous-in-hindsight) position had more to do with a deep-set need to be different, to not be following the crowd, than with any musical intuition or understanding.

However, with a little research, I've managed to trace why I might have fallen for The Dave Clark Five. In January 1964 – I was 12 – the BBC launched its new music chart show, *Top of the Pops*. The first ever episode – hosted by the now disgraced Jimmy Saville – ended with that week's number one single, the Beatles singing *I Want to Hold Your Hand*. The Dave Clark Five also performed on that very first show with *Glad All Over*. Before the month was out, *Glad All Over* had knocked the Beatles song off the number one spot.

Top of the Pops would go on to run for 40 years and more than 2,000 episodes, the world's longest running weekly music show. The Dave Clark Five would become more successful in the US, as part of the so-called British Invasion, than in the UK, and would fade away in the late 60s to break up in 1970. Dave Clark's *Catch Us If You Can* was the first LP record I ever bought; and the second was *Me* by Sandie Shaw – I recorded the purchase in my diary along with a summary of what else I was doing that Saturday.

12 February 1966
This morning I bought Sandie Shaw's LP, *Me* and then played football, it was a practice. I gave my bike a wipe over, had goulash for lunch. At 5:15 father went to the airport. He's going to South Africa. I went to club and played TT and volleyball and hockey. *Thunderbirds* and *Dr Who* I watched.

Listening to Shaw's very familiar lyrics today, resonant with the emotions of adult relationships, I do wonder quite why she appealed to a 13 year old who was still watching *Thunderbirds*. But, she did go on to win the Eurovision Song Contest the following year, a first for the UK. Shaw's trademark from the early days was performing barefoot, and some years later, I, too, would be caught by the barefoot bug during my hippy period. Was I primed, by Sandie in my early teens, to shed my shoes as soon as I left home? I have a vague memory – though there's nothing in the diary by way of evidence – that I met her years later, in the late 1970s, at a gathering in Maida Vale. This was thanks to a friend who was dating a Buddhist friend of hers.

Among my other early LPs, I recall only Bread, Dave Dee, Dozy, Beaky, Mick & Tich, Desmond Dekker (a favourite at parties).

My listening tastes evolved quickly once I'd left home in autumn 1970 and fallen under a variety of new influences. While Bob Dylan was constantly being played by my first flat mates, I was also discovering an affinity with other folky musicians, some of whom I saw live, such as Donovan, Cat Stevens, Lindisfarne, Pentangle, Barclay James Harvest (the gorgeous *Mockingbird*). Hard rock wasn't my thing, though I recall a Deep Purple concert during which my friend Phil and I took photographs for the student magazine, *Impact*. Uriah Heep crops up in my diary a few times, particularly one song which has remained a favourite for its hauntingly hopeful lyricism.

'There I was on a July morning
Looking for love
With the strength of a new day dawning
And the beautiful sun
At the sound of the first bird singing
I was leaving for home
With the storm and the night behind me
And a road of my own'

In these formative years at university, which culminated in me shedding all the trappings of Christianity (*Why Ever* – Chapter six), I wanted, needed new gods to guide me forward, and two of these were musical: Joni Mitchell and The Moody Blues. What distinguished them from many other, and more popular, musical acts, was the depth of meaning I found in their lyrics, reaching into places more spiritual, more emotional, but embraced by beautiful and original musical themes. I saw The Moody Blues live in 1971. I wrote in my diary 'really brilliant they were'. They sang my favourite song, *I'm a Melancholy Man*, one I returned to again and again for many years.

'I'm a melancholy man
That's what I am
All the world surrounds me and my feet are on the ground
I'm a very lonely man
Doing what I can
All the world astounds me and I think I understand
That we're going to keep growing
Wait and see'

And a little later came *A Question of Balance*, with this from the title song.

'Why do we never get an answer
When we're knocking at the door?
With a thousand million questions
About hate and death and war.'

It was Joni Mitchell, though, who fully captured my heart and soul; and who spoke to me in a way no one else could. It was her music, on tape cassettes, that I carried around the world with me. I'd slot these into tape players at hotels, in friends' houses, or even in the cars of people giving me lifts when I was hitchhiking, and be transported instantly to an oasis of rich feelings replete with memories, regrets, hopes. Her name appears occasionally in my diaries from 1972 on, but much more frequently in 1975 and 1976 when I was in New Zealand (where I joined a folk club – see below) and in South America when my early literary efforts were undergoing a kind of psychological and emotional awakening (*Why Ever* – Chapter eight).

10 August 1976

Yesterday, [. . .] we made heavy decisions to go to Cochabamba – nothing left for us in La Paz – but oh not a bus ticket left in La Paz for Cocha (just as now there is not a hotel bed left in Cocha). So early in the morning with distinct purpose and without cunning we hitch – we are on the edge of town, the white mountains shine – La Paz is hiding – obscure, squashed within the canyon below – oh such a first class bus pulls up with pullman seats, private lights and curtains – lots of room – and piped cassette music – I waste no time in asking for my Joni Mitchell cassette to be played into the pipe – I am very happy – the glass magnifies the sun's heat and keeps out the wind. The Altiplano is dusty dry, far fetched and speeds by, and Joni Mitchell sings melancholically.

Here are a few of Mitchell's lyrics which haunted me then – in the best possible way – and still do.

Title song on her first album *Song for a Seagull* (1968).

'Out of the city
And down to the seaside
To sun on my shoulders

And wind in my hair
But sandcastles crumble
And hunger is human
And humans are hungry
For worlds they can't share
My dreams with the seagulls fly
Out of reach out of cry'

Woodstock on *Ladies of the Canyon* (1970)
'I came upon a child of God
He was walking along the road
And I asked him where are you going
And this he told me
I'm going on down to Yasgur's farm
I'm going to join in a rock 'n' roll band
I'm going to camp out on the land
I'm going to try an' get my soul free.'

All I Want on *Blue* (1971)
'I am on a lonely road and I am traveling
Traveling, traveling, traveling
Looking for something, what can it be?
Oh I hate you some, I hate you some
I love you some
Oh I love you when I forget about me
I wanna be strong, I wanna laugh along
I wanna belong to the living
Alive, alive, I wanna get up and jive
Wanna wreck my stockings in some jukebox dive
Do you want- do you want-
Do you wanna dance with me baby?
Do you wanna take a chance on
Maybe finding some sweet romance with me baby?
Well come on'

Title song on *Court and Spark* (1974)
'Love came to my door with a sleeping roll
And a madman's soul
He thought for sure I'd seen him
Dancing up a river in the dark
Looking for a woman to court and spark'

In 1974, weeks only before I left the UK for my three year round the world adventure, I went to see *Jesus Christ Superstar*, the rock opera by Andrew Lloyd Webber and Tim Rice. As a child and teen, I'd loathed musicals on film (witness the mental scar I still carry of being forced to see *Chitty Chitty Bang Bang*), and I believe (though I can't be sure) I'd never seen one live. By the time I went to see *Jesus Christ Superstar* live, I'd been listening to the album for a couple of years, and I'd seen the movie.

> Monday 29 April 1974
> [. . .] Got on my pushbike after tea and rode to Sloane Square, but *Life Class* at the Royal Court was fully booked so rode on through Westminster to The Palace for *Jesus Christ Superstar*. Balcony seat, very enjoyable, stage made of translucent squares with lights and six of them moved up and down. Jude the best among 'em. Jesus was a bit ineffectual as in the film (same dress, same haircut) and Mary wasn't too hot either. But the general effect of the opera was very enjoyable. The latter half much the best. The Last Supper scene very good right through to the crucifixion.

Because of my own experience – faith, doubts, rejection – of being a Christian, the music and lyrics resonated with me hugely, and have remained extraordinarily familiar to me for nearly half a century. The genius of Webber/Rice to take grand themes concerning the human condition, to encapsulate them in such popular and entertaining ways, was also apparent with *Evita*. Having spent time in Argentina by then, and been in a tempestuous relationship with a beautiful Argentine singer who exuded much of the same vivid confidence and charm as Webber/Rice's Evita, I was as taken with this musical as with JCS. Indeed, no other musicals have ever come close to moving me as much.

My interest in and love of folk music was surely nurtured in New Zealand thanks to chance encounters that led to me joining the folk club in Dunedin. It's not that I have ever wanted to sing, tuneless as I am, but I liked being with folk musicians, the ambience of pub meets, and the music – often very lyrical and with a story to tell – was far more to my taste than run-of-the-mill pop.

In South America, though, I was moved in different ways. My Argentine amor introduced me (musically) to her compatriot Mercedes Sosa (La Negra) with an unbelievably deep rich voice that embodied not only her country's heritage but its troubles too, as well as to Gal Costa, a Brazilian singer associated with the Tropicalia movement.

Sosa began her career as a singer for the Peronist party, making a first album in her mid-20s. By the 1960s, she was identified with the Nueva Canción genre, a movement characterised by folk-inspired styles and socially-committed lyrics, which would become influential in the revolutionary movements across Latin America and the Iberian peninsula. Many years later, I saw her perform in London in the South Bank to a full house, and her voice was just as pure and rich and deep as the one I'd listened to so often on recordings. One of her most famous songs, written by the Chilean Violeta Parra, was *Gracias a la Vida* – this is the sixth verse (with an unimaginative translation into English).

> *'Gracias a la vida, que me ha dado tanto,*
> *me ha dado la risa y me ha dado el llanto;*
> *así yo distingo dicha de quebranto,*
> *los dós materiales que forman mi canto,*
> *y el canto de ustedes que es el mismo canto,*
> *y el canto de todos que es mi proprio'*
> *'Thank you to life, that has given me so much*
> *It has given me laughter and it has given me crying*
> *So I can distinguish blessings from brokenness*
> *The two ingredients that make up my chants*
> *And your chants, that are the same chants*
> *And everyone's chants, that are my own chants'*

Born a decade after Sosa, Gal Costa was a very different kind of singer, more pop and rock, with a powerful voice and quintessentially Brazilian. I became much more involved with her music during my two years in Rio, during the mid-1980s, falling headlong for the whole gang of Tropicalia singers – Caetano Veloso, Chico Buarque, Gilberto Gil – as well as for the samba beats that were everywhere. I particularly like Buarque's *Ópera do Malandro* inspired by Bertolt Brecht's *Threepenny Opera*. Milton Nascimento, too, spoke to me, blending jazz into his own brand of Brazilian rhythms, as did Astor Piazzolo, the astonishing Argentinian bandoneon player, whose Nuevo Tango compositions were every bit as jazzy as Nascimento's.

As I say, the likes of Joni Mitchell, Joan Baez, Pentangle had led me to folk music, and that interest had been nurtured in Dunedin, NZ, where I'd started to open up socially, in part thanks to friends I made through the folk club. In South America, I'd found myself, for the first time, letting myself be moved by the rhythms of Latin music, dancing like I'd never danced before . . . Back in London, in 1987, I was starting on a new road, becoming a father, settling down with a permanent job, yet I only had to listen to Sosa or Buarque for a few seconds to be transported back across the ocean, to Rio which has seemed, for the rest of my life, like a gorgeous colourful dream I once had. In time – and partly thanks to the tsunami of interest in World Music from the late 1980s – my Latin music collection would be expanded to include the traditional blues/folk music of Spain and Portugal, notably flamenco, fado and Ladino.

I've seen some international stars of these genres, mostly in Brighton where I live. Buika, for example, is a stunning singer bringing her own mix of jazz and soul to flamenco traditions. Yasmin Levy and Mor Karbasi both have voices that draw on their Ladino roots and which have – I exaggerate not – penetrated to my soul. Mariza was surely the first international star of Portugal's fado traditional songs and way of singing. But I, personally, was hooked onto fado by an experience I had in Madeira, in 2003, where I'd gone for a week's walking in the high mountains. I'd discovered a fado concert happening the day before I was due to leave.

Friday 5 December 2003, Funchal
I imagined the concert would start at 9:30, the time it was billed (with 9:00 being the arrival time, presumably to be there when the doors opened). More fool me! For about 20 minutes after 9:30, we all sat and watched an empty stage with four chairs and five or six portly men, all in suits, stand around between the stage and the front row of seats. They were chatting with the confidence of dignitaries – one of whom, I suppose, was the organiser – but how high the others were I don't know – mayor of Funchal perhaps. Three photographers were also milling around snapping the dignitaries in groups of twos and threes. [. . .] Four musicians finally came out to sit on the four seats, the lights went down in the auditorium and up on the stage. It must have been nearly 10:00 by this time. Now for the fado, I thought. Silly me! Speeches and a presentation took up another 20 minutes! And when they'd finished, the four musicians played an instrumental number. Something! But it wasn't what I'd come for. The main musician, who later sang also, played a guitar, two others played what looked like a banjo, the fourth played what looked like a square banjo.

When the first singer came on, Ana Moura, I was not disappointed. She was young, early 20s perhaps, tallish, slim, wearing a low cut black evening dress and a white shawl. She had frizzy hair tumbling down all around her small pretty face. She sang like an angel. Several of her songs I knew for Mariza also sings them. Perhaps she didn't quite have the strength or range of Mariza but she was beautiful to watch and listen to. Her movements were very graceful, and she smiled a lot – not in a tired stagey way but with apparent real pleasure. Twice she asked the audience to sing along with a familiar canto and all she did was to twist her hand out to the audience to hand over the lead. I suppose there was a childlike simplicity about her performance. When she came back for an encore, she just repeated the refrain from the previous song for a minute, but the audience all rose to their feet applauding her and she looked overcome, crossing her hands across her front and bowing slightly smiling all the while. Someone from the audience shouted a fado title, she turned gently to look at the lead guitarist, who nodded, and she then gave us a real encore.

I could have gone home at this point so satisfied with what I'd seen but we'd been promised three fadistas, and having paid my money and sat through all the speeches, I wasn't going to leave early. Next the guitarist sang three or four songs. His voice wasn't special but he liked to talk to the audience before each song and to win its approval (by rounds of applause) for some words of worldly wisdom. The climax of the evening's show (not for me) came next. I don't know how old the star fadista was, perhaps 55 or more I couldn't tell. Her hair was died blonde, her face round and slightly squashed like a pumpkin. This was Maria da Fé. She was covered in black clothes and looked like mutton after the earlier singer. Well known to most people there, she was given a good reception, and the applause to her songs was as good as it had been earlier. Yet, to my poor ear, her voice sounded gravelly, leathery. I was sitting there thinking how I was going to describe it – and leathery was the best I could come up with – as compared to the crystal glass of the young singer's voice. All the movements of the old woman were tired, forced, staged: when she talked to us – which she did quite a lot – she blinked her eyelids continuously, she held her head up much higher than is natural, sticking her chin upwards as if it were something she'd learned early on; and when she hit the highest of notes, in the climaxes of the fados, her whole body went into a kind of dramatic shudder which would not have been out of place in a Dracula movie. Unkind, unkind, I know.

I wondered a lot about the arrangement of the concert and how the old faddista would have allowed herself to be so upstaged by the young angel. The truth dawned on me when she closed the show by bringing on the young angel to do a closing number together: young angel was old hag's protege! Whether old hag had realised she was past it and young angel was now the star, I don't know, I doubt it. I left as the bouquets were being handed out – I could sense more speeches on the way.'

Today, as I write, Ana Moura has become an international star, with her latest albums being produced by Larry Klein, Joni Mitchell's former husband and producer. Wikipedia tells me that her 2015 album Moura is ranked as 'the 4th best-charting album of all time in Portugal'.

By the 1980s, my musical listening world was being divvied up, I suppose, into three broad strands. Alongside what I shall broadly call folk music (as described above), I was beginning to find myself attracted to certain kinds of jazz, and to various manifestations of classical music. But how and why?

Jazz first. My stepfather liked jazz music. I remember buying him an Oscar Petersen LP for his birthday one year. He was part of a jazz cafe scene in London as a young man, and may have played an instrument, though I don't know which one, nor did I ever see him with one. No, I believe, it was Mike Westbrook – pianist, bandmaster, tuba player, and composer – that brought me into the jazz fold. His name first appears in my diary in 1980, though without any details. His music has remained a significant part of my life since then for the last 40 years. As I write, he's 85 years old and still performing, mostly with his wife Kate Westbrook singing. I've bought many of their records over the years, and I've been to a dozen or so concerts. For many years, I received a newsletter – Smith's Academy Informer – put together and sent out by the Westbrooks and friends, which made me feel like part of the family, indeed made me feel like a fan, though I think of myself as the very antithesis of fan-material.

What attracted me initially was Westbrook's remarkable and original settings of William Blake's poetry – first performed and released in 1980. (Some 20 years later, though, the Westbrooks reprised the Blake work with new songs and the title *Glad Day*.)

It was music Performed with a capital P, and I don't mean like opera. Westbrook himself was on piano, occasionally narrating lines with a deep bellowing resonance. The two singers, Phil Minton and Kate Westbrook, were notable for the extraordinary way they used their voices as if they were instruments, and blending them into the powerful sounds of trumpets, trombones, but mostly saxophones – often played by Chris Biscoe and/or Pete Whyman. It was music unusual, different, exquisite at times and cacaphonic modern jazz at others. I loved it. I wasn't the only one. *The Guardian* said: 'Arguably the most majestic work to appear in recent years. It's a marriage of inspirational lyrics and uplifting scoring, performed by some of the most talented musicians in Europe, harks back to the jazz suites of Ellington.' And *The Independent* said: 'Westbrook's settings are among the greatest British music of the century... bold, optimistic and inspiring'.

Since then, and across decades, I've followed the Westbrooks. They were always, it seemed to me, ploughing their own furrow, musically wayward, literary and lyrical, experimental. Often times they were abroad, loved and appreciated on the Continent far more than in the UK. Though that said, Mike Westbrook led the first jazz band ever to play the Proms at the Albert Hall, in 1992. From my diaries.

2 March 1990

A real treat for me this week, a Mike Westbrook concert. A good few years have passed since I last saw Westbrook's gang. Abstinence has clearly made my heart grow stronger, but I cannot explain why I should have this one obsession with a band when if asked what other bands I like, I couldn't name one, not one. I like to think, of course, that Westbrook is rather unique and special, and thus I have extremely discerning taste to have picked him out from the pack; but surely he cannot be so special as to warrant sole allegiance from me. I have a number of his compositions on tape: *The Westbrook Blake, Cortege, On Duke's Birthday, Variations on Rossini, The Ass* (these last two being recordings from Radio Three). There is a tape of this latest show, *Off Abbey Road*, which I've ordered by mail.

6 May 1994

I receive my *Smith's Academy Informer* which informs me that Westbrook is playing his Big Band Rossini in Ljubljana on 28 May, my birthday. So, I write a card to Myra telling her to go and see him and celebrate my birthday at the same time. Kate Westbrook is also launching a new show later this month as part of the London Jazz Festival, so I've booked up to go and see it. I'm a true fan and always enjoy looking forward to a Westbrook concert.

14 December 2000

Westbrook's *Glad Day* plays loudly through the house – this is the reworking of the Blake songs which brought many people's attention, including me, to his work all those years ago, Often I choose to play Westbrook's music – recently *Platterback* has been growing on me and some of its melodies have been looping in my head. I am particularly fond of the lyric, 'My sum and substance stands where she stands'. It's one of those lines that, for me, evoke a hunger for deep and powerful emotions. (There's some lines from T. S. Elliot's *La Figlia che Piange* which evoke something similar in me: 'Stand on the highest pavement of the stair, Lean on a garden urn, Weave, weave the sunlight in your hair.')

We grew a little apart in the noughties, the Westbrooks and I. Here is a diary entry from 2006.

11 November 2006

Yesterday, I took a trip up to London [. . .] to attend the opening (and free) session of the London Jazz Festival – being performed by Mike Westbrook's latest incarnation, his Village Band. This is how *Time Out* billed it: 'Celebrating his 70th birthday, Westbrook remains one of our most important (and least heralded) composers. Drawing from classic jazz, English folk, brass band music, cabaret and beyond, Westbrook's music is brilliant, idiosyncratic and earthy and the MWVB featuring players from the South West where he now lives channels all his musical enthusiasms into one exuberant whole! A great start to the LJF!'

But I didn't think it was a great start at all. I thought the music Mike Westbrook had arranged for the Village Band to include his tuba/euphonia playing, was ponderous and repetitive. Although all the songs were different from those I'd heard at his last concert – *Art Wolf* (was that the one in Exeter?) – and included a package of new songs with lyrics by Kate about the links between fairgrounds and the internet!, I thought the music sounded almost identical. I struggled with this after the last concert. I'm no music or jazz expert, but I do know that once upon a time I found Westbrook's music exciting, and different and inspiring, but now it seems he's stuck in a kind of slow and ponderous groove which he can't get out of. Sometimes the music sounded as though the record was stuck.

Oh dear.

But then, as if the Westbrooks had finally got wise to the wavering of my faith, my fanhood, they turned up suddenly – this was the summer of 2015 – on my very doorstep (I exaggerate not) with a performance starting within less than one hour of my finding out about it! This was in the Dorset market town of Bridport where we have a house and spend most holidays and many weekends. Here's my diary again.

19 July 2015, Bridport

Because I hadn't yet done so this weekend, I had a yen to nip out on the bike and have a look round town, maybe to check the Electric Palace, the Arts Centre. It was 6:50pm when I discovered that that very night, starting in 40 minutes,

Mike Westbrook and band – as The Uncommon Orchestra – were performing *A Bigger Show*. [. . .]

And how thrilling it was. Having been disappointed the last couple of times I saw Westbrook in one guise or another, I was far from disappointed this time. It seemed the best of Westbrook all rolled up into one – three singers, Kate and a much younger couple, Billy Bottle and Martine Waltier, using their voices as musical instruments (but not as extraordinarily as Phil Minton used to do to Mike's music); dozens of brass instrument players (most of whom had generous solos); two drummers; guitars, double bass, and Mike himself on a small keyboard cramped into the side of the stage. [. . .] Mike, himself, now nearly 80 is rather stout and hunched, so moving about, in order to conduct individuals or groups of musicians at different points, is rather difficult. But he has a very practised stealth about him, and if it wasn't for his bright red jacket he might have been near invisible in his movements.

About half the songs had lyrics, which sounded like they had been penned by Kate and were based on the loose idea of a fairground and the show that never ends. Billed as 'an electronic fairground for the Age of the World Wide Web.' There were lyrical passages, danceable passages, and plenty of Mike's characteristic arrangements, in which every musician is playing, louder and towards a near-chaotic crescendo, before dying away suddenly to leave, maybe, a single instrument spotlighted by the absence of other sound. Kate, of course, was wearing her white gloves – never seen her without them – and pressing the microphone to her right cheek before starting to sing. What a treat it all was, and so much more exciting for the manner in which I found Westbrook was in town. Imagine, if I'd seen posters for the concert on Sunday, and found I'd missed it. I'd never have forgiven myself.

Westbrook opened the floodgates for me to experience and enjoy other jazz, of many different varieties. Top of my list, I suppose, would come John Coltrane and his *Blue Train*, Keith Jarret's *The Koln Concert*, Jan Garbarek's collaborations with the Hilliard Ensemble. My stepfather's generation of artistes, such as Louis Armstrong, Ella Fitzgerald and Dave Brubeck are surely not far behind along with Miles Davis, Wayne Shorter and Art Pepper all filling my airwaves now and then. Of home grown talent, I like Zoe Rahman's *Kindred Spirits* and Basil Hodges's *My Guardian Angel*. But, to be honest, I can listen to a whole hour of Alyn Shipton's *Jazz Record Requests* – a long-running BBC Radio 3 programme – and enjoy every track.

And so to classical music. My two young sons delight in 'which would you prefer' questions. Would you prefer a life without chocolate or one without cheese? for example. Sometimes these questions are downright silly, but other times they can focus one's thoughts and opinions. What if, for the rest of my life, I was only allowed to listen to one broad genre of music – folk (blues, world etc), jazz, or classical music? Well, on reflection, I would have to choose classical (and, with tears in my eyes, be waving adieu to Joni, Mike, Ana, Bob, John among many others). But why? What is it about classical music? Would it be superficial to suggest an answer on the basis of dimensions? I love listening to all the various folk-type music I've collected over the decades, and much of it is so recognisable, so meaningful, taking me back, almost instantaneously to other times, to earlier clones of my current self. But, I would describe it as, mostly, one dimensional, a part of the popular music culture. If so, jazz definitely could be considered as having a couple of dimensions, for providing a richer listening experience than pop, broad-ranging, exciting, improvisational, a genre full of rhythms that fill up space and time. I listen, I enjoy, but often as the backdrop to other activities (reading, chatting, games). Classical music, though, by definition is music that has stood the test of time, survived to entertain generation after generation after generation. It is three-dimensional music, most especially when played by an orchestra made up of dozens of musicians. Music with such a depth and wholesomeness that it can take over its listeners, carry them on long journeys and into dreams, across deserts and over mountains, and sweep them away into and out of every emotion.

I came to classical music in my mid-20s via two composers. Benjamin Britten and Rachmaninov are both mentioned in my diaries for the first time in 1978. I found Britten largely because of visits to Aldeburgh, a pretty fishing village on the Suffolk coast. Aldeburgh was where Britten had made his home with the tenor Peter Pears, and where they'd started up the now-famous Aldeburgh Festival, so I didn't have to spend much time in the village before curiosity led me to Britten's music. Some time later, I owned a small house in Aldeburgh (Chapter one) and had plenty of opportunity to attend concerts at the nearby Snape Maltings centre. It was, in particular, the opera *Peter Grimes* that proved so enthralling, for it is actually set in Aldeburgh, not only bringing an historic version of the village and its people to life, but thrillingly encapsulating the moods of its overpowering and temperamental neighbour, the North Sea. To be listening to one of the so-called *Sea Interludes* is to be standing on the pebbles of Aldeburgh beach on a calm winter morning with distant seagulls, or in the still of night with a cold moon, or with the waves and wind rising, threatening, or, finally, with the full force of a storm raging, ferocious, danger for anyone at sea – not least the tragic figure of Peter Grimes. It's a totally brilliant work, surely one of the finest musical compositions of the 20th century.

From Peter Grimes, I was led to Britten's other operatic stories all very different but often with young handsome misfits exposed to temptation (*Billy Budd*, *Albert Herring*), or older protagonists with repressed passions and guilt (Gustav von Aschenbach in *Death in Venice*, Tarquinius in *Rape of Lucretia*). For some years, I tried to love other operas – went to see a few at Covent Garden – but mostly they defeated me.

I've tried Wagner, for example, but simply cannot relate to his music, his stories, his characters, in the way I do to Britten's.

At the same time as falling for *Peter Grimes*, I fell for Rachmaninov's second and third piano concertos. I don't know how or why, but it was probably thanks to Harold, the South African friend who did much to bring me out of myself in my 20s. We seemed to fill our flat day in day out with the sweeping emotions of *Rach 2* incessantly, as though it were our theme tune for life. And, now if I hear it or the not dissimilar *Rach 3*, I'm transported back instantly to those times – music is so very good at that.

With the gates open as it were, I found an immense landscape of delights to explore endlessly and at will – the glorious symphonies of Beethoven, Tchaikovsky, Mahler, Sibelius, Dvorak, Mozart and Holst. Over time, I would stroll through some areas more than others, though I'd be hard pressed to explain why in words. I went to concerts, especially the Proms, more so when I was younger. I never came close to understanding the brilliance of what I was listening to, and my mind would often wander away from the music, yet I knew what took me on emotional journeys, what moved me, and what didn't. I can say that I appreciated (and still do appreciate) listening to live music (not only classical) but I must also admit that I get almost as much pleasure from listening to recorded music played at home. It never ceases to amaze me that for all of history, until the 20th century, music could only ever have been enjoyed live, and was, for most, a rare pleasure, yet I and my fellow humans, can now listen to the Shostakovitch's string quartets, Satie's *Gymnopédies* or Beethoven's *Fifth* wherever we want and as often as we want.

Evidently, music is its own expression but I am confined to words, and I'm running out of them. So, by way of concluding this chapter, I'm turning briefly to my diaries.

It's a very rough-and-ready way of looking at musical preferences, but using the magic of computers I've counted how many times, in 60 years of diaries, I've mentioned individual composers. It's very few times in fact, and brief mentions at that, but Shostakovitch tops the list (some 35 times), followed by Britten and Beethoven (mirroring, indeed, the volumes of works in my digital music collection). Here are a few choice extracts.

24 September 1978
Last night I fell asleep listening to Horowitz play Rachmaninov's third piano concerto – amazing.

16 April 1980
I went to the RFH and heard *Shostakovitch 9* and *Rhapsodie Espagnol*. Divine. Concerts are a treat.

Tuesday 24 January 1988
I tape *Shosty 5*, the last in the series of RPO with Ashkenazy at the helm. Sunday I captured 2, 15 and the concerto for piano, horn and trumpet. More than any other composer Shostakovitch communicates to me, more ever than Britten. Such a feat considering he comes from a different culture.'

Thursday 27 July 1995
The Albert Hall. What a fabulous concert. It started with the sparkling *Cockaigne* by Elgar; Maxwell-Davies unfinished ballet *The Beltane Fire* took up the rest of the first half. This was an interesting work conducted by the composer himself. He explains the music in his programme as a battle between pagan rituals and Christianity. The second half was devoted to Rachmaninov's *Third Piano Concerto*. This was one of my favourite pieces from the early 1980s, but I have never heard it played as well as this evening. The Russian pianist, Grigory Sokolov, was amazing, he melted into the music, gave it such richness and depth. Tortelier conducted with great skill too.

11 October 1998
Shostakovitch's string quartet 13 bounces through the house like a pogo stick, and rolls on its side every now and then. I am far and away from recognising the individual quartets still, although 12 is very distinctive. Part of the difficulty of course is that I never sit down just to listen to music, and so my mind is occupied by other things, and there are usually three quartets on a CD so they merge into one another without me noticing. I read the sleeve notes occasionally which help pin the music on to a moment in Shosty's life or Russia's turbulent history.

19 December 2002
Just now I've had a bath and I'm listening to Shostakovitch's 7th symphony. I'd gone into the Record Corner in Godalming in order to find a copy of Mozart's *Magic Flute* or *Don Giovanni* for [a friend's] birthday. I came out having bought a Klemperer recording of *Magic Flute*, a cheapish CD of Fats Waller music for Adam, and a complete set of Shostakovitch's symphonies. This last was a purely spontaneous purchase at the till. The set has 11 CDs – twice as many as the set of Shostakovitch string quartets I ordered and bought from the same shop a couple of years ago (I've just checked back – it was FOUR years ago!) for around £50 – but only cost £20. I had no intention of buying the set when I picked it up and commented to the shop owner at the price '11 CDs for £20!' with a rising intonation. Then, as he was packing up my other purchases, he told me how well some of the recordings had been received, and how well the set had been reviewed. He may have been telling me a pack of lies – but I bought the set any way.

27 December 2012
Shostakovitch SQ 8 is playing – it's just a brilliant musical exposition of my mind at times.

As a finale to this chapter, I'm going to invite myself onto *Desert Island Discs*, a BBC radio programme that has been broadcast throughout my life, for 10 years longer, in fact, than I've been alive. It's a classic programme, iconic; indeed, in 2019 it was given the epithet 'greatest radio programme of all time' by a panel of broadcasters. Originally devised by Roy Plumley, the programme format invites a guest, or 'castaway', to choose eight recordings, a book and a luxury item that they would take if they were to be cast away on a desert island. Many a time, I've given a half-hearted thought to what I would choose, but now I'm going to fix those choices once and for all (and if I cheat a bit, not least by choosing albums rather than songs, then who's going to blame me).

Joni Mitchell – *Song to a Seagull*

Martha Tilson – *The Sea*

Mike Westbrook – *Glad Day: Settings of William Blake*

Victoria De Los Angeles – *Cançons Tradicionals Catalanes*

Keith Jarrett – *The Köln Concert*

Sergei Rachmaninoff – *Piano Concerto No. 3*

Benjamin Britten – *Peter Grimes*

Dmitri Shostakovich – *String Quartet No. 5*

Book – The collected works of T. S. Eliot, W.H. Auden and W. B. Yeats

Luxury Item – An iPad (plus solar charger) with its memory full of my diaries, my music, my family photos/videos

Chapter seven

HEALTH
TO BALANCE MIND AND BODY

Health matters, of mind and of body. For much of my life, I've been blessed largely with physical well being, and sufficient mental stability to be able to steer clear of psychological therapists, of whatever ilk. As I write this, I am well into what is classically considered old age. For some years recently, my physical health, or various aspects of ageing unhealth, has been a mainstream topic of conversation whether internally, in my diary, or with family members. But, I wish to limit this memoir to the middle period of my life, up to my mid-fifties, say, and thus avoid the grumblings of old age.

I've always been a very active body, and I've remained naturally slim – so, no eating worries. I played a lot of sport during my school years – rugby, football, cricket, basketball, running, tennis, cross-country running – but none of it seriously, or skilfully. I like to think I was quite fast and agile at five-aside football in the park, but otherwise I was average, average, average. I began using a bicycle as my main source of local transport from early teens, a habit that's stayed with me through to my 70s.

I played no sport regularly at university as far as I can remember, though a friend introduced me to squash. In New Zealand, where I lived close to a beach, I took up swimming often in the sea. I wrote in my diary, 'Would I ever be happy living away from the sea again?' I also enjoyed plenty of skiing.

In my later 20s, I played a little squash socially with friends, but otherwise there was only swimming and walking on holidays. I had a couple of health scares, one led to a testicular biopsy (negative), and the other, after months of unusual tiredness, to me being prescribed antibiotics to clear up a rare type of pneumonia. It was this latter illness that led me to take up yoga exercises to strengthen my lungs.

I had been exposed to various spiritual philosophies and regimes during my travels and after, in London, during, let me call it, my 'alternative' period. Apart from the various kinds of yoga, there was much on offer though I partook rarely: Tai Chi, massage systems, group therapy and encounter groups (many of my friends did EST – Erhard Seminars Training), isolation tanks, primal screaming, Transcendental Meditation, free love in orange with Bhagwan and so on. The most significant investment I ever made in this regard was to attend a kind of meditation retreat one winter in the Welsh hills (Chapter three) but, essentially, I was drawn to the event not by the spiritual components but by the fact that the leader of the retreat was a well known ethologist and had authored a brilliant book on human evolution.

In general, being more scientist than hippy, I had a very healthy scepticism for all of it. Moreover, none of the other encounters (few and far between) I did have gave me any cause to seek more. As with drug experimentation, my natural caution was reinforced by anxieties, if not fears, of negative physical consequences. I do recall, for example, being prohibitively anxious about taking part in one of the EST weekends: the idea of being thrust into the spotlight in front of hundreds of people as a kind of confidence therapy was too much. Nevertheless, now that I'm reflecting, writing about these matters in what I might label as assessment mode, I can see that I have developed some kind of quasi-philosophical approach to living in a well way, one largely dependent on a variety of physical activities – the yoga, for example, swimming, cycling and rambling.

As I say, I took up yoga in the early 80s, partly because of the pneumonia, partly, perhaps, because of the activities I'd undertaken at the retreat, and also partly because of a rather strange encounter with my local doctor. Here's my diary to explain (interestingly, it seems to imply I was hovering closer to feeling a need for psychological/spiritual help than I remember).

Tuesday 21 December 1982
What an interesting talk with my doctor – Dr Richman. Because I woke up the other night scratching my head, I felt it really was time to go to the doctor about it again. Through his initiative we talked about the causes underlying my scratching, teeth grinding and headaches. I became terribly afraid and tense and tried to discover where he might be leading before answering his questions. It has only been recently that I've contemplated talking psychology to the doctor but I've been put off by the personality of the surgery, but as Dr Richman pointed out this is probably a reflection of myself. Last time with Dr Oliver I did try and suggest there might be some connections somewhere but he dismissed the idea. So since then I have not thought too seriously about returning to the subject. Dr Richman however suggested that these symptoms were caused by inner tension that needed release. He agreed that it was probably due to an upbringing without confidence being instilled in me. He said I would probably be all right if I didn't receive any major blows to my confidence. He suggested having a practical plan at the ready whenever I wanted to indulge in self-analysis, and also recommended relaxation techniques like yoga. We talked of psychoanalysis and such things. I told him I didn't see how they could do any good and he said he didn't think I needed changing and such treatment implies change. Perhaps, he felt, I should go on scratching. Now I wonder whether smoking would be better than scratching.

I bought a well-known book: *Yoga Health* by Selvarajan Yesudian and Elisabeth Haich (who ran a yoga school in Switzerland). It was more detailed and more spiritual than I wanted or needed but the text was readable, the descriptions of the Asanas clear (often with photos), and there was a good deal of focus on breathing. Over time, I conjoined a dozen or more exercises (from the book, physiotherapy experiences, and elsewhere) into a 20 minute routine. From then on, I was regularly cajoling myself (in the diaries, especially at the start of the new year) to restart my 'exercises', or do them more regularly. And so it has continued for over four decades. For long periods, I have done them every day, but there have also been periods when I've lapsed into a more haphazard regime. I've never wanted to join a yoga class or group. I've tended to believe that 20 minutes every day or every couple of days is more useful than an hour or two once a week. And, for me, there's certainly no social aspect to yoga. Mostly, it's been, and continues to be if not exactly a chore then an obligation to myself.

3 January 1988

I arrive home from work around 6pm, maybe I have a quick cup of tea, maybe not. I must do my yoga on an empty stomach. Maybe I have a bath first, maybe not. I do not look forward to yoga, it is like a task, a weight on my back. I must discipline myself to do it for the broader benefits. I settle down on the floor in the lounge, on my back, and roll backward and forward. I hear my spine crack. Then I lie with my legs up in the air supported by my hands and hips, after a few seconds I let my legs fall back over my head. When I was doing these exercises regularly, my feet would touch the ground behind my head, but now after only a few days I am still too stiff to do so. [. . .] The penultimate exercise is a headstand during which I try and breathe slowly and deeply. After the headstand I do a breathing exercise; and, finally, I lay on the ground flat for a couple of minutes. I find the deep breathing has to continue for a while, the lungs demand it – I cannot relinquish immediately the conscious aspect of the breathing.

I do sincerely believe that these physical and breathing exercises are beneficial. Immediately afterwards I certainly feel calmer, more in control, more at peace even, although this does not last long. But I think there are more permanent effects, benefits from regular practice – perhaps a more relaxed mind and body.

I say 'mostly' it's been a chore, because the chore/pleasure scale tips over towards pleasure when I'm able to do my exercises outside (rather than inside). In Kilburn, I sometimes was able to do them in the nearby cemetery, which was delightfully deserted more often than not. In Elstead, I occasionally cycled down to a quiet grassy bank by the river where, if lucky, I could be undisturbed for 20 minutes (and in the summer have a swim too). But it was after moving back to Brighton in 2006 that I discovered its pebble beach was (and still is) the perfect, and often the most blissful, place to exercise.

Let me explain briefly. Firstly, and most importantly, the area of Brighton beach I use, to the east of the Palace Pier, is wide and dips down from the promenade (Madeira Drive) in a series of levels to the sea line. There is little commercial activity along that stretch of Madeira Drive, and, in any case, beach dwellers down on the pebbles are out of sight. Still, of course, there is pedestrian traffic along the beach, swimmers and strollers in summer, and dog walkers come wind or shine all year round. I've a tendency to feel that when doing my exercises I'm making a spectacle of myself (most acutely when doing headstands, my favourite exercise), and because of this I won't start doing them unless I can feel relatively alone on the pebbles – in summer this usually means arriving very early in the morning. Once I've started, if others then come and place themselves nearby I'm usually oblivious, unselfconscious, and continue any way.

Secondly, because tides on Brighton beach are constantly shifting the levels of pebbles and gravels, I can always find a place where the beach is horizontal, flat, and where the pebbles are a good size for doing exercises on (not too small like sand which sticks to the body/clothes, and not too large which can hurt).

In summer, I'll do my exercises in swimming trunks, and swim either before or after. The rest of the year, I'll wear whatever clothes I need to keep warm. Sometimes, in winter, I'll be wearing coat, gloves, scarf, and, yes, it is a bit more awkward to do many of the exercises so trussed up, but the joy of being there, feeling the weather, hearing the waves crashing, usually outweighs the difficulties. Of course, when the weather's poor, too windy, rainy, freezing, I don't make it down to the beach – indeed, I'm making it less often as I've grown older.

I credit a routine yoga regime with: keeping my lungs in very good order; restoring one of my knees to strength after volleyball accidents; helping me develop a deeper natural pattern of regular breathing; and contributing (more or less, I don't know) to a degree of physical and mental calm.

Cycling. I'm amazed that more people don't develop, early on in their lives, the habit of using a bicycle for local transport. I was cycling to and from school from the age of 11, and have never been without a bicycle since then. For the years I lived and worked in London, I rode everywhere, to the office, to the pub, to friends' houses, to the theatre, to the shops. I worked in Sutton, south London, for a couple of years, which was too far to cycle from Kilburn, so I biked to Victoria every day from where I took the train. For years, I owned racing bikes (bought second hand), with the handlebars twisted upwards like horns, though I did gravitate to mountain bikes once I was living in Elstead. For the ten Elstead years, I didn't have much need for a cycle for transport, but Adam and I were often out on our bikes at the weekend exploring the commons and heathlands. (Before then, in Kilburn, I'd carry him around on a little seat fixed to the back of the cycle.)

Like with yoga, and diary keeping, I think of cycling as a way of life, almost philosophically so. It's a free way to travel. It's a healthy way to travel (more so since strict noxious emission laws were enacted) since it obliges a certain amount of exercise. There's no waiting around, no queuing. And it's an infinitely flexible way of moving around a city; more often than not, it's the quickest. I often used to race vehicles down the Edgware Road, along Park Lane and Marble Arch, leaving them standing helpless in endless traffic light or congestion queues. As I've written elsewhere, I was only able to take a part-time Masters at University College while working full time because I could nip backwards and forwards – five minutes travel time – between lectures and the office. Logistic super-efficiency is what a bike gives its rider.

Many years later, into old age, I'm still on my bike daily, nipping to the beach, the library, the shops, etc. And even when I'm not, I have my trousers (if I'm not in shorts) tucked into my socks, to protect flapping trouser legs getting caught in the chain, or rubbing against an oily cog. This was a habit I developed so long ago that I can't remember when. Indeed, it became so ingrained that I started wearing my trousers tucked into my socks whether on a bike or not. It's not been a fashionable way to dress, I would say, and when at work or at meetings or with friends, mostly I've given way to social convention, untucking them when not on the bike. I never have dressed in a conventional or fashionable way, and increasingly, I came to enjoy the contrariness of having my trousers snuck into socks. But, also, I came to dislike the inward streams of cold air that would rise up my calves when unsnucked, as it were. Over time, and as I've aged, I've tended to make fewer concessions to social convention. Friends/family like to mock me, but I've hardened against caring about their views. Often, in the street, when I am but a humble pedestrian, I notice strangers cannot help a slightly disapproving look as their eyes, unconsciously, drop to examine what's going on round my ankles. I keep insisting to my children that the style will come into fashion soon, and that everyone will be tucking their trousers into socks, not dissimilar to leggings. But it hasn't happened yet.

Now, dear reader, if you will indulge me for a few lines, I have one piece of advice on how to avoid having your bike stolen, and I have one intervention to make into the seemingly endless and often near-hysterical debate over the behaviour of cyclists (so often played out in the local and national media).

Advice: Isn't it strange how few private vehicles are custom-decorated, especially considering how much time and money we all put into personalising our homes. Is it because of the expense of spray painting motor cars? Or is it because cars are often traded, and customising them might compromise the re-sale value? My solution for safeguarding bikes against being stolen is exactly that, to personalise them, but not in any expensive or elaborate way. I have two cans of metal spray paint, red and yellow, and they've lasted me more than a decade, and at least three bicycles. As soon as I acquire a bicycle, new or second hand, I take it to a patch of wasteland, lie it on the ground, and spray yellow spots all over it, the handlebars, the tyres, the crossbars, the wheel rims and spokes, the pedals. I then turn it around the other way, and do the same with the red paint. It takes five minutes. The bike looks a mess, yellow spotted from one side, red spotted from the other. But, crucially, it has become – instantly – unsaleable. And if it is unsaleable, who would bother to steal it? Well, certainly not bike thieves. It's too difficult to remove the paint from so many random surfaces on the bicycle, and the spotting would put off any potential buyer. Yes, it's somewhat disagreeable to spoil a brand new bike in this way, but I've only been buying new bikes in the latter part of my life (until recently, no more than £300-400), and I never expect to sell them later. It works. I've had bikes stolen over the course of my life, but never ones covered in red and yellow spots.

Intervention: Full disclosure. I often cycle on pavements; I often ignore traffic lights. Oh, the venom that issues forth from letter writers to the local newspaper spluttering and spewing about such sins. Two facts: The Highway Code was largely written for motorised vehicle drivers. Motorised vehicles are killing machines.

Whichever way you care to look at the matter, cyclists are much closer in terms of lethal potential and individual vulnerability to pedestrians than they are to motorists, and as such they should be considered more pedestrian than driver. For example, a cyclist can usually ride to the front of a traffic queue waiting at a red light. From there, she/he can easily see if there are no vehicles moving in any other direction. She/he could hop off the bike, walk across the junction, and then hop back on, without breaking any traffic laws. But, actually, why walk across when it's quicker and easier to ride across. Moreover, there is an advantage to the drivers stopped at the red light in that when the light turns green they do not have to negotiate one or more cyclists starting up in parallel to them.

Often times, it's convenient for bike riders like me to use a pavement or pedestrian area. Cars, vans, lorries can take up so much space that cyclists are pushed into gutters or against curbs, which can be dangerous to negotiate. Pedestrian malls might be the shortest route for a cyclist, or the route across a park, yet cyclists are condemned for using them (though walking their bikes is OK).

My solution to regulating the behaviour of bike riders vis-a-vis pedestrians is simply to bring into operation a clear code of 'right of way'. Cyclists should be considered as pedestrians but when on pavements (or any non-road public area) they should give complete and absolute right of way to all pedestrians – making sure they do not inconvenience them in any way. Let's say, two pedestrians are walking side-by-side filling the path, and a cyclist is riding towards them. That cyclist should expect to have to get off his bike and walk until she/he has passed the pedestrians. But if the pedestrian areas are empty or largely free of pedestrians, cycles should be allowed to use them – carefully. Equally, when pedestrians use cycle lanes, they should give absolute right of way to cycles.

At traffic lights, if a cyclist chooses to cross when they are red for motorised traffic, the cyclist should, of course, give absolute and complete right of way to any vehicles (motorised or cycles) and/or pedestrians which are crossing thanks to a green light (or man). For me this right of way does not mean just avoiding collisions, but avoiding any inconveniencing of pedestrians (not obliging them to move out of the way, for example).

There are a lot of rude and inconsiderate cyclists out there, but there are also many many more rude and inconsiderate drivers, and dangerous ones. The rules for cyclists (non-motorised) need to be re-written. Children need to grow up understanding and benefiting from the efficiencies and joys of bike riding, but with a deep-set knowledge of how to apply 'right of way' behaviour for safety and politeness.

Apart from our (Adam's and my) scrambles around the heathlands of west Surrey, I've never particularly wanted to cycle as a way of exploring the countryside. You don't see much from country lanes; and biking rough tracks is rarely conducive for the noticing and contemplation of surroundings. No, walking – hiking if you like – is the way. Sturdy boots, a modestly filled backpack, and an Ordnance Survey map (two and a half inches to the mile). I was introduced to hiking during my school years, thanks to a history teacher who took us youth hostelling in the Lake District and Yorkshire Dales. As I've already written about (*Why Ever* – Chapter four), Colin and I 'did' the Pennine Way in the summer we finished school, three full weeks of walking.

There was often a moment during my hitchhiking trips to or from Cardiff University, along the M4, when I passed a specific view with pasture, rolling hills, copses in the distance. And every time I saw this view, I felt a huge yearning – where it came from I've no idea – to ask the driver to slam on the breaks, pull onto the hard shoulder and let me out, so that I could walk into the view, melt into the landscape. I never did do that but the idea of melting into the landscape has remained with me ever since encouraging me – on occasions over the years – to intensify a feeling of communing with nature.

While working at FT Newsletters in the late 1980s I became friendly with a newish fellow editor, Zeba Kalim. Our chat by the water cooler one day focused on the walking boots she'd just bought, and her planned hike at the weekend. I don't recall the conversation, but I do have a strong memory sense of it triggering in me a wave of nostalgia for my school day walking holidays. Almost immediately, I set about buying myself hiking boots, and organising a few days walk along Offa's Dyke on the England/Wales border.

> 20 October 1989
> Next week I am planning to do a three day hike on Offa's Dyke. I can't believe how much time it is taking to organise in my mind when to go and how to go. I have just bought some Doc Martins boots, so now I know I really will go. I must satisfy this desire to see mountains and wild open spaces.

Thereafter, I was often to be found in my Doc Martins, taking any opportunity to go hiking alone for one, two or three days. Whenever I felt that need for melting into landscapes, I'd organise myself a trek, staying at B&Bs, and hitch-hiking where necessary. (Though hitch-hiking was out of fashion by the 1980s, I've always found that one can always still thumb short rides on rural roads without much difficulty.) And when on holiday with Bel and Adam, I'd take one day for myself to do a decent long walk (though, we'd all three of us be doing shorter, circular strolls most days).

These walking expeditions were very good for the soul, I would say, ideal conditions for ruminating on one's life, on the vastness of the physical universe, and on the extraordinary beauty of the living world. They were short but perfect storms of pleasure and achievement. Being outside, walking by fields, forests, hills, rivers, lakes, being part of a constantly changing landscape with endless variation of views, is but the base pleasure of walk. There are flowers, trees, birds, mammals, insects to investigate, identify if you please, not to mention the patterns and colours of mushrooms, fungi, lichen. And because this is Britain, there is a vast network of public paths AND the most detailed, accurate maps you could ever possibly hope for to guide your way. Moreover, these maps open up a dense and fascinating world of history, archaeology, architecture to discover everywhere you go, and all so relatively close together, making for much variety on even the shortest of walks.

For me, there was still more to be had from these walks simply because they were good fodder for the diary, refreshing the often humdrum pages with deep metaphorical inhalations of landscape description, exposures to weather (whether rain-sodden or sun-drenched), and stories/connections found, whether personal, historic or folkloric.

I have walked many different landscapes in the UK, and am tempted to trawl the diaries for some extracts to reproduce here a la Robert Macfarlane. However, I can't say I'm a fan of literary writing about walking itself (though of late bookshops seem to be awash with it). That said, there are two books I consider bibles for anyone with a religious fervour for experiencing hiking as a multi-faceted adventure into geography, history, nature and science: Oliver Rackham's *The History of the Countryside* and W. G. Hoskins' *The Making of the English Landscape*.

By way of recommendation, perhaps, or to preen a little that I've 'done' a good deal of the country I was born into, here are some of the landscapes that I have loved to walk, that I have walked to love.

Snowdonia – for a decent mountain to climb
South West Coast Path – to swim every Devon and Cornish cove
Cotswolds – for thatched cottages and tweeness
Dartmoor – for pre-histories and tor stories
South Downs – for the Seven Sisters roller-coaster
Orkney/Shetland – to feel extreme calm or fierce weather
Peak District – to explore gorgeous valleys and industrial archaeology
Pembrokeshire Coast Path – for rugged rocky drama, and dunes galore

Other areas I walked with my school when still a teenager (the Lake District and Yorkshire), or know better through touring than hiking trips (Exmoor, East Anglia, Dorset, Mull, Brecon Beacons).

Abroad has beckoned me to hike only rarely, I suppose, as I didn't want to travel so far for two or three day expeditions. However, one might also ask why would I stray from my main love when she is so attractive and so bejewelled? Ireland did call me a few times, for exploring ruined castles, the wild Atlantic coast, and the mysterious Burren. I've enjoyed fabulous week-long hiking trips to Madeira and Tenerife (both with impressive mountains, superb walking, and within easy reach of beaches for swimming). Alas I've never walked among the Alps, only skied, which though fun is not the same thing.

I've mentioned swimming periodically through these pages, and I have swum often in indoor pools, but it's outdoor swimming that I love, and have always loved. It's now called wild swimming, I believe, but I cannot help thinking the term a little pretentious, especially when used by people who go in groups, once a week, to the same bit of water with infrastructure in place.

No doubt my love of outdoor swimming was born and nurtured in New Zealand where there were so many empty beaches, and rivers, often ice cold, constantly tempting me to strip off and dive in. In Chile, I was a stone's throw from the beach, whether in Vina del Mar or Horcon. During my Corsican sojourn, despite it being mid-winter, I was in the sea every day. A little later, in Rio de Janeiro, I lived so close to the water I simply needed to cross a road, climb over a couple of boulders, and dive into the blue. (Rarely, pollution drifted into Botofogo Bay, but then, if I wanted, a very short ride would take me to Copacabana beach, which faces out to the ocean, and where swimming was not the only attraction.)

Once back in the UK, for two or three years, we were in Aldeburgh every other weekend, where I'd swim come rain or shine from the long pebble beach. And always, on holidays with Bel and Adam, I would find places to swim, sea beaches, inland rivers, or, occasionally, lakes. Indeed, I would need to get in water before I could properly sense/believe I was actually on holiday.

By the early 1990s, Bel and Adam were installed in central Brighton (thanks to selling the Aldeburgh house), where I would also be at least every other weekend, sometimes weekday nights too. It was just minutes on the bike to the beach. So, why not go twice, three times a day in summer if the sun was out?

Then, we all moved to Elstead in Surrey, where opportunities for swimming outdoors were few and far between. Occasionally, we'd mess around in the River Wey, or swim at Frensham Ponds, but that would only be on hot sunny weekend days. But Adam and I were always out and about on our bikes, and walking. We swam at the leisure centre once a week for exercise, and I took up volleyball (see below). Only when I moved back to Brighton in 2006 would I be close to the sea again.

It is generally acknowledged that swimming is one of the best and most healthy forms of exercise – providing, they say, a full body work-out – and that's been a happy coincidence for me. Swimming lengths in pools feels like exercise. Whereas being in the sea, a river, a natural pool is an experience much better described as pleasure. It's not all fun exactly, outside of two or three summer months, since the water here in the UK is often a little colder than one might like, than one might find at all times of years in the Mediterranean. Indeed, as a young man, I dreamed that I'd be able to develop a lifestyle that would see me in England for half the year, and by the Mediterranean for the colder months. For a while, after Adam was born, I was able to borrow my stepfather's flat in Antibes every winter for a week alone, and indulge my need to be in the sea every day (plus I was able to drive up into the Alps above Nice for a day or two to ski also).

Like yoga, swimming provides excellent exercise for the lungs as well as for the musculoskeletal system. Getting in to cold water has grown more difficult with age, and in the late spring/early autumn months I need to spend five or ten minutes accustoming my body to the temperature, which it does eventually. Bracing, yes, but I feel so alive, never more alive in fact.

As for sports, since school, I've played little. Squash in my 20s, a little sailing (in Rio) in my 30s, and, in my 40s, I took up volleyball. We'd moved to Elstead in Surrey, and my social life was in shreds – voluntarily so, for having moved out of London, as I focused on running my business and raising Adam. I needed to get out of the house a little more, and the local leisure centre, in Guildford, where Adam and I went to swim, had a thriving volleyball club. I'd barely played the game (a few fun sessions with expats in Rio), and knew it to favour tall people, which I was not; nevertheless I press ganged myself into trying it out.

23 September 1997
On Sunday I nipped over to Spectrum centre and joined in a volleyball club. This is no have-a-laugh fun night, this is serious sport. The session lasts for two hours, and much of it is spent practising. Well, for me, that was just as well, since I haven't touched a volleyball for ten years. There are two nets set up – one is for the men who can really play, and the other is for all the others, most of whom are women. But the guy in charge did a good job of setting up the practice sessions to keep everyone busy, and even though we didn't play a proper game because there were too many people, there was enough activity to satisfy me. [The club] boasts a national team and several local league teams.

I soon learned the basics but also I was never going to make it as a hitter (the prime attribute of the best players, who are always tall). However, there is one position in a volleyball team (of six players) for which height does not matter – the setter. Each side gets three hits before the ball has to fly over the net, the aim being for it to hit the ground on the opposing team's court, or for it to be too difficult to return accurately. After the service, one of the back row of the opposing team usually 'digs' the ball up into the air, a dig being a bounce off a player's two inside forearms together. The setter almost always takes the second touch with the aim of lobbying (or digging) it up in the air close to the net so another player can jump high and spike the ball downward into the other court. An ideal team, in its simplest form, has five tall players, with strong, accurate spiking capabilities (the muscle), and one setter (the brains). The setter needs to be fast and agile to get underneath the second ball, fast-thinking to decide on which other player is in the best position for a point-winning hit, and accurate enough to place a high ball exactly right for that player.

For many months, I felt insecure at the training sessions. I was, after all, older than many of the other regulars, and almost all of the regulars were much better players. Nevertheless, I persevered every Sunday evening, and slowly became friendly with several other modest players. Nine months later, I gave myself a positive report card.

> 25 May 1998
> My volleyball is slowly improving. Two Sundays ago we had a competition evening: six teams and four or five games each. The team I was on won every single game, and, despite a handicap system, we also won overall. It was great playing with good players; they protected me a little, but on the whole I was useful, I rescued a few lost balls, and only gave away a couple of points. [. . .] I still can't control my digging, and I made a couple of bad sets. Still, I do really look forward to the sessions on Sunday evening.

And another two years on, I'm still struggling to improve but, it seems, volleyball has got under my skin. By this time, I was helping organise matches for the club's lower team (Storm), occasionally watching the sport live and on TV, and I signed up for a weekend course on volleyball refereeing.

> 23 April 2000
> Only eight people at volleyball last night, mostly all good players. I seem unable to make any improvement on my hitting or my digging, although I believe my defensive work is as good as some much better plays. I chase and predict the ball quite well, and I appear able to return a smashed ball by digging to the setter more accurately than I can a soft ball. Although in some training routines I can hit the ball with modest force and direction, I seem to lose the ability in games – I can almost feel myself over-conscious and therefore too predictive in my running and jumping. But, apart from failures to hit well, I do think I'm an asset in a team, in that I am rarely responsible for losing a point, whereas better players, who do not actually win points very often, lose them more often than I do. It is clear, though, that at any level other than beginner, the only means for winning points is to smash the ball (or occasionally tip it softly over the net).
> In June, there is to be an international match played at Guildford, the first ever it seems. Although it's a lot of work for the club (a special court has to be laid out, and proper arrangements made for the game), it is also excellent for the kudos of the club, and is an opportunity to stimulate interest in the sport.

My own interest in the sport is slowly growing. I will certainly endeavour to take Adam to see the match.

Much as I've aimed to focus on health and well being in this chapter, I've reached a crossroads (there's a pun there – as nothing makes me so angry as my own incapacities) from where all routes lead to tortuous and intricate discussions of ill-health. Nothing is quite so self-absorbing as one's own ill health and potential remedies. I'd had calf strains from playing volleyball once or twice, but in January 2001 during a game, I jumped to block a hit, and, on returning to earth my left foot found another player's foot first then buckled in the wrong direction with all my weight. I, too, buckled down on top of it in searing agony, screeching out in pain. Nothing broken, but I was on pain pills for a week, had to cancel a trip to Brussels, and was out of the game for a couple of months.

In April, though, I was back, and able to report to my diary that I'd played in the most exciting volleyball game to date – a team match against The Slayers. I was appointed setter, which wasn't always the case.

Here's my match report.

3 April 2001

We won the first game comfortably, with lots of shouting and joking and bustling between us, and the second game not quite so comfortably. But, in the third game, The Slayers finally started to get in their stride, to keep their shots in, and to block our hitters effectively at the net. They won quite closely. Because of the first two games, we were still confident of winning the fourth, but it didn't happen. We were tiring and making mistakes, they were really hitting top form, and finding our weaknesses consistently. Their top hitter served three aces in a row. They had built a strong momentum. Ian (our captain) made good use of our time-outs, though, to break their runs, but not enough to stop them winning the fourth game easily. As we prepared for the last and short fifth set (15 points rather than 25), I was fairly sure we would lose – they had stronger players, they were still fresh, and they were on a winning streak, I said so – and there were one or two critical murmurs (not very serious, but noticeable). Why did I say so? Because I wanted to express my feeling that I thought we had played really well as a team, and it had been a great match, and it wouldn't matter if we lost. I like this team, and the players in it, it works well without competitive pressure, and I prefer to put the stress on the friendly and supportive banter. I actually think it works better than placing too much stress on what one has been doing wrong. Nevertheless, Ian and Barry gave us a little pep talk. Within a couple of minutes we were four or five points down. The Slayers' momentum from the previous game was still with them. But then, amazingly (and I don't know why or how), we pulled level, and raced ahead to win 15 to 11 or something like that. It was a great victory, and a very rewarding, if tiring, match to have played.

That spring, we went on to win the Surrey third division league. My ankle injury, however, proved to be but a foretaste of how injurious sport can really be despite its reputation for being a giver of exercise, and thus of health.

April 2002, mid-game, I jumped to spike, but must have returned to ground at an odd angle: 'my knee, my leg, my body just gave way – and I was writhing on the floor and screeching in pain. It was like something had come apart in my knee – it was the worst injury I've ever had I think.'

A colleague drove me home in my car. We stopped to buy frozen peas which I held in place behind the knee. Back at Russet House, I was struck down by what felt like a terrible cramp running down the back of the bad knee and calf. But I couldn't put my foot down and exercise the calf against the cramp because of the damaged knee. I rolled around on the floor, desperately rubbing and massaging my calf, and screaming my head off in agony. The pain eventually subsided, and I was able to sleep; but, in the morning, I couldn't straighten the knee at all, and it seemed terribly fragile. I was in a dreadful state psychologically, crying quite deeply. I think this was because a) I was depressed about the short-term practical consequences of the injury; and b) because of the long-term impact the injury would have on my volleyball playing.

I went to the doctor in the morning, and was referred to A&E, for a five hour wait. The doctor thought a cyst in the back of my knee might have been an aggravating circumstance, but, after lancing it, she said there was nothing further she could do. The x-rays showed nothing broken, so I was given a bandage, crutches, and an appointment at the fracture clinic 10 days hence. Physiotherapy sessions followed, but I couldn't make progress because every exercise triggered a ballooning at the back of the knee (where the cyst had been).

Over the following weeks I moaned, self-pityingly over and over again to my diary, as if it was hyper-important to record every detail of many interactions with the health personnel. And I tired it (the diary) out with all the medical research I'd done, too, insisting it learn about cartilage meniscus tears, cruciate ligaments, and cysts. I had a theory, that I'd damaged the back of the knee by keeping the frozen peas against the skin for far too long, and ultimately the sac containing fluid round the knee had burst – which is why it felt like a cramp running down my calf. The consultant was not interested in my theories but he did, eventually, refer me for an arthroscopy (much shorter waiting list, he said, than an MRI) which I then had in mid-May. This was only a month after the accident but it felt like six months, after all my life had been turned upside down.

The arthroscopy went smoothly. I was told I had done damage to cartilage on both sides of the knee, including a bucket handle tear on the inner side, and to the cruciate ligament. The cartilage would repair itself, but physiotherapy would aim to treat the ligament damage 'conservatively' by strengthening other muscles around the knee to take over the work of the ligament. Two weeks later, I still could not straighten my leg, and I was in despair for thinking there would never be any improvement. Certainly, I knew my regular volleyball playing days were over – I couldn't possibly risk another such accident and being so dysfunctional for so long again.

> 7 June 2002
> Whatever the situation, whatever the reality, I cannot see what can happen from here to repair the situation – and whatever approach the surgeon decides to take now (an MRI scan, referral to another doctor, an operation) it is going to take many many months – of limping, worrying, trips to the hospital, almost certainly another operation with all that entails. . . I am back in distress mode this morning.

My knee did repair, in time, with physiotherapy/yoga, walking, cycling and regular swimming. But here's an amusing story – by way of a light entertainment break – about one visit to the pool.

> 5 October 2002
> The funniest thing happened to me on Thursday. When I left Spectrum and was walking back through the car park to my car, I noticed a car was blocking the aisle between two rows of parked cars. Immediately, I thought to myself what a stupid bugger, and then as I got a few paces closer I realised there wasn't anyone in the car at all, nor was there anyone standing near it, which there might have been had there been an accident. I continued to think some driver was a bloody fool. Then, a few paces nearer still, I realised with some horror that it was MY car. I must have left the handbrake off (which normally wouldn't matter, because I always leave the car in gear – or I thought I did) and it had rolled forward. Fortunately, it had stopped just a few inches before hitting the car opposite. The oddest thing, though, was that no one had apparently noticed – it was as though the universe had remained unaffected by this event. And yet I had been in the pool for the best part of an hour. Surely some driver or other must have seen my car – did they not think to report it to the Spectrum office? did no one do a tannoy call for a car that was blocking the car park? Weird, I just got in and drove away.

Recovery was a slow, slow process, not helped, in fact, by trying to progress things faster with several (counter-productive) longer walks and gentle volleyball games. In time, I also began to jog regularly. I'd never much liked running but I came to realise it was good for my knees, and the best/easiest way to help my cardio-vascular system keep trim.

In 2006, having closed down my business some years earlier, having written my magnum opus (Chapter ten), having lost Adam to adulthood, I left behind my secluded life in the heathlands of Surrey, and returned to live in Brighton. I was in my mid fifties, but felt at least 10 years younger. I wanted to re-engage with the world, be social, busy, active. I took up teaching English as a foreign language, and before long I was playing beach volleyball – at a newly built venue on the beach – with my students on a near weekly basis. I was taking adventurous trips to exotic foreign places, and hard walking trips (as mentioned above) to places like Madeira. Again, I fell in love with volleyball, the softer, gentler kind, on the sand. And I was dating. Indeed, before too long I fell quickly into a love affair, cohabiting, two more children! Life was most definitely dandy again. All of which (the joy and privilege of bringing up two more amazing sons) is potential material for a third and final memoir, though I doubt it will ever get written.

But, by way of concluding this narrative, I need to record that I had a second bad volleyball accident, leading to a second arthroscopy (same knee), and a final decision to give up the sport. Within a couple of years, I would also be in hospital for, first, a hernia op, and secondly, a triple coronary bypass. Almost overnight, it seemed, I became an old man, constantly preoccupied with health matters (I now precede any notes about health matters in my diary with the single made-up word UNHEALTH), and living to exercise to keep living to exercise to keep . . . Crinkly old bones I call myself these days as I ruminate, day in day out, on how little I appreciated health and fitness when younger.

Chapter eight

FICTION
YAH BOO SUCKS, YOU AGENTS, YOU PUBLISHERS!

During the period covered by my first memoir and before Adam was born, my fiction output was mostly confined to short stories and plays. The short stories had evolved, partly from mini character studies I'd imagined for my diary, and partly from my own literary interests at the time, such as Borges. The plays had emerged out of my involvement with and love of the theatre. I also wrote a couple of radio plays largely because I felt they would get a fair reading from the one and only market for such works – the BBC. My brief and naive hopes to become 'a writer' – along the lines, I suppose, of Lawrence Durrell, D. H. Lawrence or Anais Nin – were dashed on the rocks of the real world. I opted to become a journalist, and thus, at least, I learned the craft – if not the art – of writing.

From 1987, when Adam was born, for ten years or so, I wrote very little fiction, and what I did write was largely for Adam. I was busy through those years, being a parent, being a Euro-journalist (as I liked to describe my job), writing management reports, setting up EC INFORM, and with the practicalities of buying and selling our houses. It was only after we moved to Surrey, into Russet House, that I again sought to quell re-emerging angst – tides of existential ennui that had always, apparently, been a part of my make up – by turning my computer keyboard to fiction. First off was a collection of short stories and novellas that seemed to fit well together under the title Love Uncovered. *By this time, I'd developed some skills as a business writer and editor and in marketing, and so I was confident of being able to put together an ace sales pitch for agents and publishers. Unfortunately, I had no personal contacts in the publishing world, which might have helped, and my polished submissions achieved zilch. Short stories are very hard to sell, I was told repeatedly.*

I moved on. It was time, I felt, to write a full length novel. But my first stop was to write one for children. Since my son Adam was born, I'd become a prolific story teller (see Chapter one), and as he'd developed language and communication skills, through his infancy years, so the stories got longer and richer. Once a year, on his birthday, I would write and print out a more carefully honed story, and when he was a little older we wrote a couple of Enid Blyton-type stories together. It was, thus, natural that my first book length fiction effort would be with Adam and other young people in mind.

At a similar time, I dusted off a novel, half-written a decade earlier, about the loss (literally) of a young baby. Having spent a number of years already as a father, I was able to tap into a newly-acquired well of parental emotions. This work ended up with an unusual structure mirrored in its unusual title: Begetting, Loss, Recovery. *Once written, edited and proof-read, off went my (unsolicited) submissions to agents first then publishers – I wasn't holding my breath.*

Another – far more ambitious – novel followed (Chapter ten). There-after, still unable to find a market for my fiction, in 2005 or so I turned to non-fiction. I developed an idea I had to walk across London in as straight a line as was legally possible, and to write about the route I was walking in expansive detail. I used the internet extensively for research, and when I pub-lished the book online I was able to embroider the text with hyperlinks providing further information, explanation and sources. Ultimately, London Cross, *as I called it, attracted many more readers than I would have had for a print version – yah boo sucks, you agents, you publishers!*

The first substantial fictional work (other than plays) that I put together – around 1995 – was a collection of short stories. Some had been written or devised years earlier and they were all about relationships, love and sex, in one way or another. This led to the idea of a collection with the title *Love Uncovered* – which seemed to perfectly correspond with the underlying theme of the stories. Thereafter, I wrote one or two more to cement the collection together into a book length group.

The first of these stories is an adaptation of the (inadequate) ra-dio play I wrote in 1980 while in Corsica (*Why Ever* – Introduction): *The Brittle Rhapsody of Silence on a Winter Beach*. The lonely narrator, on a winter sojourn trying to become a writer, tells of the unusual relation-ship he or she (their gender is not revealed) develops with Napoleon, a deformed and hirsute sociopath, with limited language, living in a ruined coastal tower, more like an animal than a human. The narrator notices that he has several fingers missing from his hands. Napoleon tries to frighten the narrator away at first, but he/she returns several times, and they form a kind of friendship. Eventually, it is time for the narrator to leave the island.

This story has – like all the others in this collection – survived nearly half a century without being published so, not to leave you in sus-pense, here is the final paragraph, explaining the missing fingers: 'For the first time in my presence, Napoleon disappeared up the iron stair-case [a part of the ruined tower he'd always kept private]. He reappeared some minutes later and I watched him descend the staircase with diffi-culty. He carried a small box in one hand and some rags in the other. He came in front of me and asked if he could kiss me on the lips. I stooped slightly so he could reach. His kiss was astonishingly gentle and he made no attempt to hold it. I can still remember the sensuality of the touch and the hairs of his beard brushing against me. Then, without any further ado, he pushed the box into my hand and told me to leave immediately. I walked out without looking round, and as I made my way over the rocks past the garbage and along the track through the bushes, I looked inside the box. It was half full of blood and a finger was floating in the bright crimson liquid.'

While that story was all imagined, the second story in the collection – as chronologically written – was inspired by Robbert, a real life character I met and befriended in Rio de Janeiro. I was taken by friends to his house one morning, not far from mine, at the base of Pão de Açúcar (the famous Sugar Loaf).

7 April 1985
When we arrived at his house, he informed us that this would be his third as-sent in 24 hours. He had only recently returned from a dawn climb. Robbert does not wear this obsession with ostentation, rather it is a consuming interest in a time when there is no work to preoccupy him. [. . .] Robbert and his obses-sion to climb the rock is a good basis for a short story. Already within these few days, I've felt quite strong sensations about the Pao de Azucar and the smaller broader rock next to it because of the intense barrenness of the rock faces emerging out of the built up areas. Just at the back of me is an escarpment, al-most vertical, somewhat oppressive. I can imagine how a man could only con-trol this oppressive force by climbing the rock every day (or more should events dictate so), and I can imagine the pain that he would develop if he were denied the possibility of a climb for a day or more.

12 May 1985
I've been mulling the man and the mountain story around in my mind for a cou-ple of weeks. I liked the idea of the climber choosing different climbs according to his mood – easy ones to be able to think or savour good news, difficult ones to forget the many problems back home etc. I didn't really emerge with a rounded plot. But then I met Robbert's son in the street, Rick, on his way to climb the mountain and I realised how completely he was a victim of his father's way. So he had to be brought into the story somehow. And then, having written a well composed letter to a friend, I conceived the idea of a correspondence between son and father many years later. I imagined that a money problem had become acute so the wife left with her son to live somewhere else far away. Feeling thoroughly deceived by his father, the son becomes a dropout and ends up in prison for a short term. Likewise his father, deprived of the love of his wife and son, has only the mountain, and of course it, too, lets him down – he has a bad fall, and breaks his legs. The story starts with a letter from the father, seven years after the last contact, pleading for news from the son. The son is in prison and the father is in a nursing home, but neither reveal their current sta-tus. They hesitantly begin to communicate through their memories of the mountain. I think it has potential but can I do justice to the idea. Having written

the first few letters yesterday, I felt calm and satisfied. It's the first day I've begun to write in a very long time.

Over time – around six months and 15 letters – father and son slowly reveal long simmering resentments, even anger. Ultimately, though, they both disclose how crippled they are in different ways; and the son begins to understand that his mother might not have been such an innocent in the family breakdown as he'd always believed.

I wrote two stories for the collection with 'Roller-coaster' in the title. Each one focuses on the power and feebleness of man's sexual needs, and the consequences for those around. One – *A Roller-coaster Week* – is a very raw account, by a new mother, of her efforts to cope with the incessant bullying by her partner. The other – *A Roller-coaster Day* – is an account, narrated by a secretary, of her boss's day – in a minute-by-minute style, cynical and comical. Everything goes very wrong for the boss during the morning, until that is she gives in to his crude sexual advances (something she does occasionally and with purpose). After, in the afternoon, all the office troubles seem to right themselves. Both stories use a device I've not come across very often before or since: a kind of play script with every line of dialogue starting with 'I said . . .' or 'He said. . .'.

Some thirty years on, the stories might seem a little dated, in that we would hope our society has made progress, but has it?

Young love and old love are represented by two stories topping and tailing the collection. *Nancy's Graves* is about a distraught young woman who, left by her boyfriend, is intent on dying. This was a story conceived in Paddington Old Cemetery very near to my house in Kilburn (so named despite its position in Willesden because the land was purchased in 1855 by Paddington Burial Board.) It was one of my regular haunts, and it was always far more quiet, calm, peaceful than anywhere else thereabouts. Nancy is consumed by the sadness of her broken heart, and is intent on starving herself to death. She takes to filling the hours by visiting the cemetery, sometimes fainting, and sometimes seeing angels. She finds a grave with fresh cut flowers, and makes an effort to read the headstones. There's a Nancy mentioned as the beloved brother of someone who died, and she works out, eventually, that it must be Nancy bringing the flowers. All this she tells us in a daily diary.

On Wednesday she writes: 'Addition to my last will and testament. Please note one extra request: I would like to be buried near the graves that Nancy covers with fresh flowers. Perhaps she has love enough for me too.' On Sunday, she says she will make one last visit to the cemetery.

Then there is this:

'Later. Something extraordinary has happened. When I visited Nancy's graves, there was a newly dug patch between them with a simple cross in the ground and one red carnation funeral wreath. There was a small card and it read: 'For Nancy, who will be missed by all at the Restmore Nursing Home.'

As I was reading the label, an old lady came up behind and said: 'Dear Nancy, never missed coming here – twice a week on Saturdays and Wednesdays, regular as clockwork. Dear love, she spent all 'er money on flowers, she did. Didn't talk about family, but, reading between the lines, I think she loved 'er brother, know what I mean. Sweet old girl. Shame, the graves'll go the way of the rest of 'em now, I suppose.' And then she disappeared.

I have made a sweet tea and am drinking it now by sips as I write this. Next, I am going to wash, and then I'm going to telephone the doctor – ask for advice – I must get better. And then that job, I'll phone and tell them I'll take it. It'll be OK, I know it will. I know it will. It has to be, I have Nancy's graves to tend, and flowers to buy – twice a week on Saturdays and Wednesdays, regular as clockwork.'

I constructed *Eulogy for Igee* – the true love story of my grandfather Isaac Goldsmith (known as Igee) and his second wife the American author Vera Caspary (best known for *Laura*) – using verbatim extracts from Vera's autobiography *The Secrets of Grown-ups*. I knew Vera, not well but I'd spent time with her on both my trips to New York in the 1980s. I took all the material from her book about meeting Igee, falling in love with him, and about their marital difficulties, and then invented questions to string her words together as if it were the transcript of a radio interview perhaps. Here's the opening:

'Paul: How did your affair start?

Vera: It was not love at first sight. We were mature; we believed ourselves free of sentimentality. Nevertheless we were both aware of an immediate attraction and set about charming each other – he with the grace acquired from early association with Austrian nobility, I with the saucy gaiety that had titillated macaroni salesmen. I kept him waiting two weeks so he wouldn't think I was a pushover. Young people today declare flirtation hypocritical and a waste of time. To us it was a delicious drama, heightened by small suspense. On the night we were both aware of inevitability, but the gentleman had carefully arranged dinner and entertainment, while the lady wore lacy black undergarments.

And here's another extract.

Paul: You must have been very much in love?

Vera: I recall a scene in the pink sitting room. We stand between a swollen armchair and the Regency cabinet. Suddenly the word springs out, not as a noun expressive of passivity, in love, but the verb itself, love as active and alive as our rapid hearts. We repeat it, try it out in various tones, whisper it, croon and caress it, clobber each other with the potent word. And solemn as though swearing the oath to love, honor and cherish, we promise each other to stay together until death do us part. "Vera won't write any more; she's too happy," Graham Greene told my London agent.

Another of the stories – *Sandy* – is written as a play script, there are two women, apparently, in bed and trying to get to sleep. It is the eve of Catherine's wedding day:

Catherine: Don't move around so, the bed creaks and you'll wake up those down below.

Sandy: I can't help it, I'm uncomfortable and I can't get to sleep.'

They continue to chat, and drift into remembering a mutual acquaintance, a man, a lover they have both known. However, as Sandy seems intent on remembering all the sensuality and sexuality of the love affair, Catherine starts to focus firmly on the attributes of the man she is to marry on the morrow. Sandy begins to invoke a Keats poem (replacing the name Fanny with Sandy), intertwining it with one particular memory of making love on the sand and in the waves. Catherine keeps repeating like a mantra all the positive aspects of her husband-to-be.

'Catherine: Henry's read most of the classics and we like the same kind of books, the same kind of films, the same kind of plays. He's a bit too keen on jazz for me, but we talk about it. Christ, will you go to sleep. I'm so tired.

Sandy: And then as the tide had lapped up over your legs and hands, and was beginning to roll up between your thighs and, and you lay there thinking through the poem, and wondering at its meanings, Dan floated in from the sea – you said, he moved so quietly you hardly noticed him – and as the sea water came so he let his tongue touch you like a feather on bringing the promise of such excitement, and then as the water fell away he too withdrew, to come forward again with the next roll.

By this time, of course, the reader has long twigged that Sandy is Catherine's romantic and heart-led alter-ego. Here are the last lines:

Catherine: You see, you must see, I have no choice. I have no choice. I must . . .

Sandy: Must what?

Catherine: I must, I must look after my children, my children that are yet unborn, yet to be conceived.'

Finally in the collection, there is a story I called *Loving Alex* narrated by a New Zealand diarist, Douglas.. This also – like *Nancy's Graves* – has its roots in Kilburn. One night, I walked along the High Street and decided to drop into a large pub I'd rarely frequented. The Black Lion.

Inside, I found a solo guitarist/singer, Holly Penfield playing to an almost empty room. I fell in love with her voice, and remained an hour or more enraptured, and stunned that she should be giving her bright talent away so freely in such a downmarket drinking hole. The story began with the reality . . . In Douglas's diary as it was in mine.

'It was a damp dreary evening, twenty years ago, as I walked slowly down the Kilburn High Road in north London. The traffic was jammed with vehicles bumper to bumper. The pavement was littered with people I had never seen before or would ever see again. Lights of every colour streamed out from kebab joints and from the traffic queues, glistened on wetness wherever, and vanished like fireworks making no impression on the night.

When the drizzle suddenly turned into a downpour, I dived into a public house, it could have been any one of a dozen. My business suit was out of place among the young, scruffy drinkers yet the shelter was welcome. I chose a Guinness in honour of it being Kilburn. Dark brown stucco decorated the high ceilings and lavish mirrors reflected the dim light enhancing the baroque decor. A small stage had been erected in the corner of an almost empty adjoining room, equally lavishly decorated. As I moved away from the bar, a woman, dressed in purple robes and with purple scarves veiling her face, approached a keyboard and began to play and sing.'

Douglas is at first entranced by the singer, Alex as the barman calls her. But a moment comes when she turns her face into the light, and he suddenly realises he knows this woman – and knows her very well, it is Helen. They have both grown up in New Zealand, gone to the same school, become friends, though Douglas has never understood why when she was so vivacious and he was so dull. Subsequently she had married well, a rich socialite, while he had become a reclusive bookseller. One day, though, she had walked into Douglas's shop and they had renewed their friendship with regular once-a-month meetings at a nearby coffee shop.

Fast forward to the Kilburn pub where Douglas goes to talk to Alex in the interval. She has a few admirers around, but she whispers in his ear, 'you have surprised me but how wonderful to see you,' and 'Ssshh, can we talk later? are you busy? where shall we meet? I have so much to tell you.'

And what she tells him is this. Her (older) husband wanted children, but she, having married young, wasn't ready. She negotiated with him to have six months to herself, to travel, and together they concocted a story – that Helen was away recuperating from a serious illness – to keep the press at bay. An explanation Douglas, too, had been given.

But then comes the story-teller's favourite device – a secret. 'Douglas, I must ask you a favour, I know I have no right, and yet I know I have every right as a friend. Please, never tell anyone about my life here – not your friends, your family or any stranger – not even my husband really knows what I am doing. It would destroy him and therefore me if my antics were to be discovered.'

'It is done,' Douglas says in the story, 'It is already done, you need never mention it again. It is little enough to do in return for your friend-ship.'

But for Helen, the favour she is asking is so immense that then and there she wants to give herself to Douglas. 'And that is how it began, and that is how it has continued for the rest of our lives,' Douglas relates, until the present. 'Once every month, or six weeks, Alex – I have called her that ever since that evening – has visited my bookshop. I have moved, bought bigger shops, changed my home, but never to a location far from her, and she has given me her love, without hesitation and with-out reserve.'

With the background explained, the story returns to the present, and all has changed – for Helen's husband has died.

Douglas's diary entry a few days later closes the story.

'I have returned home early from the shop after lunching with Helen and one of her sons, who she introduced as Alex. How confusing it was with the names! But I am overwhelmed with a happiness I could never have imagined. Some men might be filled with anger, some might be burst-ing with resentment and determined to seek revenge, others might be im-ploding with anguish. But me, I am overwhelmed with a happiness I could never have imagined.

Helen and Alex arrived at lunchtime even though she knows it is the busiest time of day in the shop. I told her how sorry I was to hear about her husband. She said they had been mourning and would be mourning for some time to come, but for the moment she wanted to take me somewhere quiet for lunch. As we walked, she talked about how Alex was finishing school and would soon go to university – and I thought back to when I was a boy of the same age and had first met Helen. He was beautiful like his mother, with the same gracile facial features, and the same smile. The lunch was short and I could not stop wondering why she had brought her son. I knew about her three children but I had never met any of them. As she was paying the bill, she asked Alex to wait outside on the pavement. Then she turned to me and adopted that same serious dark expression I had seen just once before many years ago on that night in Kilburn.

'Douglas,' she said, 'Alex is your son, your son. There was never any question about it in my mind, but my husband always thought it was his. I

have no excuses for my behaviour, no excuses or explanations. All I can do is help you love him, and in time, I promise you this, I will bring him to love you too, as much as I do.' '

I had tried, half-heartedly, to sell my fiction writing before, but with this collection complete it was the first time I had sent out rafts of, what is known in the industry as, 'unsolicited manuscripts' to agents and publishers. Most of them were returned (in the sae I provided) with a fairly standard rejection letter and some combination of the following reasons: the market for short stories is notoriously difficult; we don't publish short story collections; we are not accepting new authors; your submission doesn't suit our lists . . .

I received one kind word, though it was equally discouraging. Elizabeth Wright at Darley Anderson hand wrote a note on the standard typed reply: 'You do write very well and your stories held my interest. But we simply do not handle short stories in anthologies. Good luck finding an agent who does.'

I never did. However, a quick visit now to Amazon shows there is a good market for books titled *Love Uncovered*. For example, the '*USA Today* Bestselling Author' Angie Davies has one. Here's the blurb: 'Forced to team up with Zearl Sinclair, a dangerously sexy cop, to catch a serial killer, tough detective Chenoa Campbell puts her life and heart on the line when she betrays his trust by going after the killer on her own.'

Very busy by then with my small business, and the moving to Surrey, I continued to eschew writing any fiction for adults. Instead, I turned my keyboard towards children's stories – a natural development given that I'd been making up stories for Adam since long before he could understand them (Chapter one). Together, Adam and I (he sitting on my desk) wrote an old-fashioned adventure (think Enid Blyton) about a brother and sister (Nick and Ally) getting into trouble while on holiday in Cornwall. Although I had no intention of trying to market this to agents etc., we did edit and polish the text, and then publish it at home as a 30-page A5 booklet. We even included a blurb on the back cover: '*Trapped* tells the exciting adventure of Nick and Ally as they discover a hidden cove and a secret tunnel. When they get trapped in the tunnel, events take a more sinister turn.' Ally, Nick's younger sister, narrates the story, and while Nick tends to be dismissive of her and her ideas, she's persistently caring of and for him. He gets them both into trouble, and she gets them out of it. Here's the final paragraph.

'But it wasn't the reward or the funfair or even Dad being proud of us that gave me the nicest feeling, it was that if I hadn't rescued Nick in the first place, we would never have had the adventure at all, or at least it

would have been a very different sort of adventure. But, I do think it's funny how an adventure is frightening and even horrible when it's going on, but wonderful to think about after it's all over.'

Six copies we published, and distributed to Adam's friends.

Some four years later, we revisited the siblings, and wrote a new story *Trapped Again*: 'Nick and Ally, now teenagers, are back and in more trouble than ever before! In *Trapped Again* they team up with Tom, the son of a mean fortune-teller, to do battle with the murderous Burly, who runs the fairground ghost train, and the evil Croaker, over the Big (and dangerous) wheel.' Again we published six copies, with a blue cover, and gave them to Adam's cousins and family friends. They were a joy to write and to read out loud.

So, I thought I'd try my hand at a full length novel for children. In the first place, I searched for an original setting. As far as I could tell, everything under the sun had been anthropomorphised for children's entertainment, with many stand-out characters created from the most unlikely animals. But what about cars, I reasoned, they are everywhere, and although they too had been anthropomorphised very successfully, no one had – as far as I knew – imagined and created a world INSIDE car tyres. It was virgin territory for a story-teller, and I set about the task of creating such a world. My characters would have to be made of rubber, would be born and die inside tyres, and their energy, their life-force would come from the tyres moving, from spinning – hence the name of these creatures – the tyre spinners. I realised early on readers would be asked to take a huge imaginary leap and that I would have to find a way to help them enter – and believe in – the tyre spinner world. I called the novel *The Life and Times of a Tyre Spinner by TomSpin*, and I packed a lot into a very short introduction.

'What do you think of the book's title? Not much? Me neither. That's publishers for you. Don't ask how everything in this book comes to be set down in human terms and in English, and I won't ask how you come to be reading it when you could be doing something far more useful.

But you must know three simple things.

About me. My name is TomSpin and if you were ever able to see me, I might look like a small rubber ball, or a bird's egg, but I might look like five sticks of chewing gum, chewed, stuck together and drawn out as long as a knitting needle, or drawn out even longer like a piece of thread; I might also look like an eraser of whatever shape that is sitting on your desk.

About tyre spinners. Tyre spinners do not eat, drink or breathe. We live by spinning. Our bodies are able to store energy from spinning and that is why we almost always choose to live and make our homes inside vehicle

tyres. Coincidentally or not tyres are made from the same material – rub-
ber – as we are. Our senses are not the same as yours. We have the ability
to talk, hear, see, feel but in a more complete way, something you might
consider similar to telepathy. Some aspects of our lives – the growing busi-
ness, the dying business, how we dress ourselves in different shapes, our
mental and physical games – will all seem a bit strange, so I'll try to explain
them as I go along. One other thing – time. It is difficult to tell about my
life without reference to time passing here and there. Wherever possible, I
have referred to time as you would understand it, though, in truth, our lives
are shorter and more compact than yours and we have no directly compa-
rable terms such as hour or day.

About these stories. I am a traveller and an adventurer and I don't
know if this is right or wrong but I do know my life would not be half so
interesting if I had stayed for ever with my parents, in the front offside tyre
of what I am reliably told was a blue Mondeo.'

However strange and exotic the setting, the main line of the story
is a coming-of-age memoir. TomSpin grows up, makes friends with a
traveller called Pippo, rebels against his father, and leaves home for ever.
Travelling with Pippo, he finds new friends who show him how to have
fun with games of the mind, before then becoming trapped with villains
who wish them both harm. Escaping from their clutches, the pair are
nearly killed in an accident, only to be rescued by the enigmatic Zed and
Zed. Soon after, TomSpin meets the enchanting Rosefulness, but must
compete with his friend Pippo for her favours. As the story comes to its
end, TomSpin and Pippo are reconciled, visit some weird and wonderful
people and places, and then decide to go their own separate ways.

I edited and polished the text, with Adam's help, and over several
months sent it out to publishers and agents. This was becoming a fairly
familiar pattern in my life, and it was no surprise to receive impersonal
rejection after rejection after rejection – none commenting on or acknowledging in any way the material I had sent them. It was all too easy
to feel resentment towards the individuals whose name appeared on
these rejections, and towards the publishing industry as a whole. But,
many years previously, while hitchhiking regularly, I'd learned that
there was little point in harbouring flights of rancour towards drivers
callously passing me by – my hands outstretched towards them with me
screaming '. . . you've got THREE empty seats . . .'. Instead, I learned to
reason myself into understanding the absurdity of such resentment and
rancour towards complete strangers, the stupidity. Over the years, as the
pile of rejections grew higher – my very own slush pile – feelings of frus-
tration, resentment, rancour did pop up, but, crucially, I never

experienced them deeply, or even seriously. My life was not affected. Much as I did hope, lightly, I knew deep down that any hope was hollow.

Yes, so TomSpin found his way into the dusty drawer, only to be revisited – like many of my other children's stories – when Adam's half brothers came along years later. On reflection, I've come to understand there is a structural flaw in the novel: while the story and level of writing are very much aimed at teens, the idea of cute little rubber creatures bouncing around together inside tyres would be more appealing to younger readers.

Towards the end of the 1990s, I pulled out of a different dusty drawer an incomplete work, a half written tale I'd begun some ten years earlier and abandoned. Now, I decided, was the time to make a serious attempt at completing it – a full length novel for adults, something I'd yet to achieve.

The plot came to me originally a few months before Adam was born, and was partly based on what had happened to a friend of mine. She'd fallen pregnant, accidentally, and gone through the psychological turmoil of adjusting her life expectations. Then, just as she'd done that and allowed herself to become overwhelmingly excited at the prospect of motherhood, she had a miscarriage. My character, I called her Susan, goes through the up and down cycle experienced by my friend, but then she and her husband Bill quickly decide to try for another child. And thus baby Belinda comes along. However, Susan proves herself rather unstable – indeed, the whole novel comes to revolve around her instability – and the relationship is soon on the rocks. One day, on his return from abroad, Bill arrives home to find Belinda missing and Susan distraught, distressed, extraordinarily anxious. She claims Belinda has been abducted yet she is largely incoherent, and remains so when quizzed by the police. The tension must creep in, I told my diary, as the reader is faced with mounting evidence of Susan's lies.

Unfortunately, I never had an over-riding sense of direction nor any clear idea of how the story would unfold. Moreover, I peopled Bill's narrative with barely-disguised characters from my own world, and, there was all too much recognisable of me in Bill. I mean, for God's sake, he was a science journalist while I had failed to become one (Chapter two). And Bill's joys and worries about Belinda were my joys and worries about Adam.

On my 36th birthday, I wrote: 'I spend more time thinking about Belinda, but so often draw the conclusion that I do not have the skill to write something so long and complex. I don't have the range of knowledge of basics, like descriptions of people, or techniques to involve action.'

And so, a decade past. It wasn't until 1998 that I dusted off the manuscript in my determined effort to write and finish an adult novel. I needed a rational plot, one which would tie up all the loose ends I'd created ten years earlier but also one that would be forgiving of any changes in my writing style/ability.

18 October 1998
'I've decided 'the novel' should be called *Begetting – Loss – Recovery* and be split into three such sections. The first, *Begetting*, takes the story through to the narrator's return from abroad and the discovery of Belinda's disappearance; then *Loss* takes the story through the seven days immediately after; and *Recovery* (the part I've not yet begun) will be about how Bill finds out what has happened to Belinda.

Although Bill alone narrates the tale from beginning to end, I employed an unusual device in that *Begetting* was written in a memoir-style past tense; *Loss* was written in more of an immediate diary-style past tense; and *Recovery* was written in the present. Thus, I felt, the reader would be on a journey, initially catching up with Bill's reality, then lagging just a little behind, and finally accompanying him towards a surprising denouement.

By the following spring, I'd completed and polished an 80,000 word draft. I was pleased with it: my first finished novel, good characters, an exciting story with a twist or two. But, I was also chuffed with the way I'd managed to hide the joins, so to speak, between the old and the new writing by use of the three-part structural device.

I carefully drafted a letter designed to entice agents and/or publishers to spend a little time reading my unsolicited submission. I sent out a batch of five or so, and waited a few weeks for the rejections to come in before sending out another batch. Extraordinarily, HarperCollins asked to see the full script! Within a month Nick Sayers had returned it: 'We thought that your narrative style suited your subject well, but that your plot and characterisation did not live up to its early promise.' I thought that was a little harsh, but, hey, someone in the industry had actually read one of my submissions.

Tricia Jackson at Macmillan added a handwritten note to her standard and typed rejection letter: 'I did find this extremely readable and well written but I don't feel it is one for us.' Some while later, I received another, even more positive reply: 'Well, we have received the material relating to your book, and I am writing to confirm that we shall be pleased to act for you and to enrol you onto our client list.' There were more warm words in the letter, which finished by asking me to 'see attached terms of business' overleaf. Enthusiastically, yet on my guard, I turned overleaf to read these terms – and there it was, a fee! My mistake.

I'd written to a vanity publisher. I knew all about them of course, and although the vanity route to publishing has become more acceptable in the 20 years or so since, then it was far from so.

Chronologically, *Kip Fenn* – an epic fictional biography covering the whole of the 21st century – came next in my novel-writing career. This was, and remains, the most exciting, fulfilling literary work I have ever undertaken (Chapter ten) – despite its failure ever to find a publisher.

Around the same time, there was an odd addition to my writing oeuvre, sparked by a BBC competition calling for original scripts for a first episode of a new radio sitcom. As required by the competition rules, my script contained only two speaking characters, a husband and wife team (Gideon and Avril). They work at home as freelance call centre operators (using, what was then, newish tech to have calls transferred easily). I called the sitcom *Call Us Cute* (Cute being short for Call Us Telephone Enterprises), and the first episode, titled *Save-Our-Slugs*, sees the couple hired to raise money for a slug charity. Other characters not appearing in this first episode other than incidentally were a dysfunctional teenager (Talia), Avril's yoga teacher (Rain), and a transvestite agent (Middlemax). I thought the script was very funny, and I had plenty of ideas for future episodes, but the phone call never came.

In January 2004, with a new and fresh year awaiting, I decided to give myself a few weeks working on a non-fiction project I'd devised and called *London Cross*. I quickly established (thanks again Google) that the name had never been used, not in any significant or well known way, so I made it mine. The idea was to walk across, and write about, London along two lines making the shape of a cross, one south-north, and one east-west, thus providing a kind of cross-section description of the city. I chose a south-north line, the 300 easting (rather than the 307 or 323 easting) because it's one that is drawn on most modern maps, and because it cuts conveniently through the middle of London. I would start from where the 300 easting crosses the M25 in the south and walk to where the two cross in the north – a distance as the crow flies of 30 miles. The aim was to stick as closely as possible (taking only legal routes) to the 300 easting.

I checked what other books had been written about walking in London. One expert on the city had written about a number of long-distance walks, and there was also a book written by someone who'd walked round the M25. The first of these was based on a completely different concept from mine, and the second was, I felt, flawed for being tied to such a monstrous environment the whole time, crammed full from one end to the other of hideous traffic and grisly concrete. My project felt much more interesting, and also perfect for me. It got me out of the house, exploring, which I love to do; it was very map based, and I love maps; it required lots of research which could be done on the internet and in local libraries; and it involved writing up my results in a way rather similar to my diary, only more rigorously.

I did my first walk, from near Merstham on a footbridge across the M25 to Coulsdon. This was an unusual stretch for mostly crossing countryside – the rest would be urban sprawl. But, I found a surprising amount to write about, and I enjoyed stringing my observations and thoughts together into a text, half describing the walk, and half going off at tangents about whatever I found interesting. I took a recorder, and talked to myself throughout the walk, and then used the recorded notes in conjunction with information I'd culled elsewhere. For these early sections I used my car to drive to one end of the walk, and public transport to return to it after the walk was over. But, as I got closer to inner London, and had to make my way to the northern parts of London, so I used public transport, to and from Farncombe (the station nearest Russet House).

Here's a few entries from the diary giving some flavour of my progress on the 300 easting, from excitement and enjoyment of process to anxieties and doubts about what, ultimately, to do with the text.

24 January 2004
Each walk is only about five or six miles but, if there's a library on the route, then I can spend a long time there; and my aim also is to talk to as many people as I can, even to the point of picking up local stories about particular roads on the 300 easting. Last Thursday, for example, I was talking to an old man called John on the Roundshaw Estate, and he was being so helpful I decided to test out one of my planned questions: 'If I asked you what's the funniest thing you've seen round here, what would you say?' He thought for a minute and told me it was a young man operating a road laying machine. John himself had been a road layer, and he felt that the young man didn't have 'a fucking idea what he was doing'. I won't be using that. It won't be easy trying to get strangers to talk. I've already discovered how naturally suspicious they are; and, so far, I've been reluctant to explain my purpose. It's something I'll have to consider more carefully.

If I manage one walk a week, it'll take me about 10 weeks to complete one half of London Cross. If I get that far, at that point I might start writing to publishers. I haven't yet decided what to do about photographs. I've only carried my little Olympus so far, but I didn't use it once.'

1 February 204
I thought this last section was going to be dull compared to the previous two, but, in fact, it was fascinating, through from the Carew Great Hall and Dovecote to the history of the Wandle river and its mills to the Beddington Sewage Farm, the gypsy George and his horse in Beddington Cross, a peppermint oil distillery, a unique process for manufacturing foams, a Celtic fort, and Leslie Crowther's

appearances at a local school in the 1960s. And that's only a small selection of the walk from the Plough in Beddington to West Norbury.

1 March 2004
London Cross, London Cross, London Cross is taking up all my time. This is because I've been doing the central area which is so dense with streets and buildings of interest. I was writing two or three times as much per mile so to speak, and to do so, I was having to research many more topics. My folder for the first walk has about a dozen files in, and my folder for the sixth walk, which was a third of the length, has four dozen or more. I was due to head off today for walk six, from the British Library to Archway, but there was a covering of snow on the ground, and I decided I should revisit the stuff I've already written, and see whether I can pull together a letter for publishers. [. . .] Actually, I just began this as a trial, and I never meant to speed ahead this quickly. And this afternoon, I've looked over the first 6,000 words, It doesn't seem very substantial, or very good, so – after my two or three intensive weeks on central London – I've come down to earth about it. Also trying to draft a letter for publishers has sobered me up as far as the project's attractions. It's not easy to explain them on paper, simply and quickly, and it's hard to escape the idea that no publisher will want it because they'll not be able to understand who might buy it. And I've no idea. I wouldn't buy such a book. When I write, in the draft letter, that *London Cross* is a mixture of travel writing, travel guide and *Schlott's Miscellany* (a book of random facts that was a hit last year), it only invites the thought that because it's such a mixture, it serves no purpose, and consequently no market. Although I have been having fun writing it, I got a wave today of that horrible sinking feeling I get whenever I realise that no one will ever read what I'm writing.

As the last diary entry shows, I very much got 'into' this project – walking, researching, writing. It was particularly involving and engaging in central London. Here's a short extract from the text itself which gives a flavour of how excited I was to find my walk route taking me actually through the British Museum (which has a main entrance to the south and a back entrance to the north).

'I'm thrilled that I can, according to my own rules for walking the 300 easting, actually walk through any building at all, let alone one of the greatest museums in the world. But, there are dangers here, for every gallery, every exhibition case, every exhibit could lead me to stray – metaphorically speaking – too far from and wide of my purpose. I stop at one of the kiosks in the entrance hall to look at a diagram of the layout of the ground floor, and decide on my route. If I were to follow the same rules as I stick to in walking the streets, I would be obliged to walk through the Great Court, Gallery 24 and exit into Montague Place. But, I don't do this. I choose, instead, to imagine (very roughly) which galleries a direct 300 easting line would pass through – Galleries 18, 17, 22 and 21 – and to visit these. Also, as I must pass Gallery 24 to leave the building, I add it to my itinerary.'

I completed a first draft of the south-north walk, about 75,000 words, in spring 2004. I then wrote to publishers and agents asking if they might be interested in it for publication. Generally speaking I found the replies warmer and more positive than those I'd been accustomed to receiving with regard to my fiction writing – many called the idea 'interesting' – but not one of them wanted to pursue the project further. I wasn't that surprised (as I wrote in the 1 March 2004 entry), but I did see a future for *London Cross* – on the internet.

As I've written elsewhere (Chapter ten), around this time I developed a website – pikle.co.uk – mainly to advertise and promote Kip Fenn. I soon found the need to add CONTENT that could attract visitors, and this was when I first began, literally, filling the Pikle website with information on historical and literary diaries.

However, I also used the site to promote much of my other writing, not least my journals. *London Cross*, though, was the first work that I published freely and in full on pikle.co.uk. I edited the text into 84 chapters, a page or so long, giving each one a come-and-read-me title. Here's a few samples.

> '- *Art therapy at the Netherne asylum – along Ditches Lane through the Devil's Den*'
> '- *Upper Woodcote Village, where gardens come before homes, and see-saws are lonely*'
> '- *Past wonders along the Wandle: trout, squabs, snuff and a hammer-beam hall*'
> '- *The archaeological and ornithological pleasures of Beddington Sewage Farm*'
> '- *Murder on the Ellison Road, Aleister Crowley's youthful prank and, er, Cow Gum*'
> '- *From the Ministry of Truth, past Ghandi to a legacy of Theosophy*'
> '- *St Pancras delights: Shelley's love, Hardy's tree and Soane's Mausoleum*'
> '- *York Way for a rubber factory, astro-turf, night-time flashers and a meat market*'

Navigation of the website was by way of hyperlinks. Readers could pick-and-mix, by clicking on any chapter title, or they could read through from one chapter to the next. This was still fairly early days for websites, and I found it very exciting to be making such good use of the potential of the internet. Browsing through any of the short chapters, readers could also launch off at any point via the many other links directed to further information on a topic, or my sources for that information. *London Cross* turned out to be perfect for this kind of web project.

From the start of my web life, I had no illusion that the pikle website would ever attract sufficient visitors to earn cash through advertising, and so to this day, twenty years on, none of my web pages (several thousand of them!) carries any commercial advertising. In this regard I stand shoulder-to-shoulder with the BBC and Wikipedia, and in constant battle with almost every other website in the world bombarding me 24/7 with in-your-face, pop-up propaganda.

I didn't know it at the time I was walking the 300 easting, but the type of text I was writing had a name – psychogeography: the exploration of urban environments that emphasises interpersonal connections to places and arbitrary routes. In its own way, I believe, *London Cross* was reasonably successful. I say this because, over several years, I received much positive encouragement from random readers who had found their way to the site. Without the internet, the work would never have had any audience, let alone thousands of readers. Here's a few fairly randomly-chosen emails I received.

'Have just this evening read about a third of your walk and enjoying it very much. Stumbled upon it doing research for a trip later this week to London and am staying on Tothill Street, so the Sanctuary is what got me started and then could not stop. Have been to London several times, so could follow parts of your trek in my mind's eye. Hope to finish the rest in the next few days. Thanks for taking the time. Really unfortunate no publisher would take it on. I think it is amazing.' Cynthia

'I've just used *London Cross* for the first time in order to explore the St. Pancras area. The section on the Old St. Pancras church and churchyard was particularly useful and, as a bonus, the church was open. So, thanks for providing people with such an interesting and useful site which I will certainly use again.' Pam Fray

'I have just discovered your site by accident and have been reading *London Cross*. It is absolutely fascinating. I grew up in Beddington and Croydon and can picture many of the places you describe there and which I had forgotten about. The stories behind these places I generally didn't know about – as a teenager local history wasn't high on my list of priorities but as an adult it creates such a wonderful sense of home and where I came from. Great work – thank you. I wish you luck in finding a publisher.' Martin

Happened across this while looking for info on Netherne Hospital, where my great grandfather worked as an Engineer in the 40s. I am so sorry that no-one is interested in publishing this??!! It's a wonderful idea. And there is so much stuff unworthy of being published that is swelling the bookshops . . .' Mandy

The last two comments were partially in response to an appeal on the front web page of *London Cross*. In my intro, I explained how I'd developed the idea as TWO straight line walks, but that because the south-north text had not found a publisher I had decided not to work on the second walk. 'If anyone reading this,' I added, 'is involved in the publishing world, and can see some potential for this book, please do get in touch – immediately!'

You can imagine, dear reader, how much humorous pleasure went into placing that single exclamation mark. As I write, all these years later, my website remains burgeoning with all the pages I've created, edited and amended over the years, and I can confirm that the exclamation mark remains firmly in place – waiting for, almost demanding, action.

It was not only the east-west walk I didn't do. I'd had a fantasy from early on in the *London Cross* project that if it were even a modest publishing success, I would be able to replicate the idea wherever I liked, in cities and large towns up and down the country: *Dublin Cross* seemed an attractive proposition, *Ibiza Cross* . . .

As I mentioned above, with plenty of time on my hands, it would have been a perfect model of time spent well in retirement from journalism – walking, researching, writing. In my youth, I had done a large amount of travelling around Britain, with a small rucksack, a sleeping bag, and my thumb for transport. And I'd never lost the delight experienced in exploring and finding out about new places.

As things turned out, I have only written one other 'Cross' – *Brighton Cross*. I moved (back) to Brighton in 2006, and soon decided on a straight line walk from east to west, starting on the Downs and ending at the sea. Since I wanted to walk through at least some of Brighton's centre, but, at the same time, wished for a balance, with roughly the same distance covered both east and west of the centre, I was fairly constrained as to my route line – the 450 northing.

It didn't take many weeks to complete the walk and the writing. I was much aided by excellent local history resources at the central library. The project seemed a very fitting way to re-acquaint myself with the place that had already played such a significant role in my life at different times. As with *London Cross*, I divided the text into page-long chapters, 34 of them, each one with a come-hither title, and uploaded them to my website. Sample chapters.

'- *A bosom-shaped Noddy car, a queen of dippers, and a love-sick army ladette*'
'- *Magdalene's confession time, Turner's palette, and Noble's sweet ode to love*'
'- *Yummy cakes, Egyptian fare, Bankers fish, Barracuda pizzas – and a Sanctuary*'
'- *Patrick's Shelter, RotoVision's Nudes, City Penguins – and a Regency treasure*'

'- *About a King's visits, Queen Vic's view, a boy Vic's tips, and a grandson's find*'
'- *Of cycling and lanes (long and weird), of bowling (mixed), and a rainbow of huts*'
'- *Warnings, prohibitions, shifting shingle, the flight of Charles II, and lagoon life*'

I went on to author two local history books (real ones in print!) about Brighton, both published by The History Press. There is not so much to tell about them, but, in any case, they more properly fit into the timescale of a third and final part of my life, that which I am spending happily domesticated, happily married to Hattie, and bringing up two very special boys, JG and Albert. Am I likely ever to write a third memoir to cover this last chapter of my life? Perhaps, but only when publishers develop a genre of non-fiction labelled 'Radiant Reminiscences' (to match the 'Misery Memoir' output).

Chapter nine

Diary
Five million words long, deep, wide

I have spent much time over the years and decades writing diary entries, amounting to around five million words. My diary is certainly not the longest in history – there's at least one American diary that is ten times longer, and a Zimbabwean diary that was kept for 90 years – but it is surely extraordinary in terms of, let me claim, its range: it's long, in terms of the number of words; it's wide, in terms of covering 60 years continuously; and it's deep, in terms of the variety and richness of material to be found therein. I've written about how I came to keep a diary (Why Ever – Introduction), and why and how it evolved as a means of self-expression during my travelling years. Now I want to dig deeper, look at how my diaries have evolved over the years, why I've written and continued to write diaries, what I've written in them, and who I think I've written them for. So, a bit of life writing about life writing . . . A how, what and why.

To begin, I should provide a chronology of <u>how</u> I've kept diaries – the physical/virtual entities – and how the practice of writing and keeping them has evolved over a lifetime. I will go into some detail about this, with no apologies – largely because despite having browsed thousands of other people's diaries I've never come across such specifics.

I was given a blue-covered five-year diary for Christmas in 1962. It had one page for every day of the year, with the date written at the top, each one divided into five sections with a place for the year to be inserted. I made my first entry on 1 January 1963, I was not yet 11. I wrote every day till March, then very intermittently until 25 July which was my last day at junior school. My family then moved out of London to live in Hoddesdon, and, from September, I attended Broxbourne Grammar School, where I would remain for seven years. There are no entries in the diary after that until April 1964 – none about the move or the new school. For two months, I wrote a good paragraph almost every day, then nothing until half a dozen entries in March 1965. I recorded nothing during my couple of months in hospital, but I did mention returning home, and being given the all clear by a doctor to do gym and to cycle.

Thereafter, there are only rare entries with no pattern, that I can discern. Nor do I, at any point, comment in the diary itself about restarting the diary, or about having missed out many months. Then comes a three year gap, nothing about my O-Levels, being in the Sixth Form, A-Levels, going out with a girl called Anne for four months, or my first year at the University of Wales in Cardiff. On 12 July 1971, I provide a two line summary of what's happened to me in the interim, and I continue the diary as if nothing has happened – with no clue at all as to why I've suddenly decided to restart. But something had changed, for, thereafter, I wrote a diary entry every single day (give or take the odd one), sometimes taking up two spaces in the five year diary pages, for the next three years – more or less filling the entire book.

In essence the diary entries are similar to those I wrote intermittently in my teens. I was doing more, and had a busier social life, so the entries are more detailed, a little richer. I also began to personify the diary slightly, using the phrase 'dear diary', as with this entry, which also shows not only how familiar we – the diary and I – were becoming, but that I was aware of the challenge of keeping the diary habit going.

> 13 July 1972
> 'Dear Diary we've done it, 1 whole year on the trot. [...] Might go out for a drink diary – Bye.'

Increasingly, there are entries in which I apologise to the diary for forgetting what I've done during the day, or for having to catch up with past entries that I've missed. At times, the diary becomes a 'mate' or a confessor. Intriguingly, there are a couple of references to diaries I've written elsewhere but which I've long since lost and forgotten. The back and front papers of the five year diary are crammed with extraneous notes, lists (of fellow pupils, teachers/lecturers, girls I liked, books I'd read, records I owned, etc.) and poems. After more than 10 years, I finally make a last entry in the five year diary, on 6 June 1974. There is a mysterious gap of 12 days (when I must have been very busy) before the first entry in the Asia travel diary on 18 June.

The diary book I used while travelling in Asia was a Collins desk diary for 1973, with a red cover and pre-printed lines (narrow feint) – half a page for every day, and one extra half page every week for 'notes'. Each day came with a blue banner, the day of the week, and the date. Clearly, I had to ignore the day of the week as this was 1974 not 1973. (I can only assume that excessive thrift led me to buy an out-of-date journal). I soon came to use the blue banner for either key words relating to the days entry or a headline. Every single date is crammed full with my small handwriting. When I ran out of space, which happened not infrequently, I used the 'notes' sections first and then empty pages working backwards from 18 June with a linking note – roughly a quarter of the book (from June back to March) is filled with such continuations. Indeed, the whole book is crammed full of writing and there's very little white space. As with the five year diary, there are poems squeezed into areas of the front and back. A year planner, across two pages with a tiny box for every day of the year, has the name of the place I stayed each night.

This diary – I call it Diary 1 – was my backpack's most treasured possession. I lost it twice, by leaving it on buses, in Rangoon and Bangkok, each time requiring me to chase through the city to recover it. On one of these occasions I was nearly in tears, I wrote. Otherwise, generally, I only mention the diary itself to record the tiresomeness of having failed to record several days in a row, and therefore having to catch up. And, of course, I nearly lost the diary to the cyclone in Darwin – except that I had the presence of mind to grab it, along with my money and passport, before the house exploded and all my other possessions were lost in rubble. All of which I've written about in the first memoir.

Diary 2 is a similar desk diary – with a green cover – and records my year in New Zealand. I wrote an entry for every day as prescribed by the half page spaces, in much the same way as when I was travelling, though the subject matter of this diary is far more to do with social activities than travelling. There's a fair sprinkling of what I called 'waiting poems' written in doctors' waiting rooms – as a medical rep I spent my working days visiting surgeries and promoting drugs to doctors and nurses. It was full by mid-February 1975, and then I must have started a new diary. But, I have no record of this nor any memory of it, other than that it was stolen with a bag of mine the following June. And, the only reason I know some of the detail of several months travelling in South America is thanks to a few letters I sent to family/friends which I've since recovered.

Diary 3 then does not begin until 6 July 1975, in Peru. But something has happened to my idea of keeping a diary. First of all, the book is not pre-printed in any way (other than being graph-ruled) and it is twice as thick as the desk diaries. I began a new diary life, only making entries when I felt like it, dating them as to the time of writing. Because I was no longer having to write something for each and every day, I was liberated from recording banal activities, and free, it seems, to fill the pages with poems, and, for the first time, stories – as I've mentioned in the first memoir. For the most part, however, I continued making entries almost daily, after all there was plenty going on in my traveling life which I wanted to set down.

Into the future and when much of my life was more banal, I typically wrote entries covering several days, or even a week. Occasionally, I would revert to daily entries for one reason or another, when on holiday, for example, or when I felt an urgent need to monitor why and how

I was consuming time so fast, or as a response to personal events (birth of my sons) or world events (the 2020/2021 pandemic).

Diaries 3 and 4 cover my time in South America, Diary 5 charts my re-entry into ordinary life in London, and Diaries 6 and 7 see me wearing a suit every day and working in an office, but also starting and finishing a tempestuous relationship with M. My social life is whizzing, not only with M, but Harold and Marielle and a colourful spectrum of other characters, and I'm starting to want to write more creatively – the diary is filling up with poems and literary flourishes and stories. I'm ready to throw off the grey suit. The theatre beckons, clowning.

By this time I'm becoming more picky about the books I choose to write in. Diary 5 was no more than a cheap exercise book, while Diary 8 is a beautiful journal with thick weight paper of different colours. The first eight pages are yellow, the next eight light blue, orange etc. From the start, I made the decision to forego date order and write my entries anywhere in the book according to whatever colour suited my mood that day. Some of the entries are dated, but many are not. It was an original or whacky idea at the time but, many years later when I came to transcribe the text, it was frustrating to deal with such a jumble.

The rainbow diary is the only one I've ever kept non-chronologically – thank goodness – but it is also the most striking in a physical sense. About two-thirds of the way through, the pages change from light brown to pink. On the last light brown page there is nothing but the outline of an ice cream cone shape with half the cone cut out to reveal the pink of the subsequent page. The following page has the words, written small, 'A chocolate and raspberry ice-cream'. There are doodles everywhere in this diary, as well as poems, but very few facts about my life. In retrospect it seems to be the perfect expression of the new vibrant fluorescent social life I was living.

Diary 9 is a thin volume of hand-made paper given me by a friend which, unfortunately, does not contain nearly enough about two weeks I spent in Greece living in a commune. I began a new journal, Diary 13, for my Corsica venture, in the winter of 1979/1980. It's a book with a black cover, as are the two that follow, appropriate because they chart my descent towards a breakdown of sorts (all of which I've recorded in the first memoir). My writing starts to lose its pretentious floweriness, and the entries become more serious, more angst-ridden. Diary 15 has an ornate dark green cover and, in it, the writing slowly becomes more observational and imaginative again, and less preoccupied with my emotional and psychological self.

Around this time, I landed my first job as a journalist, and after two years, I moved to work for another news publisher, and I bought my first house. I continued to be faithful to my diaries. The books I wrote in during this period no longer contain any creative writing (poetry or mini-stories), just a mish-mash of self-analysis and analysis of others, personal narratives and anecdotes, observations of the world around, surreal thoughts perhaps, commentaries, plus various other odds and ends. Many pages at the backs of the books list the culture I'd imbibed – films, TV, books, dance, music, radio plays – occasionally with brief criticisms.

I wrote in four diary books during 1984, all of them with red or green bindings, one of them written in the form of letters to Bel (though never to be read by her): we had decided to give our relationship a break, and this was my response to her absence. While on a conference trip to Rio that autumn, I bought a beautifully produced green cloth-bound diary notebook, and I started writing in it not long after. I then went to live in Rio, and during my two years there I was to buy more of these same notebooks to use as diaries – I had much to write about. And on my return to London, too, in 1987 when Adam was born.

Indeed, Diary 36 is the largest and thickest of all my diaries – called on the spine 'LIVRE D'OR', it is golden in colour with gilt-edged pages. I've used golden italic Letraset to emboss the cover with my name. I wrote in this diary for eight months, every entry is written as a letter to the new born Adam, and I often talk about 'Daddy', or briefly provide some explanatory background as if I were actually writing or talking TO him. But, at the same time, it's clear from some of the content that I never actually intended him to read it – as with the letters addressed to, but not intended for, Bel. With Diary 37, I reverted to normal style. It was a book with a grey cover, and I wrote the first entry with a grey pen.

In autumn 1989, there was a seismic shift in my diary-writing habit. Having completed Diary 39, I gave up the practice of hand writing a diary. Instead, from September, I began to write my diary directly on a computer. Since then, the only hand-written diaries I've kept – with one exception – have been during significant holidays abroad – about 20 all told. (The one exception came in 1995 when, for one diary only, I reverted to hand writing my entries, and my last entry was 'END OF DIARY – thank goodness!'.)

Here is my first computer entry, and several thereafter showing my state of mind about the change.

22 September 1989
I have bought a new journal but I have yet to tamper with it, spoil the blank virgin pages with vulgar thoughts and second hand ideas. For some time I have been considering the possibility of writing my journal notes straight on to screen. It is quite apparent that I write better on screen than in the notebooks. On screen, no matter if you choose the wrong word, it can just be changed in a jiff; if you miss a word, no awkward typesetter 'y' sign, just move the cursor

back and press the insert button; if you spell a word wrongly, no ghastly crossings out or recourse to Tipp-Ex, just retype the right spelling over the wrong one. [. . .] On screen I'm sure I will write more and more often. Whether that is a blessing or a disadvantage is tough to say, and whether or not the actual words that get written end up being better or worse, or just different, again I don't know. It may be that I'm far more likely to waffle across pages and pages of screen (just as I'm doing now), whereas when I have to laboriously record everything in long hand, I am more likely to skip it.

13 October 1989
There is a flavour about writing into a book that is entirely missing of course. This flavour has two elements: an intrinsic one that affects the very words that are written; and an extrinsic one that affects my feelings about writing. The one of course may influence the other. Furthermore, I spend so much of my time already at a word processor that adding more screen time is both physically and mentally rather boring, in a sense of the word that lies between the modern interpretation and the engineering term.

30 December 1989
I think I have decided that I will continue to write my diary entries on the word processor but not exclusively. There are two main drawbacks to writing on the screen: that sometimes I want to write when I'm not near a screen (i.e. not at the office, home or Bel's house in Brighton) and that I would never handwrite otherwise. A third drawback may be that I am less lyrical, less inclined to be poetical, and certainly unable to draw or doodle on the screen. So I shall run a journal book in parallel – if I'm at home, the office or Brighton I can write on screen, if I'm on a train or plane, or in Brussels or Antibes or Aldeburgh I can fill the pages with ink. When I print out the processed pages they can be bound as 53A and the book can be 53B. Why didn't I think of it before. [I never followed through with this idea.]

21 January 1990
Since New Year's Eve I have made but one entry into my life journal – that was on the word processor. My life has been too dull, too inconsequential, too busy with trivia to find any satisfaction in writing down events, thoughts. Partly this may have come about because over the Christmas holidays I took the trouble to print out the previous 3-4 months of diary entries – the first journal written entirely on the processor. Having printed it out, I have been rereading and editing it. I'm only half way through, even so I realise how uninteresting so much of the matter really is – the details and trivia of my daily life are not worth the value of the laser printer print-out. What the narratives lack is description – description of people, places, things, rooms, faces, events. Such writing takes more thought, more work. Experience shows that if I set my standards too high vis-a-vis quality of input then volume declines sharply.

In April 1990, after some hesitation I invested £1,500 (£4,000 today) in a Toshiba portable computer, a tiny machine weighing just 6 lb. This was a real innovation, a computer so lightweight that it could easily be carried in a small backpack, to Brighton, to Brussels, away for the weekend, down to the coffee shop, or simply to another room at home.

How useful for work, but also for the diary, and for any literary endeavours I might have been working on at the time. Typing my diary on the very machine, I wrote, 'I have a suspicion we (me and Tosh) are going to be very happy together.' And we were; never again would I NOT have a lightweight laptop to supplement my desktop computer.

Then, within in a year came another very important milestone in my diary life: I began transcribing the older, hand-written diaries into digital files on the computer. I started with Diary 1 and it took 20 years 'in odd bursts of determined energy' to digitise all 39 main diaries (plus the five-year diary). Some time later, I went on to type up all the holiday diaries too.

Over the years, I've struggled with various aspects of how to manage the diary books and files, but eventually I arrived at a stable, numbered chronological system. So, I have a full run of computer files (Diary 0 – Diary 118) and matching hard copies, being either the hand-written journals (39 main and 21 holiday) or bound books I created from the computer files. I went to some lengths to make these bound books of the computer-written diaries (slim A5 ones at first and then fatter A4 ones later). Each of the A5 books carries several months' worth of diary entries, and were designed and produced to be in chronological sequence with the holiday diaries. Latterly, though, I've printed and bound my computer-written diaries on an annual basis, with any holiday diary in that year being numbered in succession and before the next year. (By way of example, the computer-written diary for January-December 2016 is numbered 109, and the hand-written holiday diary for a trip to Malta in April 2016 is numbered 110.)

The hard copies and bound originals of all my diaries sit tightly packed together in two cardboard boxes; the digital forms of all my diaries (0-118) also sit cheek-by-jowl in a single folder on my computer (with back-up copies, of course, on a different hard drive).

The benefits of having transcribed my diaries into digital form have been and are prodigious. From the very start of the transcribing process – I hadn't read my diaries since they were first written – I found myself enthralled by the process, finding out what I'd done and where I'd been and who I'd met. I was rediscovering myself, and I relived, to some extent, all the years from 1974 to 1989, and all my substantial holidays. And I did this again – reliving my past – when I published an edited version of my diaries on the Pikle website.

The other main and more substantial advantage of having transcribed my diaries is that they are searchable. I was not aware, early on, how useful this would be, how dependent I would become on word searching my past – for people, places, books, films. Whether I want to flesh out a faint memory, recall what I did on my 50th birthday, see what I thought about a film the first time I saw it, or count how many times I've had gout in the last decade, all I need is a reasonably effective search term or phrase. Indeed, I've become so used to consulting my diaries, I cannot understand how the rest of the non diary-keeping world manages without.

By around 1980, I'd established a routine for making entries in my diary, one that has remained more-or-less constant since then throughout my life. I make my entries intermittently, each one dated according to that particular calendar day. There is no pattern to when I make these entries, no time of day, no regular gap between entries. In essence, I suppose, I sit down to write an entry when I feel like it. I might check the date of the last entry (usually between one and seven days previously), and then most of what I write will relate to the days that have passed since then, as well as to the current day if there's anything to say about it. Thus, the dates to be found in the vast majority of my diaries have much less specific relevance than the dates found in most published diaries i.e. which refer to what the author has been up to on that date. My way of keeping a diary has some disadvantages, notably that without a daily routine I do miss out stuff that I might have wished to record. A less significant disadvantage is that sometimes, when looking back, it is difficult for me to pin down the exact date of some event (though I can usually work it out). By contrast, I believe, my much freer way of keeping a diary has allowed it to flourish over the years.

However, I need to qualify the idea that I only write my diary when I feel like it, or rather I need to qualify what makes me feel like doing so. The passage of time is definitely the main driver, a kind of self-discipline in that I sense mild pressure building up when I haven't made a diary entry for some while. But there is also a qualitative aspect to this in that I find myself wanting/needing to record certain thoughts, news items or events, and once I've made a mental note of them, the pressure to get to the keyboard increases.

So, that's all the prosaic details about the <u>how</u>. What about the <u>what</u>? What have I written about, what do I write about? What is in the five million words that make up 'my diaries'.

In short, I'd have to say there is selection of almost everything in my consciousness. I don't know about your consciousness, or anybody else's for that matter, but mine is a busy newsroom, and although I don't manage to write about a fraction of what goes on inside it, over time, I believe, my diary has come to hold a good and representative sample of the 'everything'. Indeed, it wouldn't be too far off the mark to claim my diary provides a comprehensive cross-section of my conscious life.

I do have a couple of caveats, though, to this idea. Firstly, although I've always aimed to write as honestly as I can, I do – slightly – censor what goes into the diary. So, to be frank, and as one example, there is and has been more sex in my life and my head (aren't we men supposed to think about it some 20 times a day) than there is in the diary. I have, though, fought against this particular restraint from time to time, not wanting to be so prudish, And, as another example, I am probably more prejudiced about some kinds of people than I am prepared to set down in ink, as it were. And, as a third, I can be careful about what I say concerning my children (though not always) – not least since they are the humans most likely ever to read my diaries in an uncensored form. A second caveat is that there are times, not frequent but not infrequent either, when I only discover what I think about something or somebody (i.e. what is in my SUBconscious) through the act of writing. In other words, I don't have a particular opinion when I start making an entry about X, but I do have an opinion by the time I've finished – I know I do because there it is in black and white.

That said and stated, I still wish to take a punt at making a list of what can be found in my diaries – categorise my entries in some way. Let's see if I can.

- Snapshots of my activities and of those I'm living with. Occasionally I deliberately spell out the banal routines of a day or an activity just for the record – as if I were making an entry for Mass Observation. Until 1987, I wrote exclusively about myself. Of course, I wrote about my parents and siblings, friends and girlfriends, but what I wrote was largely focused on my interaction with them. When Adam came along I filled my diary with details and more details about his activities and development, and I would also record what his mother was doing when not with us. Since Hattie, JG and Albert came along (starting in 2007), I've found myself having to be almost as attentive – in diary terms – to their lives as to my own.

- Commentaries on those activities.

- Problems with the house or car or computer, or with organisations/administrations.

- Thoughts, plans, hopes for and about the future.

- Self-analysis, self-criticism, angst, excruciating details of arguments (as if to document both my wrong doings and self-justifications) and exasperations with the world around me.

- Local, national and international news. This is a variable feast of briefs and longer items. The key world events usually get a mention as do big national stories, though this depends on whether I happen to be in writing mood at the time. I sometimes refer directly to articles in *The Economist* if they've peeked my interest for one reason or another. Local stories get into the diary if I find them quirky or they affect us in some way. I often also mention top-level sporting events. I love the Olympics, the World Cup, cricket internationals, and, as I follow the competitions, so my diary does too. Now and then, I like to mention golf, tennis, rugby, snooker matches, but only at the highest level, and especially if there's been remarkable performances.

- Science developments, particularly to do with brain sciences and evolution, along with my own views on particular theories.
- Day trips, special events.
- Travel/tourism – I often aspire to Travel Writing, capturing scenes, people, feelings, thoughts. In 2000, while on holiday and keeping a holiday diary, I devised a slightly different way of writing, one that I have continued to use regularly on holiday – a kind of scene setting, describing where I am, what I can see, hear, and sense right there, in the moment. I call it writing 'Al Vivo', and to distinguish this from the rest of the holiday diary (in which I'm usually writing about the recent past), I sometimes use a different colour pen.
- Brief reviews of the books I'm reading, the TV dramas I'm watching, films I've seen, shows, theatre, exhibitions.
- Coverage – direct from the author's brain – of current or planned fiction and non-fiction projects.
- Details of colourful dreams in as much detail as I can remember.
- The status of and changes in my health and well-being. I do this fairly scrupulously as it helps me understand and manage my ailments.
- Examples of synchronicity. I love to find coincidences of all shapes and sizes in my life which seem to occur remarkably often. Sometimes, I jokingly give them a random number in the thousands as if I've been keeping count of them my whole life long.
- And other minutiae of daily life

There, that's the <u>how</u> and the <u>what</u>, and now what about the <u>why</u>. Why do I write a diary? I need to go back to the beginning, to my five-year diary, started when I was 11, and kept very intermittently until I was 18, and then more regularly through my university years. I would say that the near sum total of my reasons for writing in that diary was to record my life as it was passing. At the very beginning, it was probably a bit of a novelty, I was probably lonely (we'd moved to a new area, and I'd started a new school), and it seemed a worthwhile thing to be doing. Every now and then I must have come across the blue-covered diary book and thought I really should carry on with it, but then I'd lapse again. By the time I got to university, and was starting a new life, free of home restraints and responsibilities, I must have thought it would be useful to keep up the record of that new life. Habit probably provided a momentum to keep it going. (I write about this in more detail in *Why Ever*.)

Then, when I went travelling and started my first proper journal, I know for sure that it was meant to be nothing more or less than a record of my travels. And I recall, for example, telling people that I chose not to carry a camera, partly because it would be expensive/difficult to develop/store/post the films, but mostly because I wanted to write the pictures of where I went and what I saw. In New Zealand, during the period of the second proper journal, I tentatively jotted down the odd poem; and then in South America I began including more descriptive creative content and composing very short stories. By then my reasons for writing a diary had become more complex, the diary had become not only a record of my activities (increasingly imperfect in that regard) but a vehicle for self-expression. However, this latter motive – self-expression – faded over time, in my 30s, largely in response to a busy life as a working journalist and, a few years later, my becoming a parent. My need to write creatively, or as a mechanism for self-expression, hadn't gone away, the opposite, it had become a fairly major part of my life – but one that was entirely separate from the diary.

From fairly early on, the diary became a confessional, a place for safe self-reflection and self-analysis. For example, I'm confident that when I was heading for a breakdown in 1980 it was partly through keeping a diary that I was able to identify what was happening to me; and, eventually, the diary writing helped me discover remedies too. In the depths of other depressions through my life, I've found it hugely helpful to write analytically about their possible causes, and to use written logic to work out the best ways forward. This in itself would have been justification enough for keeping a diary all these years. It may also have saved me a fortune in potential therapy costs!

I also keep a diary for the joy of writing: using language to communicate accurately and efficiently and playfully what's going on in the grey mass of neurones up there in my skull, somewhere behind my eyes.

I have, of course, occasionally come against the 'why question' in the diary itself. Here is one attempt to answer it from 2001.

171

18 January 2001
I think [Adam] was asking me about why I write a diary, and then hit on this question as a way of helping me answer it: 'If you had a few hours spare, Dad, assuming you knew you were going to die in a few hours time, and you had a spare hour before you died, would you spend it writing in your journal?' After some explanation, I said yes, I probably would.

I told him, as I'm sure I have before, that my journal writing has become a complex part of who I am, and that I can identify several different reasons for it. One important reason (and this is why I have encouraged him to do the same), I said, is that it helps me to sort out things about life in my head. In order to write things down, it's necessary to arrive at some clarity of thought, and this can be an extremely useful process. It can often force a kind of objectivity. It helps one argue a case through, and perhaps see the flaws; it helps concretise what one might like or not like about a film, a person, an event, a plan, a wall-paper . . .

Secondly, I said, I love to read my diaries, probably more than anything else – and this pleasure has certainly fed through into one reason why I keep writing. In particular, a journal entry written Al Vivo is one that can serve particularly well to bring back a memory that might not otherwise be recoverable.

Thirdly, my journal provides a record of my life, which, I think, is actually valuable. It is certainly valuable to me – it serves as my memory – and it may be valuable to you one day, or to your children, but more than that, I think my diaries, with the right editor and publisher, could be publishable. And, for this reason, I probably would want to write something on my death bed.

The idea of the diary being a good read comes up again in another diary entry two years later. But this one also illustrates the active way I've used the diary as a tool 'to help sort out things about my life'.

29 October 2003
I get a lot of pleasure from reading my diaries. I don't know how to explain it: they kind of fill me up, remind me that I'm a person with a deep rich past. But, at the same time, they also remind me how impoverished my life has become; they tell me that I should be capable of having a life with more in than I now have. They show me a person I've lost; and spur me to find him again. And yet, unfortunately, they don't tell me how to do that. They can't, because I'm a different person now; and an older man. I can't reproduce the experiences or the relationships; nor would I want to; but I feel sure there must be a way to get somewhere where I am more of whom I was. This now requires not only finding a partner, more of a settled social life, but also an occupation too. It seems to me – and has done for a long time – that these things are now out of reach. Reading my diaries is like a tease: come on boy, you've done good before, you can do good again. Although this period now feels like a full-stop in my life [I'd turned 50 the previous year], surely it can only be a semi-colon, I just have to find a way of moving the sentence (the life sentence!) on.

Until I was in my mid-late 20s, I only ever wrote the diary for one person, myself. But, as my ambitions turned towards being a writer so I began – very vaguely – to consider that the diary might have some literary value one day. To put this in perspective, I also considered that much else I wrote – plays, short stories, novellas – might attract a publisher (Chapter eight). Though, of course, there was a significant difference, all my other writing projects were developed with the idea of finding an audience, whereas my diaries definitely were not. I don't believe I've ever composed a diary entry FOR some future audience, but over time, I suppose, I have imposed slight self-censorship (as described above – and see diary entry below) in fear of audience judgement of the writer.

An exciting moment arrived in 1997 when my diaries came to the attention of a producer making programmes for Radio 4. To this day, I remain proud of this fact, not that the programme was made but that it was nearly made! (Which is to give away the end of this anecdote before I've begun.)

'Do you keep a fascinating diary?' ran a headline towards the back end of the *Radio Times* in a section where the BBC occasionally calls for viewer participation. The ad asked for four pages of extracts giving a flavour of the diary – for a programme called *Messages to Myself.* Well, I decided that I had to include something from the Asia travel diary, and from the diary written to Adam after his birth. I also chose extracts from 1981, the year after my depression, and about speaking to my father Frederic for the first time in 23 years. I confided to the diary itself: 'I was determined not to spend long over this, but, in the end, it took me all morning to get the four pages together. Even then, I wasn't happy with the potpourri. [. . .] I found it difficult to find truly entertaining passages to divulge, and I would be hard pressed to call them fascinating. I think I could put together a book which one might be able to describe as fascinating, but I would need the scope of a book to develop themes and cross-references, and allow the reader time to build up a picture of my confused life.'

Six weeks later, I received a letter from the Bristol-based producers, Martin Weitz Associates. It said: 'We thought that your diary was very well written and interesting to read.' I was overwhelmed by this, it felt like my whole diary writing life – and all the time I'd spent writing – had suddenly been acknowledged publicly.

12 August 1997
The truth is, of course, that I have never written my diary with a view to publication. That is not to say that I have not considered that a good editor could turn it into a good read. I have always said that I probably represent an interesting example of an ordinary screwed-up guy trying to making his way in the world. However, it is also true that, apart from an early period, I have never been unaware of the fact that somebody might read the diaries one day, and I do, therefore, conceal a little (although I would argue that the little I do conceal

is rather unimportant and there is never complete concealment any way). My diary, therefore, represents, in my view, probably one of the most sustained and personally honest and self-analytical accounts of a life that exists anywhere.

Weitz asked for more extracts, and I ended up spending an entire day selecting a new batch. Nearly three months later, by chance I had the BBC World Service playing on the radio, and on came the programme – *Messages to Myself*. I was astonished to realise that the programme was not a compilation of extracts by different diarists but a whole half an hour devoted to one person and his or her diary, interweaving extracts from both the diaries and an interview with the diarist. Wow, a whole half an hour about me and my diaries!

But months and months passed by with no further contact from Weitz, until March 1998. A young-sounding woman, Susan, called me up, told me the BBC had decided to go-ahead with a new series of *Messages to Myself*, and she asked me for yet more extracts. However, she gave me no guidance other than that she was quite interested in the relationships with Frederic and with Adam. I sent a further 20 pages of diary extracts, and I was soon forced into a closer analysis of my relationship with the diary. I'll let the diary explain.

Sunday 22 March 1998
I am almost tongue-tied. I don't quite know what to say. My diaries have been the centre of some attention, and I find myself a little embarrassed – embarrassed by the content of the diary, its omissions and its repetitions, and by my own relationship with the diary, as though it is a friend, or a substitute for a friend, because on closer examination, on reflection, this seems to me like a weakness, the word pathetic comes to my mind, though not absolutely appropriate, it is not entirely inappropriate either.

The reason for all this is that it now looks almost certain that the BBC will run a half hour programme about my diaries in May or June. The producer, contracted by Weitz, a 25-year old woman called Susan, has now visited me twice – once the Friday before last, and once last Friday. Outside of my immediate family, and B, there can be no one who knows quite so much about me now and I doubt I shall ever see her again.

On her first visit, she spent most of the day simply quizzing me about the people and events in my life, particularly about Fred and Bel, taking copious notes. By then I had provided her with four lots of extensive extracts, and now she has five or six. I found it really disappointing that so many key points in my life were not properly recorded, or not recorded in a useful way. Several times, I resorted to sending the producer letters – the letter I wrote to Gail about Fred's papers and photos, the letter to Bel's parents about the decision to have a child. Why? Because, I had thought out what I wanted to say more carefully, with someone else's listening in mind. My diaries are not written to be read by an outsider, they're meant to be read by an insider who knows all the people, what all the references mean, and who can put everything into context in an instant without tedious explanation. There was, for example, no satisfactory report on the break with Frederic, nor on my meeting Bel, not even on why I keep a diary. Why do I keep a diary?

Then, this Friday, she came back again with her tape recorder and taped an interview with me for more than two hours. I found this really quite stressful. She covered most of the personal events of my life, particularly the difficult year in 1980, but hardly touched on my professional life or achievements. Once or twice, I had to decline to talk about a subject – Harold, M wanting to get married, and the feminine side of my nature (which I had mentioned to her previously simply to explain something). I never really relaxed with the microphone on, I found myself composing and sometimes inventing answers, I even had to stop myself once or twice.

What I fear now is that Susan will have the stories of my life – Frederic's treatment of me, the romantic but strange relationship with Bel, and my overwhelming joy of being a father – to take over the programme. My initial interest in having my diaries used was because I thought they might be interesting in themselves. But, in the three weeks since Susan first contacted me, the interest in and focus on these personal elements has escalated. And all the time, Susan has been as honest and straightforward as possible, and she's promised me time and time again, that she will not use anything I don't want used. It's as though I've led myself into my own trap. The diaries have trapped me.

In our two meetings, Susan was very enthusiastic about my diaries, and how well-written they were. This was music to my ears. A couple of weeks later she emailed me to say she was working hard on the programme and looking for an actor to read the extracts. I couldn't believe it, I really couldn't believe my diaries were on the cusp of becoming, if not famous, then well known about. I imagined – as one does – the amazed reaction of friends and family members. Most knew I kept a diary but this part of me carries no weight with them, no importance, no relevance. The radio programme would, I dreamed, give my diary-writing activity real status.

I didn't hear from Susan for several weeks after that. The silence felt ominous, and I wasn't mistaken. I emailed her a couple of times before she replied. Weitz's company had researched six programmes but were only going to make five, mine was to be dropped. She told me she and another of the Weitz team has argued strongly to include a programme on my diaries, and that they'd been angry at their boss's decision. The only explanation she could give me was that my 'themes' weren't strong enough, and I recalled how, while being taped, Susan had pressed me to be more expansive about my feelings towards Frederic, and about when he kicked me out of his house. But, I'd had none, as I've explained elsewhere (*Why Ever* – Chapter twelve), and there was nothing to say. Obviously, I thought a lot about all this after the fact, and I stuck with the belief that I had been right – morally – not to invent some media-friendly emotions that fitted the situation. Now, many years later (years in which the Misery Memoir arm of publishing has flourished) I regret that that radio programme wasn't made, possibly because of my scruples.

My diaries never made it onto the airwaves but – during the process – I had got accustomed to the idea that I, myself, might not be, should not be, their only audience. Within five years, I had launched my own personal website, and in April 2004 I began the long process (it took three years) of editing my diaries for the period of my life pre-Adam (1974-1985) and uploading them to the website. I established a simple format for the web using 13 text files/pages per year: one introductory page (with a biographical summary, and a description of the diaries themselves) and 12 pages (of variable lengths) one for each month. The Home Page carried a general introduction including the following two paragraphs which go some way to explaining why I had decided to make my diaries public.

'Each published file here relates to a particular month. Although these files are edited (and reduced), I am not making any changes to the originals, other than to remove errors, and make the text more accessible and/or readable. On telling friends about this project in preparation, it was not unusual to be asked why I was intending to make my diaries public. The obvious answer would be that I, like most writers, want to be read (even though, of course, my diaries were never written to be read, or with an audience in mind). I do wish to make it clear, though, that I am not net-publishing because I think my diaries are good writing or valuable in a literary way. Thirty years ago my writing was poor and immature (it took me several attempts to pass English Language O-level).

In fact, I hope my writing has developed over the decades, and I do not wish to disregard or disguise this development. On the contrary, one of the main reasons for publishing these diary entries is to demonstrate and reveal change, whether this is through the writing itself, or, much more broadly, through what I have to say about my own life, and how I've coped with the physical, emotional and psychological trials and joys of being alive, of being a conscious human being.'

Ten years later, I edited and uploaded diary extracts for the years 1986-2005. And for these files I wrote a second general introduction with an explanation of my editing priorities.

'It is nearly 10 years since I first published some of my diaries online – covering the years 1974 to 1985. At the time, I stated that my published diaries, here on the Pikle website, were reduced and only edited for corrections or readability. But, I did not explain why parts of the diary were edited out altogether.

Consideration of other people's privacy, of course, was one motive for cutting text, though by using pseudonyms and initials I kept more in than I might have done otherwise. One specific area of concern was my writing about intimate matters. Guided by the fact that I, personally, like to read about other people's private lives, and have always much admired, for example, the diaries of Anais Nin, I tried to include as much of what I wrote about love and sex as I felt comfortable with. But there is, inevitably, much I left out. I cut material that I felt was too dull, too self-absorbed, too off-the-wall to make any sense; and, though I tried very hard not to delete writing that made me out to be arrogant, childish, foolish, uncaring, etc., I did not always succeed.

The difficulties with publishing my diaries from this later period of my life were more daunting than those for the earlier period. This was for the simple reason that I became a father, and so there is much in my diary about my son (Adam), about my relationship with him, and with his mother. While there is little that I personally would be unwilling to publish, there is much, I imagine, which would be considered private by the others involved. Over the years I have had various conversations with both Adam and Bel about making my diaries public, and neither of them like the idea, and I have no problem understanding their points of view.

Thus, in taking the decision to make public my diaries from this point on, i.e. from 1986, I have edited them with due consideration for the feelings of my family – which is not to say I have left them out, for without them nothing would make sense. Being a father to my children (as I write this I have a young family and two young boys) has been such an enormous privilege and such a great joy I cannot imagine what would have become of me without them.'

There are now over 400 month-long diary web pages on my website. At the time of writing I have no plans to upload any further files.

I never expected my web-published diaries to attract any attention from the random public or media. I thought that some friends might dip in, and strangers might land on them occasionally through Google searches. But it was both surprising and very gratifying to receive, every now and then, emails from past friends and acquaintances who had come across their names in my diaries (one of these I mentioned in *Why Ever* – Chapter ten).

Since the radio programme anti-climax, my diaries have had a couple of lesser opportunities to shine. In 2011, The History Press published my book *Brighton in Diaries*. It covered 26 diarists across the ages, one to a chapter, starting with Samuel Pepys, and including the geologist Gideon Mantell, and the writers Virginia Woolf and Arnold Bennett. I also included several unknown diarists found through the Mass Observation project. Because of my long and varied history with the city, I included by own diaries for the last chapter.

And then, in 2019, I published the first memoir – *Why Ever Did I Want to Write* – crammed full to bursting with extracts from my diaries, as this very one is too.

Chapter ten

KIP FENN
MAGNUM OPUS OR WHITE ELEPHANT?

17 March 2001
'More rain, more puddles in my garden. Moss is taking over the lawn. The concrete
in my drive is falling to bits, and the fence is falling down. I've typed up another
old diary this weekend, from October 1978. In a truly spooky moment, I was lis-
tening to something on the radio when the place Berkeley Square was mentioned,
at that very moment, that exact moment, I was turning a page in the diary, and
the first line of the new page was entitled 'Berkeley Square'!

Because of my newsletter schedule I am faced with very little to do in the
forthcoming week, so I decided to try and give some thought to a new novel. I've
come up with the main character, Thomas aka Kip Fenn, and I've written an open-
ing two paragraphs, only another 2,000 to go.

That was the day Kip Fenn *entered my life. Rarely can an un-*
published fictional character have come to dominate one person's life as
much as Kip Fenn *came to dominate mine. I say 'unpublished' though in*
reality the novel Kip Fenn – Reflections *(subtitled* One Man's Journey*
from the beginning of the 21st Century to its End) was published twice,*
hardback and paperback. However, both times were by my own Pikle pub-
lishing empire (that's facetious aggrandisement if you were wondering)
and neither edition sold more than a handful (literally) of copies. A failure
it was, pure and simple. Nevertheless, I remain immensely proud of the
novel, the writing therein, the epic stories, the imaginative ideas, the large
cast of characters, many of whom the novel followed throughout their
lives.

My aim here is not to reprise Kip Fenn's story since you can order
it directly from Amazon or find second hand copies aplenty on Abebooks
(all of which would originally have been copies I sent to reviewers) but to
tell the tale of why and how I came to write the novel, and of how nothing
I did – and I did much – could attract a mainstream agent, publisher or
any sales. I couldn't even give it away.

Yet, to tell you the truth immediately, I thought, when I had first
written the book, it was brilliant, original, special; I still think so today. I
believed, and also still believe today, that given the right publishing treat-
ment it would have attracted widespread media interest, a significant
readership, and, consequently, profit for a publisher. But it proved to be
too big a book, too ambitious; and, because I had no connections to the

industry, no track record, no publisher or agent was prepared to invest the time, take such a risk on an outlandish work, genre-busting – not with their slush piles already stacked high to the ceiling with ready-made genre-perfect crime, romance, coming-of-age lookalikes.

I'm not bitter, I'm not. I can honestly say, though, that still – 20 years later – barely a day goes by without me thinking about, or referencing Kip Fenn and his story. Thus, I'm hoping that by writing this full and unexpurgated story of my failure (to bring Kip Fenn – Reflections *to its right and proper audience) I will find closure.*

I had an original idea for *Kip Fenn* – the name and the arc of the story I wanted to tell – in March 2001. By May I'd made very little progress. (Throughout this chapter I refer to Kip Fenn, meaning either the novel or the character, sometimes interchangeably. Where it's clear I'm referring to the novel I've italicised *Kip Fenn*, otherwise I've left the name Kip Fenn un-italicised.)

18 May 2001
'Why do I find creative writing so very difficult? It is now 10:40am, and I haven't yet started to think about *Kip Fenn*. Admittedly, I went to bed late (about 1:30 after watching a recorded edition of *West Wing*), and therefore I lazed around in bed until 8:30 or so this morning listening to the radio, then I listened to the radio a bit more until 9:00, then I read a novel for 45 minutes or so, then I played a bridge computer game for another 40 minutes, then I took a walk around the garden which I do several times a day, then I made another cup of tea, and now I'm writing up my diary. It's a deep feeling in me, that I recognise, but which I don't understand or control. It may well be linked to another feeling I get which obliges me to stop when I've actually done some creative writing for a couple of hours. I have never been able to work long hours uninterrupted on writing, in the way that I can on accounts, for example, or production, or resolving a computer problem. There is a kind of mental or physical energy cut out which stops me simply getting on with it. I've wondered if these feelings are connected to a fear of not being able to do the job, not being able to come up with anything, of not being able to produce the goods, or, if I've produced some goods, a fear of drying up and not being able to produce any more.

Perhaps I am being too harsh on myself. I mean it is difficult, very difficult, in the early stages of a new project, especially one which starts from absolutely nothing – as does *Kip Fenn*. I don't really know how to start, where to start, I don't even know how to begin to start, or to begin to begin to start, or to begin to start the beginning of the planning. I have tried three or four very broad chapter headings to provide a framework for my thinking, but each one is just a few lines of notes. Because I may have decided to tell Fenn's story roughly chronologically, I spent some time yesterday starting to work on his background. I now have another page of scrawled notes but this bears little relation to my other notes. [. . .] This is a very ambitious novel, and I should not be undertaking it in the odd week here and there around my main job. This is preposterous, and yet I've spent most of this week coming to the decision to use my free time over the next 18 months to work on *Kip Fenn*. I should really be choosing a less demanding project for these spare weeks, and leave *Kip Fenn* until I've closed my newsletter business down. Oh isn't it easier to have these circular arguments with myself than to get on with it. And this is the fun part, the creative imagining part, wait until I have to sit down and start writing – then my ability to prevaricate will multiply xfold.

A week later, I seem to be edging towards a beginning.

24 May 2001
'I continue to struggle with my imagination over *Kip Fenn*. I've sketched out, very roughly, the main themes for about half the book. Tomorrow, I shall try and type it all up into some sensible notes (rather than rough hand-written notes, covered in squiggles, boxes, arrows) so that, when I eventually get round to returning to it (one month, one year, two years . . .), I'll be able to re-engage, so to speak, with my ideas. I talked to Adam last evening about some of them. He said he thought I was trying to squeeze too much into one book, but I explained about 'Reflections' being a term coined, in the late 2080s, for autobiographical books which skim on the detail, while any real autobiography would have to be full of endless detail, with names and places, which, when not real, would be boring to invent, and even more boring to read.'

Come summer and several weeks free of my newsletter, I'm still hesitating.

10 August 2001
Although I have a structure and some characters, I don't have a clear idea of how the writing will be, how the style will work. I mean will it work if I just start writing at the beginning and keep writing and writing and writing. What I've written so far appears to be nothing more than an introduction – so I may make it just that, which means this morning I should be trying to get going on the first chapter. But what can I possibly do in a week – and surely I can't write this book in the work gaps over the next year and a half. Shouldn't I be trying to write something simpler in the meantime, some short stories? I'm not committed to *Kip Fenn* yet, which is why I'm dilly dallying a bit, and why I can't decide to focus clearly and exclusively on it during these days.

16 August 2001
So my two weeks on *Kip Fenn* have gone up in smoke. I failed miserably to do anything constructive during the summer [. . .]. But, I must say, it is very very difficult to get going on *Kip Fenn*. I have made a start on chapter one, but only out of desperation to get something done. I don't really believe I can do this novel, I think it'll turn out to be another *Rats* [my first, and failed, attempt at a novel], an exciting idea, but beyond both my ability to write, and the detailed knowledge of many different kinds of facts I would need to make the story work. I started writing what I thought was chapter one, but it soon transpired that it was too general, too reflective, and so I've assumed it could be a kind of prologue. I then took a while to come up with a more specific scenario for chapter one, which I have started writing. But I don't have much confidence in myself, and I've taken every opportunity I can, not to write it. Now my time is up, my summer spare time is over.

And now I must pause – as the world did not – to reflect on the events of 11 September 2001. The following diary entry hints at how those events underpinned and strengthened the broad sweep of political ideas I was trying to develop in the novel.

15 September 2001

It's Saturday now, and so far I haven't written about the events last Tuesday which have so shocked the Western world. The crashing of the planes into the buildings, and the loss of life was bad enough, but the subsequent crumbling and total destruction of the two World Trade Centre towers in New York made the terrible and horrific attack ten times worse – not least because so many more people (including hundreds of firefighters) were killed by the falling buildings. But also, in a way, because of the symbol created by the changed Manhattan skyline, and the great loss of physical property. During the first two days, no one paid any attention to the fact that the hijackers, teams of three-six, had not only been prepared to die, but knew they would definitely die, and that these teams must necessarily have included highly trained (pilots) and intelligent people. This is quite extraordinary in itself. President Bush used the word 'cowards' to describe the terrorists. What a stupid thing to say. They may be detestable, evil, murderous, corrosive, poisoned, loathsome (I've resorted to the thesaurus) but they are not, were not, cowards. What can lead people to act in such selflessly destructive ways: only a passionate belief in something, usually religion or nationality. I strongly supported the UK action in the Falklands and the West's response to Iraq's invasion of Kuwait (against much popular opposition), but I am not convinced that the apparent worldwide response – at least that collected and reported by our media – to this tragedy is the right one (involving some kind of military action in Afghanistan, and, possibly, Iraq). First, it is really important to try and bring perspective to the issue. It seems that around 5,000 may have been killed; and, yes, it is the most terrible terrorist attack, with more victims than any single event of its kind in the modern world, only outdone, so to speak, by natural disasters and actual/ongoing wars. (Ah, but, as I write this, I recall the Bhopal tragedy in India, which may well have been bigger in terms of deaths and injuries and generational birth defects – I would need to check – but not of course in terms of financial loss or the loss of such famous buildings.) But, as one commentator pointed out, one quarter of Afghanis (i.e. millions of people) are currently in danger of starvation; and another one asked where was all this outpouring of anguish when 20,000 people died in India earlier this year as a result of floods. And, I wonder, how many people die on the US's roads, or are murdered by guns, in any given day. Most of those are senseless, selfish, greedy murders, but Tuesday's murders were in fact driven by people with passion and self-less objectives. I believe the world should not be considering revenge or vengeance, or not only, but should be looking deeper for the reasons why this terrorism exists. Parts of the world have, after all, accepted that some terrorists – the Palestinians and the IRA for example – have had legitimate arguments that needed listening to, or dealing with. Just because the terrorism is on a global scale, does not mean we should be trying to patch up the problems, we should be searching in a global way for the underlying causes, in the same way that the UK is now trying to solve the Northern Ireland problem.

I believe (and this is one of the themes I've already identified for *Kip Fenn*) that the underlying causes must be traceable back to the extraordinary divide that still exists between the rich and the poor in this world, more specifically between the rich nations and the poor nations. And, it so happens, that the Muslim/Arab nations are the ones most likely to be able to rally fanatics and armies to assault the rich West. The fact that, despite huge divides within the Muslim/Arab nations, one part of the Muslim world has managed to shake-up the west should not be taken as a call to arms, but a call to peace, a call to a greater understanding of what divides the world. The US has reportedly decided to devote an extra $20bn to fighting terrorism – if there are five million Afghanis hungry, that $20bn could be used to give each one $4,000 each – that would surely defuse Osama Bin Laden's power.

And now, finally, I am fully engaged in the process of writing *Kip Fenn – Reflections*. This is clear from how my diary entries start to include more details of the futuristic ideas I'm working on, and how the structure of the novel might evolve.

3 October 2001
I have just listened to a debate on globalisation on Radio 4. I've also recently read a number of articles in the *Economist* on the same subject. I'm interested because this is going to be a theme that I must tackle in *Kip Fenn*. George Monbiot, a writer in the *Guardian*, was one of the people on the programme. His main aim was to promote the idea of a world parliament. I think that is naive. Interestingly, there does not seem to be much evidence about whether the inequality in the world is growing or not, and what impact globalisation might be having on whether it is or not. If I remember right, I have already planned in *Kip Fenn* that a report will be published in the 2020s or 2030s which demonstrates how much of the world's wealth has been sucked into the first world in the previous 50 years, and that this, extraordinarily, starts off a chain of events which eventually leads to the formation of the ICCO [this ended up in the novel as the IFSD]. I haven't given much thought to it, but I know already that ICCO is not a world government. [. . .] One speaker in the debate argued that it would be impossible for a central worldwide organisation to be able to divide up how money should be distributed between a village in Chile, for example, or a town in Africa. He said there needs to be much more local (and in his view voluntary) involvement in deciding how development monies should be shared out. Sometimes, a couple of times a week maybe, I get such an urge, such an itch to sink into *Kip Fenn*, and get going, but I simply can't go in and out of it on a daily or even a weekly basis. I will try now, through until Christmas, to use my spare weeks.

20 October 2001
I've been working on *Kip Fenn* all week. I wrote about 9,000 words, more than doubling its length. But this is the first week, I suppose, in which I have really got to grips with writing it. I wrote every day, not as much as I would have liked – but still every day. I am in sight of the end of the first draft of the first chapter. This part of the book is probably the easiest to write, because it's set in the small world of Kip's childhood, which is in the very near future. For later chapters, I am going to have to invent and predict much more than in this first one. I have already begun to realise there are limitations to the novel's structure.

There can be no plot as such, which may severely undermine its publish-ability. And there are limited ways in which one voice can keep linking ideas and anecdotes to sustain a narrative. [...]

Kip Fenn keeps crossing my mind – which is good – but I expect he'll vanish over the next couple of days as my business journalism takes over mental space. I thought today, for example, (and I need to note this here or else I'll forget it) that I should intersperse email dialogues throughout the book in order to help break up Kip's voice, and to allow me, the author, a wider scope. In chapter one, for example, it occurred to me that I could use an email correspondence between Kip's mother and her brother to allow more comment on his mother's teaching methods, and on how she brought Kip up. Kip could explain that he 'inherited' the correspondence from his uncle. There could be at least one email correspondence in every chapter, perhaps.

In November, I visited The Photographer's Gallery in London where I viewed an exhibition of Eugène Atget's photos of turn-of-the-century Paris which led me to ask in my diary: 'Is Kip Fenn keen on 19th century photography?' I already owned books of Atget's works, and many others about the beginnings of photography, and it suddenly seemed like a natural hobby for Kip to be a collector of early examples. I had no idea at the time how I would weave this into the novel, but old photographs did, in time, become central to several stories in the book, and to Kip's productive retirement years.

At the same time, I was transcribing my Brazil diaries onto the computer, and it was no coincidence, therefore, that the second chapter (which I'd just started work on) saw Kip as a young man adventuring in Brazil – adventuring that would have serious consequences much later on in his life.

Here are two paragraphs from the book's short prologue which give a very brief idea of the themes and ideas that are to come:

'I lie here, all these years later, reflecting carefully back over my life, editing and dictating, editing and dictating to the wallscreen in front of me. I have a wealth of personal and more general material to help the process, not least a lifetime of email communications which, from my 20s, I collated and stored. One day they may be net-published along with this, the bare bones of a biography - or, more accurately, my Reflections,- which I am preparing in these last months of my life.

You may have heard of me, Neil or Kip Fenn, thanks to my career within the United Nation's International Fund for Sustainable Development, the IFSD, (especially during the First Jihad War), or my modest efforts within an organisation called REACH in the aftermath of the Grey Years. You may also have heard of me in connection with my daughter Crystal, who fell victim to the suicide epidemic of the 2040s, or my son, Bronze, whose idiotic caper in the 2060s disrupted both our lives (his tragically more so than mine). Or, possibly, you may recall my name in connection with a sexual weakness, but which was, essentially, a private matter and should never have been exposed in public. I will not ignore the personally painful and embarrassing, but I hope other areas of my private life, for which I am thankful, will take precedence: my co-op children, Guido and Jay, for example, or my role in launching The Josephine Collection archive of 19th century photographs.'

Notice the reference to co-op children – yes, I found a way to bring in my ideas on that too. It might be true to say that I filled *Kip Fenn – Reflections* not with any actual events from my own life but with fictional hyper-versions of social, cultural, political, biographical ideas I'd experienced, touched on, or imagined. After all, I had a century of future time to invent, and through which to navigate my anti-hero civil servant, Kip.

By the end of January 2002 I had finished a draft of the first two chapters, totalling over 23,000 words, and it seemed I would need ten chapters, roughly one for each decade of Kip's life. The book was already on course to be far longer than most published novels, and would end up running to over 200,000 words. But was I happy with the story, the writing? I asked myself this very question at the time.

25 January 2002
But, am I pleased with it so far? I don't know. I really don't know. [. . .] On the whole, I'm pleased that I've managed to take Kip's story the places I wanted it to go. I'm less pleased to find that it's impossible for me to weave more general themes and grander ideas into the overall arc of the story. I had a vague idea, for example, that over and above the story, I could focus each chapter on a topic, say memory, or change, or love. But, the narrative is too strong, and varied, and constrained, as it is, largely by chronology. Also I worry a lot about telling the reader, rather than showing him/her (which is quite difficult in the pseudo-biographical style I've chosen).

And a few months later I wrote this in the diary: 'Although I always thought *Kip Fenn* was too ambitious a project and I would never manage it, I'm surprised that I have made such good headway with the first two chapters, but I'm beginning to worry just a bit that it may yet become too difficult. But I don't think so, I just need the time and mental space to focus on it.'

It took me more than six months to finish the third chapter (I was still working full-time, and would only close my business at the end of this year). But, by this time, I had a fairly clear plan of how Kip's life (and the world!) would unfold into the latter decades of the 21st century. I barely mentioned in my diary many if not most of the themes and stories that found their way into *Kip Fenn*, but here is one I did.

20 August 2002
Solidly into chapter four now. I've spent the whole day writing about Kip's trip to Dracula Park with his two children. I thought up the idea of a Dracula theme park some while ago. At the time, though, I didn't conceive any direct link with Kip's story, I just thought it would be a good idea for something imagined about the future. But then, while doing some research on the internet for a possible site, I found the Romanian government already had such a project and had been studying various sites for years (and that the chosen one was being opposed by environmentalists). Without really planning it out, I found myself writing that Kip had a busy autumn in 2032, involving three trips, and somehow Dracula Park became one of those. [. . .] To make it work, I'd have to give the trip some meaning. The two other trips Kip takes that autumn – to Malta and Manchester – are there so he can embellish on his relationships with Tom and Alfred respectively. After some careful thought, I decided to stick with the Dracula Park trip and use it to say a bit more about Kip's daughter Crystal.

It took me the rest of the year to complete that fourth chapter, and in the New Year – with EC INFORM no more – I had far more time to spend on Kip.

14 January 2003
Starting work on Kip Fenn again is always a slow process. Every time I restart it gets slower: there's so much previous material to take into account, so many characters, so much history. In first considerations for chapter five, for example, I find the list of people that will need to be mentioned (along with reasons for mentioning them and their stories) is already long, and yet I don't want the chapter to be a simple record of what's happened to Kip's friends and family. The main new theme for the chapter is the suicide epidemics that are to take place in the 2040s, and the genesis and consequences of this trend. This will link in and lead up to Crystal's suicide – I hope. But I have to deal with Arturo's arrival, too, Guido's growing up, Kip's relationship with Diana, etc. all against a backdrop of growing religious conflicts around the world, conflicts which will lead to war in chapter six (the God War as it becomes known, or the Holy War to end Holy Wars or whatever, I haven't found a suitable name yet). But I have thought a bit about this war, and I realised today that it will, of course, have to be like the cold war in the sense that it will build up in stages, and take place all over the world, in those countries which are shared by Muslims and Christians. It will have to lead to major successes for the Muslim world both in terms of territory and power in international organisations.

But it's so slow at the beginning of a new chapter, my head is always racing off trying to follow every lead at once, trying to resolve every unresolved situation in one go. I've given myself a full three weeks to write this chapter, starting yesterday, so three or four thinking days shouldn't go amiss.

In fact, *Kip Fenn* was now taking up most of my daily life. I'd set a schedule of completing one chapter – 20,000 words – per month. At the end of January, I was able to record the following: 'Today I worked well from 8:00 to 12:30, from 1:30 to 3, from 5 to 7, and from 8 to 9.' Through that

spring I worked hard and regularly. Here's a few more diary entries recording my progress.

8 April 2003
At 21,000 words, I must be close to finishing chapter seven, but Kip is only 65.
The chapter is supposed to cover a whole decade. I'm not sure I know why this
happened – the stories I wanted to tell in the chapter took too long. I've decided
I need to take a rain check, which means rereading the whole manuscript up to
this point, before carrying on with chapter eight.

12 April 2003
Back to work on *Kip Fenn* [. . .] Now I must press on to chapter eight. I need to
make a big decision before starting: whether to have a planetary crisis such as
a meteor hit or a major volcano eruption which blackens the sky for several
years. If I don't, there won't be too much to write about in the last chapters; and
if I do, I might not be up to the business of thinking it through and writing it.

20 April 2003
Chapter eight is coming along; I've cracked the back of it, I hope. I know what I
have to write today, and tomorrow I'll do the letters for the annex. I lie awake
in bed sometimes thinking of all the things the book is not. Just in the last few
days, for example, I've worried that there's not enough science fiction stuff vis-
a-vis the war; that the style of the writing in these latter chapters has changed
from the early ones; that there's not enough demonstration of how Kip loves
his partners or why they love him; and that there's not enough interweaving of
themes in these final chapters with the earlier ones.

Six weeks later

8 June 2003
Kip Fenn: I am so very nearly at the end of the first draft. It's scary. I may finish
tomorrow. Which is not to say there aren't hundreds of things to amend. But to
have got to the end, to have written the whole damn thing (I once called it a
'ridiculously ambitious project'), to have invented a 100 years of history, and a
man's whole network of family, friends and jobs . . . I'm going to be walking
around with something of a glow on my face once this first draft really is finished. My god, have I really done it? written a 220,000 word novel covering the
whole of the 21st century? No, I can't have done. What on earth will I do next?

Of course, I had plenty to do next. I had a first draft of a very long
and complex novel that needed editing, proof-reading, checking for con-
sistency, and so on. On my first read through, I marked many a grammar
or spelling mistake, but I would invariably avoid new wording/rewriting
where it was required by preferring simply to leave a pencil squiggle
down the side. But when I come to be doing the corrections on screen,
I'd arrive at a squiggle, have a momentary think about why the squiggle
was there, and then leave the computer – to do some weeding in the garden or washing up in the kitchen. Half the time, the sentence or

paragraph rewrites were required because my language was clunky or I was trying to cram too much in, or I was trying to express something mildly difficult and not succeeding. Thus, I needed to get my head back into the psychological or geographical or political or factual or whatever place I had been writing about. And it was hard, much easier to have a tea break. Another tedious procedure was to deal with, what I called, verbal weeds. I found I had overused words and phrases like: 'I know', 'I think', 'I found', 'perhaps', 'at least', 'of course', 'sometimes'. I made a list of 30 of them, and a grid with a column for each chapter, and I went through rigorously weeding them out, or replacing them with alternatives, better phrases – a task made much easier thanks to computers, but tedious none-the-less.

On 30 August 2003, I was able to report to my diary: '*Kip Fenn* is finished, finished, finished. I've worked my way through a final proof read and corrections. I'm sure I've made errors doing the corrections, but I can't proof read it again. I've got to call it a day. I mean it's a job for a copy editor now. If someone wants it, I might get motivated to clean it up some more at a later stage, but I can't do it now.'

I was very hopeful for *Kip Fenn – Reflections*. I'd been disappointed by the publishing industry for years and years, never managing to sell any of my fiction to agents and publishers alike (Chapter eight), but at heart I believed in the publishing world, and I believed in its judgement of my work. Yes, of course, I knew the industry was made up of imperfect humans who had their own preferences and prejudices, but as a whole, surely, I argued to myself, if the writing was good enough it would succeed. Again, it didn't help my cause that I had no useful connections with any agents/publishers, but wasn't I always reading about manuscripts being plucked from the slush pile and being auctioned among ever-keen publishers for piles of gold? *Kip Fenn – Reflections*, I told myself was too good to be ignored, too interesting and full of ideas, too rich in characters (more than 200 that appear more than once) and stories, too unusual – unique in fact – to sink in those slush piles rather than effervesce to the top.

Here was the basic pitch I included in all my submissions.

'*Kip Fenn is the fictional autobiography of a man who lives throughout the 21st century. He is born on 29 December 1999 and dies in January 2100. This book is most definitely not science fiction, but nor is it conventional fiction. I think of it as an original and thought-provoking novel, one rich in ideas, political and cultural, with a complex web of stories and themes. It does foretell a dark scenario for much of the century, which might be thought controversial, but not without strong expressions of hope towards the end. Kip Fenn's career, first as a British civil servant working*

with internet regulation and then later as an international official working to alleviate the rich-poor divide (up to and including being the Director
General of a major new UN agency), sees him involved in key events of the
century.

But this is also a personal story, the reflections of a man, weak in
his personal relationships but evidently successful in his chosen career. At
least half of the book is taken up with stories about his three partners (not
shying away from matters intimate), five children, friends and interests
(including volleyball and 19th century photographs). These tales weave
through Kip Fenn's life and thus through the novel, in a realistic way,
largely driven by the characters themselves or the events around them.

While never losing sight of the fact that the potential readership
for this book is actually living now in the early part of the century. I've tried
to ensure it reads authentically as if written in 2100, its audience familiar
with the events and culture of the 21st century. I hope I've managed a reasonable balance. For example, by using the imagined publishing concept of
'Reflections' I've been able to allow Kip to pick and choose personal and
historical information which fits together like a jigsaw puzzle without the
usual (for a genuine biography) footnotes or references.

The book contains ten chapters (215,000 words), very approxi-
mately covering one decade each of Kip's life. Seeds for many of the issues
and stories later in the book are set in the early chapters. Given the con-
straints of the biographical framework, I was particularly conscious of trying to ensure that there is a narrative drive to impel readers from one
chapter to the next. Moreover, although most of the book is written in look-
ing-back mode, there are interludes in the present (which increasingly
weave in with the biographical narrative), and there is also a real-time
surprise for Kip in the final chapter.'

I made a list of about 20 authors' agents, and gave each one a
rating out of 5 as to how likely they were to be interested in *Kip Fenn*
(based on their website and the *Writers' and Artists' Yearbook*). I rated
one agent 4, four others 3/4, and five 3. I wrote to my one 4-rated agent,
A.M. Heath. A return letter, signed on behalf of one the directors, arrived
promisingly quickly (oh yes, I was happy to ride my hopes high on the
thinnest of premises) confirming my material had been received. Unfortunately, within less than seven more days, the manuscript had been returned with an unsigned, photocopied rejection letter! By mid-Novem-
ber, the rejections had piled up, I was running out of agents to contact,
and I confessed all to the diary

29 December 2003
Kip Fenn may well prove to be my swan song – I think I was preparing to give
up 'trying to be a writer' after *BLR*, but I've never been able to quite dump the

ambition in just the same way (this is a hard thing to acknowledge) that other people can't stop buying lottery tickets. It's a damn sight easier to buy lottery tickets than to write novels; but there is also the ongoing quest to add a touch of meaningfulness to one's life – and writing has always given me a feeling of trying to do something significant, get somewhere significant. I can't imagine writing a book any more significant than *Kip Fenn*. And so I'm neutered really – I've nowhere to go down this line.

Well, I did have somewhere to go, I had a list of publishers, and I proceeded to write to them directly. Did I get a friendly word, an encouraging phrase from any one of them? No. Standard rejection letters from every one of them.

By the time I ran out of publishers and agents to write to, I was fairly certain I couldn't shovel the manuscript into the same drawer – the dusty dark place – as all my other unwanted writing. I began a plan to form my own publishing company (I'd already done this once with my business newsletters) and turn the manuscript into an attractive printed hardback with a dust jacket. If I did that, surely, *Kip Fenn – Reflections* with so many unique aspects and newsworthy features would be irresistible bait to reviewers. One review in a mainstream publication, I reasoned, could make all the difference.

There is a long entry in my diary in which I summarise the feedback I'd had so far from publishers/agents and friends who'd read the book, as well as the arguments either way, for and against self-publishing. There was little evidence in favour of publication. It would be fair to say that Adam was *Kip Fenn*'s greatest fan (after myself of course). He had been unbelievably supportive of me all through the writing (willing to chat about every aspect of the story as it unfolded in my head and in my words); he had proof read the book for me (I paid him for this); and once the book was finished he continued to let me vent about all the frustrations of trying to get it published. But when it came to this decision to print and publish myself, he expressed concern.

15 June 2004
'Adam has been brilliant. Not only was his enthusiasm for *Kip Fenn* so important during the two or more years I was writing it, but he continues to be interested in the project, and happily talks to me about it when-ever I bring up the subject. I asked, for example, the other night whether he thought I should self-publish. [. . .] His immediate response was to express concern that the only force leading me towards the idea of self-publishing was that he, himself, had been so positive about the book. He knows I've not encountered enthusiasm from anywhere else. [. . .] He also knows that he is just 16, and hardly the best judge in the world. So, I can well understand his concern. It is surely based on knowing the practical consideration that no one has backed my view of the book, but also, perhaps, on not wanting to shoulder any responsibility for my decision. It hadn't occurred to me, until that moment, that he might worry

about this. So, I reassured him – absolutely – that I would still be in the position now of considering self-publishing, whether he liked it or not.'

About this time, I had a very late but interesting reply from an agent. It was a standard rejection, but included with the letter was a six-month old 'reader's report'. I'd never seen one before, and I'm fairly confident its inclusion was a mistake.

'The accompanying letter is not an accurate reflection of this author's writing talents – he is capable of sophisticated writing. The idea of a fictional character attempting to write his own autobiography, is also good. I like the way Paul Lyons looks intelligently at autobiographical writing. On p2, for example, he says: Writing in the Reflections mode means I am less constrained by time . . . and I can embellish the facts more generously than in a formal biography . . . I need not worry where failures of memory . . . leave me struggling to fill in certain . . . gaps.

Perhaps this comes close to Rousseau and his belief that autobiography need not be factual in order to relate the truth of a person's life. His writing can strike at you at points. The author's description of this mother's reaction on p11 to Kip telling his mother his Dad is not his real father, is perceptive and I like the recollection of his father's funeral on p2. However, ultimately he does not grip the reader's attention with either the story (his searching for evidence of his real father through his mother's love letters, girlfriend's death by fishing rod [sic] in chapter two) the character's internal life or his writing style.

Conclusion – good enough to stand out, but probably not good enough to seriously consider.'

Despite being very confused about the opening sentence, I took some reassurance from the reader likening me to Rousseau and from her comment, 'His writing can strike at you at points'. But what struck me most was that although this 'reader' had been tasked with assessing my novel, she'd made her assessment on a dozen or so pages, and hadn't come close to realising any of its ambitions, its grand themes or complex characters. So, if she wasn't taking the time to approach the substance of my book, then less-motivated slush-pile clearers were never going to.

Neither Adam's doubts or enthusiasms nor this letter influenced my decision. I had to proceed, of course I did. I set up Pikle Publishing and purchased 10 ISBN numbers for future use. I worked on proofing the novel, putting it into book format (450 pages), researching printers, types of paper, book sizes, etc. I designed a dust jacket, one which I would eventually deem a failure. It was grey and purple, with 'Kip Fenn' writ in very large letters filling the front cover. I'd expected it to have a matt surface, but I'd made a mistake with the printers, and it turned out glossy. Nevertheless, I liked it a lot, I thought it was cool, sophisticated and different (like the book itself), and that it would stand out on a book shelf against so many other brightly coloured offerings. But Kip Fenn never got onto bookshelves, and at a glance, without special attention, the book simply looked dreary.

Apart from the novelty of the story itself – I mean it's not every day one comes across a fictional (and non-SF) autobiography with an invented history lasting the whole of the future century – the narrative has several structural quirks.

1) Each chapter begins with an invented quotation, many of them from characters that appear in the book.

2) Each chapter ends with a selection of (fictional again, of course) extracts of correspondence to and from Kip and close friends or family (thus allowing albeit brief comment from third parties on the events in the book).

3) The narrative written by Kip is largely about his past, but occasionally at first, and more often later in the book, he writes about what is happening in his present (i.e. in a care home, where he chats to a nurse about his writing, and where he is visited by relations), indeed right up until his death day.

In preparing the book to be published, I found several ways of potentially enhancing the reader experience. So often when I read a novel, I come across a character that I can't quite remember, and I find myself scuttling back through many pages looking for the last reference to that name. My readers, I decided, would have an index that could lead them straight to the first mention of that character. This index would also include a very brief description of each person. Secondly, I included, at the back, several family trees each one based on Kip's wives.

And, thirdly, I thought it would be helpful to have a timeline of major events through the century, and this fitted very neatly down the inside front and back flaps of the dust jacket. Fourthly, on the back cover of the dust jacket, I included, as publishers do, some favourable advanced reviews of the novel. Naturally, these had to be invented as if around the time of publication, i.e. after Kip's death. I created highly realistic quotes (if a tad hyperbolic, but that IS the publishing norm) provided by characters mentioned in the book, ones who had known Kip personally or professionally.

Here is one of them, for example, by the niece of Kip's third wife: 'At first glance, you might wonder why an apparently uninspiring character such as Mr Fenn – a volleyball-playing civil servant – bothered to write his Reflections. And you might want to slap the young Mr Fenn across the face because of his attitude to women and sex. Yet there is nothing dull about his story, or the way he tells it. I even cried here and there towards the end. An extraordinary life. An extraordinary book.' 'Irene Sanderson writing in *Guardian Women* (October 2101)'

And here's another: 'Few today have heard of Kip Fenn but he deserves to be better remembered. He was a good friend to Nigeria, Africa and all the developing world. In this remarkably honest book, Mr Fenn tends to skim too quickly over his long career in the IFSD, and I for one would have liked more about his achievements and less about his personal life.' 'Chidi Naiambana writing in Nigeria Economic Gazette (March 2012)'

Also, I maintained the conceit of Kip being a real person (as in the reviews) by including at the front of the book a dedication to his children (and grandchild). I also included a (working) email address in his son's name for any reader that had a question or comment.

In August 2004, I received some 800 copies of *Kip Fenn – Reflections*. Why so many? It seems laughable in retrospect, but before print-on-demand was available, one needed a sizeable print run to keep down the unit cost. It was a judgement call, and I must still have had some hope – however slim or fanciful – that sales would take off.

I suppose here is as good a moment as any to explain that, hitherto, I had felt that I had never fully committed, fully invested in my writing. People spend thousands, tens of thousands of pounds on their hobbies, holidays, interests, but I had always balked at investing in myself when it came to such matters, partly out of a lack of self-confidence, and partly out of a vague feeling that I shouldn't have to 'sell' my creative writing (unlike, of course, my business writing which I'd proved very capable of selling). But now, here I was on the threshold of finally 'pushing' my work forward: I could well afford a few thousand pounds.

Spoiler alert. Some 20 years later, I still have two unopened boxes of freshly minted books, though I've disposed of many along the way. I can honestly say that, over time, the cardboard boxes which the books came in – very sturdy they were and a good size for packing heavy books – have brought more benefits (when moving for example) than their contents.

I sent out more than one hundred review copies – the book was quite heavy so postage was another significant cost. I sent them to daily and local newspapers, magazines, and even to various individuals I thought might be interested. And then I sat back and waited, and waited ... needless to say (as if I didn't know, deep down, that very little would happen) I managed to attract but three reviews, all in local newspapers. *The Farnham Herald* and its sister the *Surrey & Hants News* ran identical pieces entitled 'Author foresees planet's dark future in his fictional debut' with a photo of me holding the book to my chest. The author of the piece, Zoe Wright, cribbed most of it from the press release I'd included with the review copy. However, she added a short paragraph of opinion near the end: 'There is no doubt that this is a thought-provoking, and refreshing idea for a fictional book. It should be a compelling read for anyone sick of standard futuristic reads.' Hmmm.

Weeks later, in a fog of disappointment I composed a letter to send as a follow-up to all the reviewers who had received review copies. Here's a flavour of it.

'Don't you personally hope for something new and exciting in the world of fiction? Don't you ache for novels that have something real, important and perhaps controversial to say? Don't you long for books that can't be pigeon-holed into a genre the moment you pick them up? And perhaps you worry – like I do – that fiction, as an art form, has become so inward-looking, so obsessed with descriptive content and emotional navel-gazing, that authors have lost the will to comment, to stand on a rostrum and shout out about big issues that affect our lives today and will affect them tomorrow? Can I ask you this: how would you know if a truly original novel – especially one that might need time and effort to appreciate – arrived on your desk?

I received eight replies. Suzi Feay at the *Independent*, in her email, sounded both apologetic and cross at my letter, so I ended up sending her a longer personal email. And a man named Christopher Arkell, at the *London Magazine*, returned my letter with a note scrawled on, saying he'd like to meet me. I rang him, and it transpired that he wanted to teach me a lesson (this is my interpretation). He'd invited me to come and help him choose which books he sends out for review. He said I should have a look at the *London Magazine* before I respond, but, if I don't, he'd like that even better because he'd be very interested to know how I'd go about choosing books for review!'

I had another potential source of feedback, which proved equally depressing. This was still fairly early days for the internet, but I'd set up a personal website earlier that year – www.pikle.co.uk – with information about my writing projects, especially *Kip Fenn*. I'd mentioned the URL in all my letters and press releases. By dint of a free service from a website called Statcounter I could keep count of any visitors to my pages. I'd hoped that there might be some following the promotional mail outs. There weren't.

It took a while but eventually I had to conclude, reluctantly, that reviewers were in the same club as the publishers and agents, and to ask myself rhetorically, why on earth would they spend their valuable time on a random, rather long and somewhat complicated book, one not fitting into any genre, and authored by someone outside the club? For decades I had accepted the club's judgement that my books simply weren't good enough (whether in the writing, or the story), but I couldn't and wouldn't accept this about Kip Fenn.

Barely a day went by when – dispiritingly – something in the news didn't chime with a *Kip Fenn* theme.

> 17 January 2005
> The news today highlights a major report on world poverty, and the fact that the rich world needs to provide much more development aid in the future. It makes me sigh with such great regrets. What with Britain holding the Presidency of the G8 and publicising the need for more attention to Africa's problems, and the tsunami disaster, and the report on poverty, this would have been such a good time for media reviews about *Kip Fenn*. And yet my book still rots at the bottom of the ocean, unseen, unheard, unsmelt, unfelt.

About this same time, I had the first inkling of a new way to find readers for *Kip Fenn*. Websites were becoming all the rage, but their owners were beginning to understand that they were not magic marketing tools in themselves, customers would have to be led there, whether by advertising or other methods. Google rankings were becoming important but the key for someone without huge resources, I worked out, was CONTENT. Provide useful content (as many bloggers were soon to do) and punters will find their way to your site. What could I supply the world that it didn't already have?

Information on diaries, that's what. I set about creating *The Diary Junction* (a name inspired by a radio programme I'd been listening to for some years – *Late Junction*), a web-based database of 500 diarists, complete with biographical information, internet links to further information, and, crucially, links to where diary texts could be read online freely and without much advertising. Back then, I was still in a state of wonderment about the internet and its potential, and it felt great to be working on a project that helped fulfil that potential. Behind my efforts, though, was the key aim of directing traffic to the Pikle website where I could expose visitors to Kip Fenn advertising.

It took several months to learn to build a website, to compile the data, and to publish it online – at www.thediaryjunction.co.uk. For each diarist I provided dates, nationality, content descriptors, etc. The website also included pages of listings: alphabetical, chronological, by nationality, by profession, and by content tags. Once launched, I sent out hundreds of emails to addresses that I'd collected while researching the diarists and their texts. I garnered a few supportive comments, the best was from Michelle Pauli at *The Guardian*: '. . . this amateur (in the best sense) attempt to document historical and literary diarists is a great browse. Truly a labour of love by one individual, over [500] diarists can be accessed through a variety of lists, including alphabetically, chronologically and by profession, and for each there is a brief biographical summary, journal dates and a few links. This isn't the site for in depth information on any of the diarists but it does provide a good overview of journal-writers from 838 right up to the present day.'

My Google ranking increased considerably, but the *Kip Fenn* advertising on every page of the site fell totally flat. As I write, all these years later, I can confidently say I've not sold a single copy thanks to demand generated by my website despite nearly a million 'visitors'.

Pleasingly, however, I did get an insightful write-up (with a cursory mention of *Kip Fenn*) in a very successful blog run by an ex-publisher, Grumpy Old Bookman. He wrote in November 2005:

'Only yesterday, I remarked that perhaps the best way to publicise a book via a blog or web site is to provide some material of value or interest to a particular group, and then to plug your book in passing, so to speak.

This is a technique being used to good effect by Paul K. Lyons. Paul has developed an impressive web site called The Diary Junction. *It's pretty self-explanatory. It provides a vast amount of information about historical and literary diaries and diarists. Picking a name more or less at random from a list of 450 diarists (so far), I chose Dora Carrington. There isn't a vast amount of info provided, and it is not cheerful, because it seems that the lady's diary records how she decided to kill herself. Nevertheless, the Diary Junction would be a useful starting point for a researcher. As for Paul Lyons's other work, he does give us links to his novel* Kip Fenn – Reflections, *and to some of his other fiction and non-fiction projects. See what I mean? All you have to do to get readers for your blog/book is be able and willing to put in hundreds of hours of work on (a) your book, and (b) a web site which provides useful information. Quite simple really. Then you get to be rich and famous. Maybe. . .'*

A couple of years later, Grumpy gave me another write-up, ending with this: 'Take a look at the novel, for instance. [. . .] The prologue is really rather intriguing, and far more so than many a self-published novel. The 'dust jacket' (in pdf) also provides a taste of what is inside, which is more than can be said for many of them. All in all, the Paul K. Lyons empire is an impressive one.'

Hardly.

I must skip on, this last chapter is already consuming too many pages.

The following year, I was thrust back onto the *Kip Fenn* hope machine by a new online venture from HarperCollins called Authonomy. This allowed users to submit their manuscripts for discussion, critique and ranking by fellow site members. Those manuscripts most highly ranked would be ensured consideration by HarperCollins editors. The system depended strongly on mutual backscratching, and so comments had to be taken with a pinch or two of salt. Nevertheless, I found the process very involving, feverish at times, and made efforts to see *Kip Fenn* move up the charts – but not enough.

Here are three of the scores of comments made by author-readers, almost all of whom seem to have 'got' the novel (unlike the agent's 'reader'). Ali Mair (whose book *Daisychains of Silence* rocketed to near the top very quickly) wrote: 'Well, how to say I'm in love with your writing without looking a complete fool? I don't know and I don't care. I am. This is wonderfully inventive, clever, truly accomplished writing. I'm in awe of your towering imagination and your astonishing achievement. Enough superlatives. I read some of the first chapter then curiosity led me to chapter ten, and I found myself immediately empathising with Fenn – the knowledge of his deathday, his doubts – all beautifully portrayed. This is stunning, masterful and probably the best work I have come across on Authonomy. Bravo. I want the paperback version so I can read the entire book over and over again at my leisure. Please let me know when this is published – I mean that.'

And Maria (aka Bluestocking, who was very busy on the site, and was the author of *Dorkismo*) wrote: 'Truly amazing. What an exquisite gift you have, I mean this guy is *real*, his parents are real, his friends are real, his experiences are real. And I am absolutely sick to death that I can't get 'Trumpet Boy' on Netflix for the foreseeable future. One of the loveliest books I have seen here and I have seen hundreds and hundreds. I'm all set to read the lot as time permits. I absolutely love it; I have no suggestions for you – this is a fully realized work of the most rarefied quality. I hope it gets into the hands of the right editor at some stage. Oh wait I do have one suggestion, which is to break the book into two so that you don't have to change anything. I hear that they like a first novel to be under 100,000 words. Very best of luck.'

mn73 wrote: 'Speechless. Directed here from the outstanding praise you have received in the forums and can only echo the sentiments. If you had printed copies in your house my cheque would now be in the mail. This is amazing, just the thing I would buy and I love it. I cannot find anything negative to say. Beautiful. Exquisite.'

It was heart warming that *Kip Fenn* was taken up so positively by the Authonomy community, but saddening too, for it only re-awakened the disappointment at not having managed to promote him more successfully.

And so, years passed, the cardboard boxes were used more than once, and the books themselves were slowly trickled out of the house to charity shops. Adam had long since moved, first to Brighton to study economics and then to work in London. *Kip Fenn* was a regular visitor to our conversations over the years, especially when climate change was in the news, or internet regulation, or world poverty, or cloning, or . . .

I too moved to Brighton, though this had nothing to do with Adam being there. I'd lived in a Surrey village for ten years, run my business, been a parent, and now I wanted more happening, more colour, and the sea, so I moved back to Brighton. There I met and married Hattie, and had two children all of which I do not mean to write about in this memoir. But I do want to complete the story of *Kip Fenn*, which went on for some time, chronologically, into this new period of my life.

I should explain that around 2010-2011, I'd had another wave of regret about *Kip Fenn* and decided to re-edit the work into three separate books, of roughly equal length. What made this idea less mad than it sounds was the emergence of Amazon's print-on-demand publishing arm, CreateSpace, and its availability for UK customers. In essence all one had to do was upload a formatted text and a pdf of the cover (front, spine and back). It took a little trial and error to use the CreateSpace software but the whole process was relatively easy, and, crucially, astonishingly cheap – there was not even an obligation involved in the process to buy a single copy.

I renamed the work *Not a Brave New World*. Yes, this was a shameless attempt to take advantage, if only by (mis)appropriated association, with Aldous Huxley's famous novel. I'd adapted the structure so there were now 10 'Parts' (equivalent to the old, and over-long, chapters) with three each in the first two books, and four in the final one. Each Part was now broken up into much shorter chapters, every one with a title starting with the word, 'In which . . .'. (This was a technique oft used in classic literature – *Three Men in a Boat*, *The Pickwick Papers* – though I later found out, annoyingly, that it had also been used by the Booker prize winner in 2013). I retained the original prologue in the first book, and wrote short new prologues for the second and third books. I subtitled the whole work *A Trilogy in Three Wives*, and named each book after Kip's three wives, *Gillian*, *Diane* and *Lizette*. I retained the family trees and the index (signalling who each person is and in which books they occur), but abandoned the timeline that had been on the dust cover of the hardback. I hoped these changes might make the novel(s) more palatable for publishers. After designing three new covers, far more attractive and intriguing than *Kip Fenn*'s original dark dust jacket, in January 2014, I had CreateSpace print a first (proof) copy of each book in the trilogy (for a few pounds). I re-proofread them, and finally purchased 20 copies of each paperback.

I went through the whole process of writing to agents and publishers again. This time I received snippets of feedback (rather than none), mostly positive, but no one wanted to take the project on.

I did though have a couple of flirtations with agents, which I'd like to mention briefly.

Hattie, when much younger, had herself published a memoir, successful in sales and with reviewers. She was writing again, and had found an agent with a very reputable agency. This agent had also taken a shine to a draft book manuscript of mine (about London and diaries) and so I'd signed up to be a client as well. This was exciting for two reasons. Firstly, I felt confident she would find me a mainstream publisher for the diaries book; and, secondly, I'd be able, in time, to suggest she take a look at the *Kip Fenn* trilogy. Within a month or two, very unfortunately, she had left her agency for another job, leaving both Hattie and I adrift.

For some time, I'd also been having an intermittent dialogue with a very well-known agent who'd also shown an interest in the diaries book and was prepared to take a look at the trilogy. In May 2011, he wrote: 'Dear Paul, I've only dipped into this, but I'm certainly very intrigued. I hope you can bear with me for a week or so more while I take more time to get across it? All best.'

After six months, I'd heard nothing, and I wrote to the agent again. He replied: 'As you may have guessed, *Not a Brave New World* didn't click for me – just too ambitious, I think. Very tricky to get the balance between the 'now' references and the 'alternative future' and keep the whole thing grounded and the reader engaged. I'm afraid I couldn't add it all up.'

Here, then, is me still outpouring to my diary.

29 June 2012
And as for Kip. Oh dear, oh dear. My endless efforts on his behalf continue to go completely unrewarded. Having revised the whole book into a trilogy, and revamped the promotional blurbs, I exhausted the agencies and moved onto publishers some time ago. Most publishers these days – four-fifths – will not accept unsolicited fiction submissions. I devised a letter, acknowledging this, but still trying to woo them. Only one in four or five of my letters has even been acknowledged with a rejection slip. Most recently – six weeks ago – I wrote to four publishers that do still accept unsolicited material, and only one has bothered to reply. This is Myriad Editions in Brighton. Very sweetly, they wrote 'All three books sound very interesting but unfortunately I think the project may be too ambitious for us overall'.

It was very satisfying to have hold of the paperback versions, but I had no illusions that I would be able to sell them any better than the old *Kip Fenn*. I gave copies away to friends, and I mailed a set to the British Library (under the legal deposit requirement). I revamped the *Kip Fenn* part of my website, and I posted images of covers and info on Facebook and any other websites I could find.

A year or two later, I wrote in the diary, '*Kip Fenn* did for me. I put everything into trying to get it published, marketed, distributed . . . and twice published it myself . . . all to zero, zero, zero result.'

And so, I must draw this story to a close. A word search of my most recent diaries shows that I've mentioned 'Kip Fenn' but half a dozen times, usually in a similar context to that of the above quote. I thought I would never write any fiction again (other than stories for my children), what on earth would be the point; and yet I have. I've self-published a satirical novel, and I'm a third of the way through another trilogy based on three characters growing up in the sixties and seventies. As so much of this memoir and my previous one (*Why Ever Did I Want to Write*) demonstrate, I must have writing in the blood, nothing else seems to come close in terms of purpose – even if no one reads what I've written. In closing, a metaphor is raising itself before me. It's as though I've climbed the highest mountain. Does it matter that no one knows? Surely the climbing is the thing, not the accolade for having done so. Can I, then, refer you dear reader again to a very early paragraph in the introduction to *Why Ever Did I Want to Write*.

'Much of my writing has been so-called 'life writing' [. . .] I've also written novels, plays, short stories, poems, local history, psychogeography, and children's fiction. I am not society's idea of a 'writer', a published author with a portfolio of commercial or literary books behind me. No, I am my own idea of what a writer is: someone who enjoys the process of writing, the translating of thoughts and ideas into communicable language; someone for whom writing infuses their daily life; and someone whose mind and soul is affected – infected even – by how and what they write, and by the need to use words to explain, to expose, to imagine, and to play.'

www.pikle.co.uk

Printed in Great Britain
by Amazon

37337894R00116